TOWARDS MODERN PUBLIC FINANCE:
THE AMERICAN WAR WITH MEXICO, 1846–1848

FINANCIAL HISTORY

Series Editor: Robert E. Wright

TITLES IN THIS SERIES

FORTHCOMING TITLES

TOWARDS MODERN PUBLIC FINANCE:
THE AMERICAN WAR WITH MEXICO, 1846–1848

BY
James W. Cummings

LONDON AND NEW YORK

First published 2009 by Pickering & Chatto (Publishers) Limited

Published 2016 by Routledge
2 Park Square, Milton Park, Abingdon, Oxfordshire OX14 4RN
711 Third Avenue, New York, NY 10017, USA

First issued in paperback 2015

Routledge is an imprint of the Taylor & Francis Group, an informa business

British Library Cataloguing in Publication Data

Cummings, James W.
Towards modern public finance: the American war with Mexico, 1846–1848.
– (Financial history)
1. Mexican War, 1846–1848 – United States – Finance 2. Finance, Public –
United States – History – 1801–1861
I. Title
336.7'3'09034

ISBN-13: 978-1-138-66378-7 (pbk)
ISBN-13: 978-1-85196-988-3 (hbk)

Typeset by Pickering & Chatto (Publishers) Limited

CONTENTS

LIST OF TABLES

INTRODUCTION

At noon on 11 May 1846, following clashes along the Rio Grande River in south-west Texas, President James K. Polk forwarded a war message to Congress claiming Mexican troops had 'invaded our territory and shed the blood of our fellow citizens on our own soil'.[1] The violence followed months of military and diplomatic provocation on the part of the American government and frenzied anti-American rhetoric by the Mexican press and people. News of the fighting arrived in Washington at a propitious time. The belligerency of the Polk administration had created a crisis on two fronts. Though anxious to compromise, the British were greatly aggrieved by demands for the termination of the joint occupancy of the Oregon Territory and American occupation up to the 54° 40' line. They were prepared to defend their rights by force if necessary. In spite of the possibility of hostilities with Great Britain, the administration had resolved on war as the only way to break the impasse with Mexico. The failure of John Slidell's mission had recently dashed hopes of settling the Mexican claims issue and purchasing all or part of California. Fortunately for Polk, the British submitted a proposal to the American minister, acceptable to most Americans, on 18 May 1846, ten days before news of the hostilities along the Texas–Mexico frontier reached London. By this narrow margin Polk avoided the possibility of engaging his nation in a two-front war.

The attack by Mexican cavalry on United States dragoons east of the river provided an excellent opportunity to blame Mexico for the crisis. The American public's indignation came from the portion of the message regarding the shedding of American blood. Many of Polk's fellow citizens, much of the international community and, certainly, every Mexican doubted whether the scraggly land between the Neuces and Rio Grande Rivers had really become part of the United States on the annexation of Texas.[2]

Polk could, and did, argue effectively that war existed and, therefore, Congress must recognize that fact and 'place at the disposition of the Executive the means of prosecuting the war with vigour, and thus hastening the restoration of peace'.[3] Under relentless administration pressure, after only two days of debate, Congress passed a joint resolution recognizing that a state of war existed between the United States and Mexico. The resolution also included a general provision authorizing the necessary troops and supplies. Timing allowed the United States to avoid the possibility of one disastrous war but engage in another that held the promise of immense territorial gains.[4]

Who or what caused the Mexican–American War remained, and remains, an important question to contemporaries and historians, but regardless of responsibility the war had to be fought and won and the men and money to accomplish this task had to be found.[5] The endeavour took place during a period of great change in American history. The market, transportation and financial revolutions were in full flood and preparing the conditions for the American Industrial Revolution. Slavery, not economic policy, was beginning to dominate political discourse and sever the intersectional institutions, such as the churches and political parties, which held the nation together. At the same time the country was becoming wealthier and its economy and financial institutions more mature and specialized.[6]

Politically, Polk's presidency culminated the Jacksonian Age.[7] He brought to the presidency a thirst for territorial expansion and a determination to implement the main planks of Jacksonian economic policy. For better or worse, he accomplished his goals. By 1849 the size of the United States had increased by 50 per cent and the Twentieth-Ninth Congress, with the active encouragement of Polk and his Secretary of the Treasury, Robert J. Walker, had passed some of the most important economic legislation of the nineteenth century. The war did not even prevent the administration from demanding and securing passage of a revenue tariff, the Independent Treasury and a warehousing system. Successful implementation of the first two was essential to the war effort.[8]

Ideologically, the programme advocated what modern historians have labelled 'republicanism'. This demanded the promotion of the interest of the common man and divorcing the people's government from the corrupt moneyed interests. According to James McPherson 'the core of Republicanism was liberty, a precious but precarious birthright constantly threatened by corrupt manipulations of power'.[9] The goal was a virtuous republic which emphasized community interest instead of capitalism with its pursuits of self-interest and profits. Such a republic needed yeomen and artisans possessing sufficient productive property to retain their independence and provide a buffer against the powerful and their dependents. The belief system rejected the granting of monopolies or special charters or the allocation of federal monies for development. Inevitably, it was believed, such grants favoured certain classes or sections and fortified growing inequality.[10]

The rhetoric's main challenge came from the desire for economic growth and individual betterment shared by both the Jacksonians and their opponents. If economic opportunity is opened to the masses they cannot be blamed for seizing it. The Democratic Party was replete with its share of economic thrusters, whether small-scale land speculators perched on 160-acre tracts near the frontier, southern yeoman farmers seeking to enter the slave-owning planter class, Philadelphia artisans striving to convert their workshops into small factories, or Tammy Hall politicos energetically working their Manhattan districts. For fifty years political purity had faced off against practicality. Growth demanded transportation facilities, credit, capital, commerce, development – and then more credit and capital. In other words, it needed all the accoutrements of capitalism. Here lay the paradox for the Jacksonians. In the end they adopted a policy of spreading opportunity to the widest possible segments of the white male population. They chartered more state banks, spent state (not federal) money on internal improvements and attempted to restrict monopolies and economic privilege.[11]

After considering Polk's and the Jacksonians' objectives it may seem illogical to discern significant advances in the ongoing evolution of the American financial system in a middling-sized war and this last quixotic effort to hold back the progress of capitalism and modernization. The solution to this dilemma lies in a constant of American history reaching far back into the colonial era. The urgent demands of warfare have consistently led to change and innovation in public finance.[12] There is much truth in Richard Sylla's assertion that 'virtually every major innovation in financial institutions and markets arose in response to governments' financial needs and policies', usually war.[13] The Mexican–American War, like previous and future conflicts, required adaptations and actions not envisioned by its makers. Financial reality, not Jacksonian rhetoric, proved the dominant force.

The historical importance of America's war financing lies not just in its contribution to victory or defeat in the field but also to its impact on the unique way the country developed. This becomes critical if one accepts, as the author does, the premise that wars, and cleaning up the debris afterward, have first periodically transformed government finances and then by extension the financial system of the nation. When this is combined with the certainty that finance made major contributions to the growth that transformed the United States into the world's foremost economic power during the nineteenth century, the need to understand elements of this phenomena becomes clear.[14]

The objective of this book is to contribute to our knowledge of the economic, financial and political history of the United States during the mid-1800s by providing information on the financing of the Mexican–American War, a little studied but important aspect of the era. It is also a fascinating story for those interested in how the resources for great enterprises, such as military campaigns, the East India Companies, the transcontinental railroads in North America or internet companies, are secured. This work combines existing scholarship with research into the records of the Treasury Department and Bureau of Public Debt. Many of the government records from the period have not been inspected since they were moved to the National Archive and Record Administration's new facility at College Park, Maryland, in the early 1960s. These records provide an opportunity to view the war's financing from the government's perspective.

No attempt is being made to resolve, or seriously enter, the ongoing scholarly debate concerning the relative importance of the economic changes that buffeted nineteenth-century society. Scholars advocating revolutions in finance, the marketplace, transportation, management and industry are numerous and quite capable and willing to defend the differing viewpoints. The fact that most scholars do concede finance a place of consequence (if not that of the wellspring or igniter) in the nation's economic progression suffices to makes the Mexican War's contribution towards a modern financial system worthy of study.[15]

Given the importance of the nation's public and private financial systems the question becomes what long-term effects did the War with Mexico have on their development? First, it ensured that no all-powerful central bank sprang up to direct public and private finance. Next, it helped restore America's commercial reputation. Last and most important, it provided the opportunity for investment bankers to emerge and fill the void in marketing government debt.[16] As Fritz Redlich once remarked, this development is critical because 'modern investment banking originated in the field of public credit'.[17]

Though Andrew Jackson killed the Second Bank of the United States, the Polk administration made certain it never rose from its grave. Because the war financing was in the main successfully executed, the administration ensured the survival of the Independent Treasury for seventy years. With prosperity and strong government credit, the Whigs, even after their success in the election of 1848, lacked the strength to replace it with a national bank. Such an institution did arise after the two prior wars. Without a dominant central bank, the American financial system emerged as a widespread, fractured, competitive and aggressive conglomeration. Risk-taking, innovation and entrepreneurship permeated the entire economy. Independent financial institutions of all sizes serving local, regional and national markets arose. Access to financial services became widespread and almost a right. State governments, in particular, responded to the needs of their constituency by opening up credit. Recent scholarship makes it clear that access to credit and the services of financial intermediaries are strongly correlated with capital accumulation and burgeoning economic growth, such as characterized nineteenth-century America. Further, eliminating the possibility of a new national bank in a city outside New York assured the financial dominance of Wall Street.[18]

A successful war and its funding contributed significantly to restoring the nation's international credit standing. This tended to fluctuate throughout the

nineteenth century. The default of a number of state governments on debt obligations sold abroad in the late 1830s and early 1840s had brought American credit
to a low point. The sale of a large part of the Mexican War loans to British bankers such as the Rothschilds and Baring Brothers helped restore the credit of the
federal government and faith in American commercial honour in Europe. The
successful effort by defaulting states, particularly, Pennsylvania, Maryland, Indiana and Illinois, to restructure their debt and resume interest payments helped
substantially in this resurrection. With American credit again strong foreign
investors willingly helped fund the great expansion in railroads and manufacturing that began in the 1850s.[19]

The financial community scored its greatest single achievement of the 1840s
in the successful floatation of the Mexican War loans. It reinforced and sped
up a crucial developing trend, the marketing of securities, both governmental
and non-governmental, by a specialized group, the investment bankers. The war
proved to be their great opportunity. The 1840s was a crucial decade in their rise
to the top of the securities industry. In the future, commercial banks would invest
in government debt obligations and arrange medium- and short-term credit for
their customers, but the investment bankers became the intermediaries between
the investing public and both governments and corporations seeking to market
long-term bonds and equities. Success propelled them on to railroad promo-
tions, the marketing of Civil War loans and, finally, the financing of American
industry. In the end they made their home, greater Wall Street, synonymous with
capitalism.[20]

A review of the financing effort also provides an opportunity to inspect
the operations of the Independent Treasury during its formative years. The
Sub-Treasury remained an essential part of the nation's financial system until
establishment of the Federal Reserve System in 1913. Beginning under the stress
of war and with the hostility of the nation's banks, it survival was by no means
assured. Its operations were intimately associated with, and to a great extent
formed by, its need to support the military effort. During the first two years,
war financing constituted its most important duty. Though it survived the Independent Treasury never met the expectations of it proponents. Divorcing the
Treasury from the influences and risks associated with the American financial
system proved impossible. In fact, the Independent Treasury ultimately became
very sensitive to the needs and interests of the financial community.[21]

The late 1840s were a favourable time for the financing effort. The economy
was recovering from the Panic of 1837 and the depression that followed. Heavy
exports of grain, cotton and especially breadstuffs in 1846 and 1847 brought
prosperity to all levels of society. National wealth was doubling every fifteen
years, and in that sense the country was four times stronger than in 1812. Unlike
in the previous wars with Great Britain and its powerful navy, American ports

remained open and the vital customs revenue unimpaired. The Mexican conflict, unlike the Civil War and the War of 1812, was relatively short with limited needs in men and money. The government's credit at home, though not abroad, was high and investors and financial institutions possessed surplus funds.[22]

Three large loans totalling $49 million, authorized by the Acts of 22 July 1846, 28 January 1847 and 31 March 1848 provided the money necessary to wage the war successfully. In devising this legislation, Congress drew on the experience gained in financing prior wars and the deficit incurred between 1837 and 1843. The Treasury's effort to market the first loan, particularly the treasury notes, produced mixed results. The undertaking provided valuable lessons, including the need to consider market conditions and the desires of the financial community.[23]

The second loan, totalling $23 million, was sold in three separate contracts during 1847 and the first half of 1848. The successful flotation of this issue ensured the availability of the material, men and money for the conquest of Mexico. The legislation again authorized a combination of treasury notes and bonds. At the urging of the Treasury Department, in an effort to increase the marketability of the treasury notes, Congress made the short-term notes convertible into twenty-year 6 per cent bonds at the election of the note holder. In the past the Treasury had generally redeemed the notes by selling long-term bonds and using the proceeds.[24]

The third loan of $16 million was floated after receipt of a peace treaty and the funds used for demobilization, bonuses and treaty payments, as well as to increase the Treasury's cash reserve. Congress abandoned the use of treasury notes and authorized the issuance of twenty-year 6 per cent bonds. Much of the issue was sold abroad, helping to re-establish American credit. The saleability of the bonds to foreigners was increased by giving the purchaser the option of coupon or registered bonds. Coupon bonds were more appealing to Europeans because ownership was more readily transferable and the interest could be obtained by the bearers or their agents by presenting the coupon at an office of the Treasury Department.[25]

The American government's successful financial effort contrasted sharply with that of its opponent. Mexico entered the war with an empty Treasury, weak credit, a civil administration in disarray, and a populace divided by class, wealth, geography and political outlook. The inability to implement an orderly financial plan and to obtain sufficient funds proved fatal to Mexico's ability to resist the invaders. The army consistently went into battle ill-trained, ill-armed and ill-supplied. Mexico's problems were further compounded by the Polk administration's effort to tax the Mexican people in order to reduce the burden on its own constituency and to weaken Mexico's ability to wage war. In the end this effort – called the Mexican assessments – proved more frustrating than profitable to the Americans.[26]

Historians have chiefly studied the period 1845–9 in light of Manifest Destiny, territorial expansion, military history and the developing sectional conflict. Scholars who have addressed the economic issues of the Polk administration have concentrated on the congressional struggle over the tariff and Independent Treasury. No in-depth study of the financing of the war has been made. The one serious attempt to address the subject appears in one chapter of Justin Smith's two-volume work published in 1919.[27]

Biographers have displayed more interest in war financing, but solely in the context of their particular subject. In the only recent biography of Robert J. Walker, James Shenton treats Walker's time as Secretary of the Treasury in a general way. The main thrust is the era's politics. Shenton does develop the theme of Walker's efforts to secure the confidence and support of the business community at the expense of Jacksonian principles. In his 1947 study of Walker's political and economic policies, Frank Tick gives a more in-depth look at war financing from Walker's perspective, but Tick's interest in the financing is restricted to the acts of his subject. Henry Cohen provides an interesting and extremely well-researched study of the business career of William W. Corcoran, the major figure in marketing the Mexican War loans. Again, Cohen's main interests are Corcoran's political and financial activities. Polk's biographers likewise overlook war financing and focus on expansionism, his managerial style and legislative accomplishments. What is lacking is a broad, overall view of the fundraising activities and their impact on the Treasury Department and the nation's banking and securities industries. Hopefully, the present study will meet this challenge and shed additional light on American public finance between the Panic of 1837 and the Civil War.[28]

1 FINANCIAL AND ECONOMIC BACKGROUND

By 1846 the United States possessed a rich history of war financing and economic development reaching back over two hundred years. Both successful innovation and abject failure crowned the efforts of the colonists and early Americans to develop a financial system capable of funding public endeavours and private enterprise. In the beginning, colonial governments relied on sources as varied as paper money, taxes paid in kind, tobacco warehouse receipts and loans from local merchants to finance military campaigns. Lessons were learned, forgotten and relearned. One lesson absorbed early by colonial officials was that current means (taxes) were insufficient for the massive outlays required by warfare and, further, likely to be rejected by the populace as too burdensome. Like European states they turned to various schemes of borrowing. The provincial officials also observed that some methods used to finance military efforts were admirably suited as economic stimulants during periods of slow trade. The financial and economic environment in which the Mexican–American War was financed was shaped by past experimentation and evolution. This chapter is devoted to placing the process in a historical context.[1]

During the colonial period the British Americans funded their military efforts against the French and their Native American allies largely with bills of credit issued by the provincial governments. Massachusetts pioneered this method in 1690 and, as warfare became more extensive and expensive in the eighteenth century, one colony after another found it necessary to follow the Bay colony's example. The paper money, the first in the British Empire, passed as currency alongside the gold and silver coins then in circulation. The value of the bills, other than faith and trust, lay in the provision making them receivable for provincial taxes and other public dues.[2]

As the eighteenth century advanced the wartime expediency became a technique to stimulate trade by increasing the money supply and by financing agricultural expansion. In a raw and developing country like North America, capital, if it does not exist or cannot be imported, must be created. The colonial governments loaned capital to merchants and farmers in the form of paper money and accepted mortgages and other debt obligations as collateral. As long as the bills remained in circulation the governments stood to reap a tidy profit as they exchanged non-interest-bearing instruments for interest-bearing obligations.[3]

The huge emission of paper money for war, commerce and agriculture led to a steady depreciation of the currency that accelerated in the 1740s, particularly in New England. The colonists were learning what Alexander Hamilton was to stress half a century later. Hamilton believed that 'the creation of debt should always be accompanied with the means of extinguishment'.[4] Without adequate assurance to creditors and note holders, debt depreciates and rampant inflation permeates the economy. Eventually, Massachusetts's currency fell to one-twelfth its face value in silver. Fortunately, a parliamentary reimbursement of military expenditures allowed the colony to redeem its paper money at that reduced rate in 1749.[5]

The monetary depreciation suffered by the colonies eventually forced the British Parliament to abandon its policy of benign neglect and take action. The impetus for change came from British merchants in the American trade who were being paid, or feared payment, in the depreciated currencies. The sting in the colonial legislation lay in the provisions requiring acceptance of the bills as payment for all public *and* private debts. The Currency Act of 1751 restricted new issues to a life of two years and eliminated the legal tender provision in private transactions. Initially the law only applied to the four New England colonies, but in 1764 it was extended to the remainder. Despite Parliament's concern it is estimated that paper money made up 50 to 60 per cent of the $12 million in currency circulating at the time of the Revolution.[6]

Who controlled the currency and the economy became a very divisive issue during the 1760s and early 1770s. As the American economy became larger and more self-sufficient the greater the resentment against parliamentary control grew. The colonials, in particular, wanted to control the money supply. They repeatedly made their demands known. For example, in 1764, in what Michael Kammen regards as New York's opening salvo of the Revolution, the legislature petitioned the King and Parliament for four policy changes, among which was the repeal of the Currency Act of 1764. Robert Wright points out that those policies favouring the home market in Britain tended to force up colonial interest rates and decrease profits and asset values. In the end, economic problems, ideology and political concerns led to rupture and war.[7]

As delegates to the Second Continental Congress assembled in Philadelphia in May 1775 the supreme crisis of early America broke. The Congress constituted what passed as a national government but possessed little real power and only limited resources. The delegates inherited a war already in its early stages and an army of militiamen surrounding Boston. Whether the conflict ended in peaceful negotiations or was fought to the bitter end this army needed supplies, pay and munitions. To the bitter end proved to be the case. The Revolutionary War's scope, intensity and financial demands were unprecedented and at times failure loomed.[8]

The lack of the power to tax gravely handicapped Congress's ability to prosecute the war. Without this capacity the simplest recourse was to follow colonial precedent and issue paper money redeemable by the States. On 22 June 1775 Congress authorized the emission of bills of credit with a face value of 2 million in Spanish milled dollars. The notes ranged in value from $1 to $20 and bore the imprint of the Continental Congress. Military expenses quickly consumed the first $2 million and it became necessary to make further emissions. During the first five years of war, paper money constituted the main source of funding. A total of $200 million was outstanding by early 1780. Over-emission and inflation reduced the value of a dollar to 1.5 cents in silver.[9]

Congress also attempted to sell long-term bonds directly to the public. For this purpose a loan office was established in each state to collect the proceeds, issue the certificates and pay the interest. The public found the 4 and 6 per cent loan office certificates with interest payable in continentals unappetizing. In spite of this the loan offices continued to issue certificates through 1781. Of the $67 million issued most went to army contractors who preferred them to paper money. They did have one advantage that became important in the future. The Continental Congress and the government of the Confederation acknowledged their legal liability to the holders at the specie value (not face value) of the obligation at the time of issue. This reduced the liability from $67 million to $11 million.[10]

After 1779 and the collapse of the currency, America's ability to resist depended on two funding sources. First, the army increasingly maintained itself by requisitioning supplies and services and 'paying' with certificates drawn on the quartermaster and commissary departments. Because of the poverty of the continental and state governments it proved difficult for the person supplying the goods and services to obtain reimbursement. Second, Great Britain's traditional enemies supplied loans and subsidies. Benjamin Franklin managed to negotiate loans totalling 34 million livres from the French crown and a further million from the Farmers General. In 1782 John Adams secured 5 million guilders in Amsterdam. This loan, the first of many in Holland, was the Americans' initial exposure to loan contracting by investment bankers.[11]

As the war neared its end the Continental Congress did take one step that held great portents for American finance. In May 1781, it chartered the country's first bank, the Bank of North America. The government supplied $254,000 of the $400,000 in capital and deposited $462,812 in silver obtained from the French. From this firm base the bank initiated the outstanding feature of nineteenth-century American banking, the issuance of specie-backed bank notes.

Since the bank stood ready to redeem its notes in coin on demand the notes circulated at par (face value). The bank assisted the government in paying its bills and with short-term loans. It quickly became profitable and doubled its capital.[12]

The Revolutionary War's cost in specie exceeded $110 million and probably approached $135 million. Despite the importance of foreign subsidies and loans the citizenry of the thirteen states bore the main burden. This fell, not in the shape of equitable taxation, but through the depreciation of the paper currency. Soldiers and suppliers who retained the promises to pay constituted the real losers. In addition to repudiating the continentals, the Continental Congress wrote down the other debts to what it deemed their specie value at the time of issuance. At war's end the national government recognized a domestic debt of $27 million consisting of $11 million in loan office certificates, $11 million in paymaster notes issued upon demobilization of the army, over $1 million in quartermaster certificates and $3.7 million in final settlement certificates for the remaining sums owed the public. Around $80 million dollars for supplies and payroll simply disappeared.[13] Not all patriots agreed with Benjamin Franklin's assertion that

> this depreciation though in some circumstances inconvenient, has had the general good and great effect of operating as a tax, and perhaps the most equal of all taxes, since it depreciated in the hands of the holders of money, and thereby taxed them in proportion to the sums they have and the time they held it, which generally is in proportion to men's wealth.[14]

In spite of their chaotic and confused nature the mass of paper emissions allowed the nation to maintain the war and survive until victory was achieved. Americans emerged from the conflict with their independence and a deep distrust of paper money that plagued the body politic until the election of 1896 and the creation of the Federal Reserve System in 1913.[15]

Funding the residue of Revolutionary War debt after adoption of the Constitution in 1788 represents one of the most important moments in American historiography. Historian Richard Sylla believes that in addressing the disaster that represented the fiscal landscape of American public finance Alexander Hamilton and his Federalist allies initiated a financial revolution.[16] Robert Wright argues that Hamilton's efforts led to the emergence of 'a modern financial sector that laid the basis for America's ultimate political unification and economic development'.[17] According to Ron Chernow, Hamilton's latest biographer, Hamilton really sought to use the government's fiscal machinery to implement his vision of the new nation's future as a commercial and industrial power.[18]

What happened in the early 1790s to bring about this financial miracle? First, the Constitution gave the new federal government the all-important taxing power. Congress quickly placed duties on selected imports and an excise tax on distilled spirits. With a secure source of income Hamilton managed to fund the Revolutionary War debt. He only funded the legally recognized amounts and made no attempt to resurrect the continentals or other obligations previously written down or off. To assist the government he secured legislation creating a national bank and a mint.

To Hamilton the debt represented a great opportunity. He urged funding because he believed 'a national debt, if it is not excessive will be a national blessing. It will be a powerful cement to our nation. It will also create a necessity to keep up taxation to a degree which without being oppressive will be a spur to industry.'[19] Using fiscal policy and public finance Hamilton proposed the creation of a powerful commercial, financial and manufacturing nation that contradicted the limited government and agrarian society envisioned by Thomas Jefferson. The benefits Hamilton cited from funding the debt included securing the support of the influential debt holders, an improved credit standing that allowed borrowing in time of war on reasonable terms and increased respect abroad.[20]

Hamilton proposed to fund $65 million in depreciated domestic debt by exchanging this mass of paper for new government bonds. The debt consisted of Congress's legal obligation of $27 million, $13 million in accrued interest, $4 million in interest on the unpaid interest (indents) and an estimated $21 million incurred by the states (assumption) for war expenses. Bonds of 6 per cent were exchanged for two-thirds of Congress's debt and two-thirds (final amount $18 million) assumed from the states. Deferred 6 per cent bonds (interest payable after 1800) went for the remaining one-third of Congress's obligation and two-ninths of the states' obligation. The interest, remaining state debts and various odds and ends, including a small amount of continentals at 2 cents on the dollar, were funded with 3 per cent bonds. In the end the Treasury issued $30 million in 6 per cent bonds, $14.7 million in deferred and $19.7 million at 3 per cent. The bonds were callable at the government's pleasure.[21]

What Hamilton really created was $50 to $60 million in capital for the expansion of trade, financial institutions, agriculture and manufacturing. According to Stuart Bruchey, Hamilton forced the public to increase the nation's pool of savings through taxation and then used the revenue to create capital by restoring the value of the debt obligations. The new bonds represented solid, liquid assets that could be sold, used as collateral for loans or exported abroad in lieu of specie. Along with the restored public credit and additional capital came renewed commercial and economic confidence. Hamilton also successfully argued that the current holders of the old debt should reap the benefits from any price rise. Ron Chernow believes this attitude established the moral and legal basis for American security trading. This principal, the free trade of securities with the buyer assuming all rights to profits and loss, to Chernow, laid the foundation for America's future financial prominence.[22]

In addition to funding a national debt the Federalists created a powerful new bank headquartered in Philadelphia. Its advocates advertised its major usefulness as a source of short-term loans for the government, paying its expenses, storing its surplus and being a fount of strength during war time. In the broader economic sense the bank represented another $10 million in capital to finance commerce and other enterprises. Its bank notes and power allowed some control over the three state chartered banks existing in 1791 and later over the ninety-seven others that opened between 1791 and 1811.[23]

The new bonds and bank stock became the mainstays on the embryonic securities markets in Philadelphia, New York and Boston. Robert Wright sees in Hamilton's acts the key pillars of a modern financial system – a negotiable public debt, a secondary securities market and a central bank. The securities markets and a portion of the debt remained but the bank's enemies allowed its charter to expire at the end of its twenty-year life.[24]

Because of its demise a year before the second war with Great Britain began, we cannot assess the bank's wartime performance. Even without it the Treasury possessed several advantages over conditions existing in the Revolutionary War. A fairly extensive system of state banks and security markets existed and a policy of fundraising through the sale of long-term bonds was established. On the reverse side, American security markets lacked maturity.[25] According to Edwin Perkins they were especially 'devoid of prominent merchant banking houses or any specialized firms that engaged in underwriting new securities offerings or in related investment banking activities'.[26] The Jeffersonians who succeeded the Federalists in 1801 specifically sought to prevent the emergence of a powerful network of loan contractors.[27]

The Treasury Department's efforts to finance the War of 1812 (1812–15) by marketing long-term bonds in the old manner of opening subscription books and waiting for orders to pour in proved ineffective. President James Madison's insistence that the bonds be assigned an interest rate of 6 per cent caused much of the problem. It would be some time before the government realized that the market, not it, controlled interest rates and security prices. To supplement the reduced bond sales the Treasury issued treasury notes. These instruments became a major feature of American public finance. The notes paid 5.4 per cent interest and were redeemable in one year.[28] If the owner elected, the notes could be used to 'pay all duties and taxes laid by authority of the United States and all public lands'.[29] Their real benefit lay in the ability to pay government suppliers and creditors in script.[30]

In 1813 one innovative transaction showed the potential for investment banking in public finance. Anticipating difficulty in marketing the $16 million loan of that year, Secretary of the Treasury Albert Gallatin announced his willingness to consider proposals directly from capitalists on any unsold portion. In response to this appeal a syndicate headed by David Parish, the son of a Hamburg banker and the American agent for Baring Brothers; John Jacob Astor, fur trader, China merchant and real estate mogul of New York; and Stephen Girard, banker and leading merchant of Philadelphia, submitted a bid for $10 million of the 6 per cent bonds at a price of 88. Payment was to be made in ten monthly instalments. Parish, Astor and Girard pledged to place the bonds on a 'best effort' basis with other investors but made no unconditional commitment. The Treasury authorized a 0.25 per cent commission. The syndicate obtained $9.1 million on its terms and disposed of the majority to smaller investors and institutions willing to follow its lead. The transaction had many of the attributes of investment banking in that a syndicate was formed, bids made and accepted and the bonds sold to investors. On the other hand, no binding commitment existed to take all of the bonds. Importantly, the transaction stands uniquely alone and the federal government did not repeat it until the 1840s.[31]

The Treasury managed to muddle through the remainder of the war by selling bonds at a deepening discount. It emerged from the war with a national debt totalling $127 million and a new national bank, the Second Bank of the United States. The debt included $37.8 million of pre-1812 obligations, a $73 million increase attributed to the War of 1812, a floating debt of $9.3 million and $7 million in new 5 per cent bonds issued to pay the government's 20 per cent share of the new bank's capital. The difficulty in adequately funding the military effort provided the proponents of a national bank with the arguments needed to convince the public of its benefits.[32]

In the two decades following the war state governments dominated the field of public finance as the federal government concentrated on reducing its indebtedness. New York State started the internal improvement mania by successfully financing and building the Erie Canal. This waterway eventually provided relatively cheap transportation between the Great Lakes and New York City. In the beginning the states relied on the chartered banks within their borders to finance the projects either through direct loans or the purchase of equities or state bonds. The banks served a loan contracting function and resold many of the securities they obtained. As larger amounts became necessary the states tapped the London money market either by negotiating with the American agents of British investment bankers or by sending their own representatives to London. A small number of American private bankers and brokers such as Prime, Ward & King, Rathbone & Lord and Thomas Biddle & Company also began to experiment with investment banking and loan contracting during this period by bidding on portions of the bond issues and reselling them to American investors or sending them abroad. Regardless of the original purchaser, two-thirds of the state securities ended up in Europe.[33]

By the 1840s the United States possessed an extensive and far-flung banking system, a vibrant insurance industry, active securities markets and entrepreneurs seeking new sources of profit. These financial intermediaries were quite capable of tapping any available savings and investment funds. The existence of such funds depended on the country's economic conditions. As noted, in the Revolutionary War and the War of 1812 the young nation either lacked or failed to mobilize the material and financial means to battle adequately its opponent. The economic health of the country in 1846 would determine whether it had overcome these problems. Additionally, since Mexico's ability to resist largely dictated American military requirements, it is important to consider the means available to the Mexican government. The remainder of this chapter provides a review of the status of the two economies, the revenue available to each and their ability to borrow.

The economic and political landscape that the new Polk administration entered in March 1845 was forged by President Andrew Jackson's war on the Second Bank of the United States and the subsequent Panic of 1837. The struggle between Jackson and Nicholas Biddle, the bank's president, over re-chartering the institution came first and in the view of many contemporaries caused the second. After some initial difficulties, the bank under Biddle's leadership had by 1829 become a powerful and rich institution. To Jackson and others its size and privileges constituted a threat to democracy, the well-being of the people and the government itself. Several features of the bank's operations did leave it open to a populist attack: private management, a privileged monopoly, use of government funds, a large foreign stock ownership, the ability to expand and contract the money supply and significant political influence. In its favour it maintained a sound currency, restricted excessive lending, expanded and contracted the money supply in response to economic activity and transferred funds around the country cheaply and efficiently for the government and merchants. From a commercial standpoint it was a useful tool.[34]

Jackson planned from the beginning of his first administration to radically overhaul the bank and shear it of those attributes he considered dangerous. He personally disliked banks and, in spite of clear precedent to the contrary, doubted Congress's authority to charter such an institution. Further, he favoured the use of specie in everyday transactions (below $20) and sought to restrict bank note usage to large commercial transactions. Jackson appeared willing to compromise and allow a national bank in some less invasive and far-reaching form to continue. For political reasons, and on the advice of Martin Van Buren and others, he held his fire during most of his first term. The bank's numerous friends outnumbered its enemies. The machinations of Jackson's political opponents brought the issue to a head. Though warned by Jackson, Biddle allowed a bill extending the bank's charter to be introduced in the Senate in January 1832. When the bank emerged as a political issue in the election of that year, Jackson determined to destroy it.[35]

In his message vetoing the charter's extension Jackson called upon the public to support his efforts to slay the 'monster' by appealing to class interest. The bank was an instrument used by rich Americans and foreigners to oppress ordinary citizens. It stood for economic privilege and served as a barrier to egalitarianism and equality of opportunity. Jackson acknowledged that certain inequalities resulted from varying degrees of talent, education and inherited wealth but believed these advantages should not be further increased by governmental favour. Jackson observed that 'many of our rich men have not been content with equal protection and equal benefits, but have besought us to make them richer by acts of Congress'.[36] The message resonated with those farmers and workers concerned with the march towards an aristocratic society dominated by bankers and merchants. The message was not well received in all quarters. Jackson's opponents effectively attacked his constitutional interpretation, the omission of the bank's real benefits and his assertion of new and expanded presidential powers. In the end, Jackson's popularity ensured his re-election and the bank's destruction.[37] The leading historian of the bank war, Robert V. Remini, argues that between the two proud, stubborn men, Jackson and Biddle, 'they crushed a useful institution that had provided the country with a sound currency and ample credit'.[38] Remini believes that because of its power and the potential for the misuse of that power the bank needed to be curbed, not killed. Failing to curb it, Jackson was right in destroying it.[39]

In 1833 Jackson followed up his veto by withdrawing government deposits from the Bank of the United States. Actually the Treasury deposited all new receipts in a small number of state banks and paid government expenses from its accounts at the Bank of the United States until they were exhausted. In reaction to the withdrawal and political defeat, Biddle contracted credit and brought on a minor panic. Jackson refused to yield and eventually the crisis passed. In 1836 two further actions impacted the financial system as the Bank of the United States was winding down its operations. The Deposit Act curtailed the Treasury's discretion in selecting deposit banks and increased their number from twenty to ninety, thereby reducing control over the 'pets'. The act also provided for the distribution of any surplus over $5 million to the states. In an effort to increase the use of specie and damp down a speculative mania in western lands Jackson issued the Specie Circular requiring payment for public land to be in gold and silver coins. All of these measures became political issues when depression began to sweep the nation a year later.[40]

The Panic of 1837 slowed, but did not stop the headlong expansion during the nineteenth century that took the United States from a small, insignificant backwater to a world class economic power. By the mid-1800s the population of the United States was doubling every twenty-three years and its economic output every fifteen. Not only the nation but many individuals were becoming wealthier. However, this long-term trend provided little immediate comfort to those Americans who lost jobs, farms, businesses and income during the late 1830s and early 1840s. Naturally, this dissatisfaction found expression in the political arena as the monetary and credit crisis of 1837 developed into a full-blown depression by 1839.[41]

Most historians now reject political action as the primary cause of the 1837–42 economic distress. They trace the financial and economic contraction to international forces over which the small American economy had little control. Contemporaries, however, searched for answers closer to home. Politicians of the time found the source of the hardships in the actions of their opponents, and their rhetoric dominated economic and monetary policy for the next decade. Henry Clay and the Whigs attributed the crisis to Andrew Jackson's attack on the Second Bank of the United States. Clay believed the failure to re-charter that institution, along with withdrawal of government funds in the bank's possession and the Specie Circular, undermined a strong currency and produced speculation, inflation and eventually the failure of many state banks. John C. Calhoun concurred in part of Clay's analysis. He conceded that unwarranted expansion of the currency induced reckless speculation, particularly in western land, and brought on the Panic. Calhoun argued, however, that it was not the withdrawal of the deposits from the Bank of the United States, but their redeposit in selected 'pet' banks that brought the inflation about. The new funds allowed the 'pets' to increase the money supply by issuing more bank notes. The Specie Circular, in Calhoun's opinion, compounded Jackson's error by draining specie from the East causing the overextended banks there to fail.[42]

The Democrats acknowledged the importance of inflation and overexpansion but attributed the disasters to the actions of bankers and speculators, not Jacksonian policy. Polk, then Speaker of the House of Representatives, denied any governmental responsibility. To Polk, a limited federal government possessed neither the power nor the responsibility to oversee the private sector. Since the government held no mandate to control or prevent 'the rage of wild speculation and over-trading, which are in fact the causes of their present sufferings and complaints', it should not shoulder any blame.[43] The real villains were the panic-makers whose efforts to embarrass the Jacksonians had got out of hand. Polk astutely recognized the international scope of the crisis and rightly pointed out that Great Britain, with a national bank, was experiencing the same liquidity problems as the United States. Senator Thomas Hart Benton's villains were bankers and politicians seeking to discredit the administration. He blamed the immediate crash on an over-issuance of bank notes inadequately backed by specie reserves.[44] The major effects of the initial phase, 1837–8, were primarily monetary and financial. Though produce prices and wages dropped sharply, they recovered and by 1839 signs of expansion began to appear. The unravelling of a large-scale cotton speculation by the United States Bank of Pennsylvania in the spring of 1839 forced that bank, the largest in the country, to suspend; it plunged the nation into depression. The main feature of the depression was severe deflation that reduced prices by 33 per cent. Americans continued to plant and produce at the old levels but received less money for their efforts. The decrease in the value of exports and internal trade reflect price adjustments, not changes in output. On a more positive note, the decrease in prices made American products more competitive and set the stage for a later recovery. In the meantime, the end of British investments stopped many large internal improvement projects underway in the western states. Cotton planters and labourers dependent on public works suffered most severely.[45]

Economic and financial hardships weakened both political parties and wrecked the two administrations preceding Polk's. As Martin Van Buren settled into the presidency in the spring of 1837, the storm broke. Among other problems, eighty-two of the eighty-eight banks holding government deposits ceased redeeming their notes with gold and silver coins. The suspension froze government funds and placed the depository banks in violation of the Resolution of 1816. This joint congressional resolution defined legal currency as notes of the Bank of the United States, specie, treasury notes and notes of specie-paying banks. With the demise of the Second Bank of the United States and retirement of the treasury notes, only specie and valid bank notes remained. Now, technically, the deposit banks' notes no longer constituted legal tender for the payment of taxes or government debts. Restricted by his philosophy of limited government and bound by prior Jacksonian policies, Van Buren took little action to address the problems faced by the economy as a whole. His primary goal devolved into protecting government funds and revenues by divorcing the government from the banks. Only in his last year did Van Buren, over strong opposition within his party, succeed in passing the Independent Treasury Act. Disaffection and recession proved too much for Van Buren's re-election bid in 1840. The Whigs now assumed responsibility for dealing with the crisis.[46]

The death of William Harrison within a month of his inauguration, and the accession of Vice-President John Tyler, ended any Whig chances of addressing the country's ills with a united front. Tyler, an anti-Jacksonian with conservative Democratic roots, rejected Henry Clay's economic activism. He signed the bill repealing the new Independent Treasury, but resolutely opposed efforts to charter a new national bank. Tyler believed that in the three prior presidential elections the people had condemned the national bank, 'pet' banks and the Independent Treasury. This left little else. Faced with the loss of government revenues he did, reluctantly, sign the protectionist Tariff Act of 1842. Fortunately, time proved to be an economic healer. The economy bottomed out in 1842 and began a recovery in 1843. Many banks in the large money centres also resumed specie payment allowing the government to return to the deposit bank system. By 1846 the American economy had sufficiently recovered to support the war effort.[47]

The revival of trade proved particularly beneficial to the government and dramatically restored its revenues. Receipts from custom duties, land sales and miscellaneous fees increased from $19,643,966 in calendar year 1842 to $28,504,519 for the fiscal year ending 30 June 1844. A further increase to $29,769,134 occurred in fiscal year 1845.[48] Customs duties provided over 90 per cent of all ordinary income. Americans disagreed whether the tariff should be protective or for revenue only, but they had long ago resolved that levies on imports should be the national government's main support. In 1845 duties were being collected under the protective tariff passed under Whig auspices in 1842. Democrats had attacked what they deemed its unfairness. Whigs, however, proclaimed it the saviour of the nation and the primary factor in the ongoing economic recovery. The surplus grew so rapidly in the latter part of his term that Tyler, in his final message to Congress, recommended investing excess revenues in a sinking fund to repay the new national debt incurred to finance the 1837–42 deficit. Tyler feared a large surplus would remove too much money from the private sector, thereby disrupting the money market and hampering trade. A sinking fund proved unnecessary as the redemption of maturing bonds and treasury notes absorbed most of the surplus.[49]

Robert J. Walker, Polk's new Secretary of the Treasury, lacked the Whigs' confidence in the continuing income-producing qualities of the existing tariff. By the first quarter of fiscal year 1846 (30 September 1845) it was evident to Walker that the tariff's protective features were restricting imports and lowering custom receipts. He noted a $2 million (20 per cent) drop in duties when compared to the same quarter in the previous year. Additionally, he estimated a decrease in revenue for all of fiscal year 1846 of $3 million and a further drop of $2 million in fiscal year 1847. The protective tariff was accomplishing its objective by encouraging American consumers to substitute domestic products for foreign imports. Walker noted a fall in the average duty rate from 37.84 per cent in calendar year 1843 to 29.9 per cent in fiscal year 1845. Political partisanship framed many of his assumptions and they proved unduly pessimistic. Duties fell only by $545,445 in fiscal year 1846 and increased land sales offset half of this, leaving a total decrease of $269,887. Increased military expenditures, not lack of revenues, unbalanced the budget.[50]

In the last full year of peace, fiscal year 1845, Congress appropriated $9,533,203 for the War Department and $6,228,639 for the navy. The army received $3,155,027 of the War Department's share with the remainder going for pensions, Indian Affairs, fortification, ordnance and the militia. In the fiscal year ending 30 June 1846, the War Department's expenditures climbed to $13,579,428 and the Navy Department's to $6,450,862. The Treasury Department estimated that $3,404,648 and $147,619 respectively of the increase was due to the onset of hostilities with Mexico in May 1846. Sufficient funds were on hand to pay this increased cost without borrowing. However, after reviewing the Treasury's deposit reports for June, July and August of 1846 the *United States Magazine and Democratic Review* concluded this could not continue. Beginning in July expenditures began to exceed revenues by over $2 million a month. The Treasury's cash reserves were fast disappearing.[51]

In March 1845 the new administration inherited $5,748,764 in available funds deposited in forty-five banks or other financial institutions, the mint in Philadelphia and branch mints located at Charlotte, North Carolina; Dahlonega, Georgia; and New Orleans. Deposits ranged from $35 at the Bank of Sandusky, Ohio, to $669,898 at Washington's Bank of the Metropolis. Except for Corcoran & Riggs and Francis Dodge, both of Washington, and Oliver Lee & Company of Buffalo, all the banks were corporations chartered by the states or, in the case of the District of Columbia banks, by Congress. New York City banks held $1,347,108 in deposits and the District of Columbia institutions a further $1,323,552. The government, at the mints, physically controlled only $390,199 of its own money.[52]

From March 1845 onward Walker strove, mostly by cutting back on debt reduction, to build up the Treasury's cash reserves. By December 1845 government funds on deposit, after deducting outstanding drafts, amounted to $8.3 million and peaked on 27 April 1846, at slightly over $12 million. Polk defended this action in his first annual message of 2 December 1845. He expressed sympathy with the desire to extinguish the existing public debt rapidly, but because of the unsettled relations with Mexico, he believed now was not the appropriate time. Prudence demanded an unusually large Treasury balance (see Table 1.1 for the Treasury's quarterly balances for March 1845 to March 1849).[53]

Rules set out in the Deposit Act of 23 June 1836 governed relationships between the deposit banks and the Treasury. Receipts were deposited in selected banks spread across the country. To receive government funds banks were required to maintain specie payments and to provide security adequate to protect the deposit. This additional security was usually in the form of good state or federal bonds deposited with the treasurer in Washington. Both the government and banks received significant benefits. Banks earned interest on the deposited securities and from commercial loans that were based on government money.

The deposits, being considered demand deposits, earned no interest for the government. The substantial services rendered the government at no cost reduced profits considerably. The banks paid government creditors, cashed treasury drafts, made the interest payments to holders of the federal government's debt obligations, stored coins in their vaults and transferred government funds around the country as needed. Whatever the advantages, Jacksonians such as Polk and Walker resented the use of government funds for private gain and were anxious to make changes. It was an open question, however, whether the Treasury could dispense with the assistance of the financial services industry.[54]

Table 1.1: Treasury Deposits[55]

Date	Amount ($)
24 March 1845	5,748,764
23 June 1845	7,344,934
30 September 1845	8,378,981
31 December 1845	8,299,686
30 March 1846	10,995,787
29 June 1846	9,310,258
21 September 1846	4,815,297
31 December 1846	2,947,163
29 March 1847	3,531,959
21 June 1847	6,144,196
20 September 1847	4,328,790
27 December 1847	4,200,339
27 March 1848	1,944,643
24 June 1848	1,638,112
25 September 1848	3,446,796
25 December 1848	4,314,165
26 February 1849	5,568,268

In many respects the financial environment had changed significantly by the mid-1840s. The destruction of the Second Bank of the United States and the discrediting of many incorporated banks in the wake of the 1837 Panic left a void in domestic and international exchange, note discounting and the marketing of securities. The country's lack of a standard paper currency and a national banking system compounded the problem and complicated the mercantile community's ability to transact business. Notes issued by the state banks served adequately for local trade, but not for long distances. Value of the notes varied according to a bank's reputation, its perceived ability to redeem its notes in coin and its distance from where the transaction was taking place. There was also a natural reluctance to ship specie all over the nation. Trade of any distance required acceptable credit instruments and bills of exchange.[56]

A new group of financiers operating as private or merchant bankers began to capture a large portion of the exchange, note discounting, stock brokerage and loan contracting business. Occasionally they accepted deposits and, on rare occasions, issued their own bank notes. Security for the bankers' clients rested on their reputation and honour. Most of these bankers, like William W. Corcoran, the House of Brown and George Peabody, began as wholesale merchants and evolved into banking by allowing other merchants, for a fee, to use their credit facilities. Typically, a merchant banker sold a domestic bill of exchange payable at a distant point (e.g. New York or Boston) to a merchant (in, e.g., St Louis, Chicago or Charleston) who owed money to a eastern manufacturer, importer or merchant. The local merchant then sent the bill of exchange to his creditor who presented the bill to the merchant banker's correspondent in New York or Boston and received payment. The bill of exchange might be payable on presentation (sight) or a specific number of days or months after presentation. In another scenario, the buyer gave the seller a note payable in the future. If the seller needed ready cash the note could be sold at a discount to a merchant banker. The banker could retain the note to maturity or endorse it and sell it to a commercial bank or other financial institution. The additional security provided by the endorsement increased the value of the note and provided the merchant banker with a small profit to compensate for his risk. In another situation, the merchant banker might, for a fee, issue a potential purchaser a letter of credit that most manufacturers and wholesalers accepted as cash and for which they gave the appropriate discounts. Since specie and capital were limited in the United States, most of its trade moved on credit with settlement months or years in the future. Merchant bankers served as a clearing house for the vast amount of bills of exchange and credit instruments moving across the nation. The cancelling of bills of exchange against one another greatly limited the amount of specie needed for the final settlement in both domestic and foreign trade.[57]

The financing of foreign trade was more specialized and limited to a relatively small number of large firms such as the House of Brown, Baring Brothers and that of George Peabody. The capital that financed most of America's foreign trade, particularly the important cotton exports, originated in London. That city was the international financial centre and clearing house. Foreign exchange meant the pound sterling and almost all bills of exchange to finance foreign trade were drawn in it. Typically, an agent for a British importer or cotton factor bought cotton in New Orleans and paid with, or allowed the seller to draw, a bill of exchange or other credit instrument payable at a future date in London. The bill might be payable by the importer or a British merchant banker specializing in the American trade. At the same time, a British manufacturer was selling goods on credit to a New York importer. The New York importer sold many of the goods in New Orleans. To complete the various payments the financial community, in essence, moved the New Orleans bill of exchange to New York in order to pay the New York merchant. The bill was then forwarded to Britain to pay the manufacturer. Actual collection from the original issuer, the British cotton importer, could be made at this time. In practice, the mass of bills of exchange on London were being commingled and bought and sold at every step. A thriving market for good bills existed.[58]

The most successful of the private bankers evolved into investment bankers and began to rise to the top of the securities industry. The Mexican War proved to be a major step in this process. It should be pointed out that investment banking was not a term in general use until the 1880s. Those engaged in the practice tended to continue using the old terms of private or merchant banker. However, by the end of the 1840s a portion of their business had moved beyond the scope of business practiced by other private bankers. In this study, an investment banker is defined as a professional middleman who purchases securities directly from the issuer and resells them to investors. He assumes the risk of any fall in price before resale and conversely, stands to gain if the securities are sold above the contract price. By contrast a broker or agent sells the securities on a commission basis and assumes no risk.[59]

The commercial banking industry was also undergoing change in the 1840s. The banks realized that if they were to survive crises such as that of 1837 and to prosper, they needed good professional management and liquidity. Presidents and cashiers, not the board of directors, began to assume responsibility for day-to-day operations. Also, every effort was made to maintain a reasonable specie reserve. Commercial banks in the eastern money centres were fast becoming deposit banks instead of primarily note issuers. Most of their borrowers were accepting deposits on which they drew drafts instead of walking out with bank notes. By 1855 deposits exceeded notes as the foremost bank liability in the nation as a whole. New York banks had passed this threshold a decade earlier. Except as an investment, the banks were abandoning government finance to others and concentrating on serving local merchants, manufacturers, speculators and businessmen. Bank officers as individuals, however, would prove enthusiastic participants in war financing.[60]

In addition to secure revenues and a viable financial system, the ability to adequately fund this new war on satisfactory terms depended on the federal government's credit-worthiness, its ability to carry additional debt and its credit history. The federal debt, before the Civil War, peaked at $127 million in 1816. Following the War of 1812 the nation made a strenuous effort to pay off its indebtedness. Nineteenth-century Americans attempted to abide by Thomas Jefferson's admonishment that each generation assume responsibility for its own public debt. Congress, in the Sinking Fund Trust Act of March 1817, mandated that $10 million a year be set aside to pay principal and interest. Occasionally a drop in revenues or the lack of government securities in the market at a reasonable price limited the ability to meet this goal. Despite drawbacks, the Treasury succeeded, between 1816 and 1829, in reducing the debt by $65.2 million. Additionally, funding operations successfully replaced the old securities with new ones paying a lesser interest rate. The John Quincy Adams administration, in particular, made great strides. It retired over $33 million of outstanding obligations in four years.[61]

As of January 1829, the national debt stood at $58 million divided into four major bond issues ranging from $13 to $19 million dollars and bearing interest at rates of 3 to 6 per cent. Liquidating this remaining debt was one of Andrew Jackson's highest priorities. In 1829, for example, almost half of the government's receipts went to pay $9,841,024 in principal and interest of $2,542,843. Helped by a healthy economy, large public land sales and peace, the Jacksonians, for all practical purposes, eliminated the debt in 1835. The Secretary of the Treasury reported in that year that only $291,000 remained outstanding and that the Treasury possessed sufficient funds to redeem the remainder, when and if the securities were presented. It appears some of the debt certificates were lost or destroyed. This was the last time the national government would be debt-free. The exhaustion of the Treasury after the beginning of the Panic of 1837 and accumulated deficits over the next five years of $31 million brought a new national debt.[62]

Believing the crisis in 1837 to be temporary, President Van Buren and Congress agreed to alleviate the government's cash shortage by issuing $10 million of one-year treasury notes to be sold at par or issued in payment to public creditors. The Treasury was authorized to pay up to 6 per cent. The usual provision making the notes receivable for public dues allowed the notes to retain their value but further reduced actual cash coming into the Treasury as importers made use of the notes instead of specie. From 1837 to March 1843 Congress authorized eight treasury note issues in an effort to fund the deficit and redeem maturing short-term notes. In all, $51 million in notes were authorized and $47 million actually issued. Interest rates varied from 0.1 per cent to 6 per cent, but $28 million carried the highest rate.[63] In an effort to retire the short-term obligations and place the finances on a more solid foundation, Congress authorized three bond issues totalling $21 million (see Table 1.2). In marketing these bonds investment bankers began to emerge as a factor in federal finance. John Ward & Company headed syndicates that purchased part of the second loan and over 90 per cent of the third. Commercial banks, however, remained dominant, even in the syndicates headed by Ward.[64]

Table 1.2: Bond Issues, 1841–3[65]

Legal Authority	Amount Authorized ($)	Actually Issued ($)	Length (years)	Interest Rate (%)	Price Received
Act of 21 July 1841	12,000,00	5,672,977	3	5.4–6	par
Act of 15 April 1842	17,000,000	8,343,886	20.67	6	2.5% discount
Act of 3 March 1843	indefinite	7,004,231	10	5	1–3.75 % premium

Economic recovery allowed the rapid retirement of the first of these loans, the Loan of 1841, and most of the treasury notes. To facilitate the redemption of the notes Secretary of the Treasury J. C. Spencer issued a public notice on 6 April 1843, advising of the Treasury's intention to redeem all treasury notes issued prior to 1 July 1842, or becoming due by 30 June 1843. The notes were to be redeemed with money, not bonds or other treasury notes. Interest ceased on those not presented by 30 June 1843. Spencer followed this announcement with another on 28 June 1843, notifying creditors that interest would cease on all remaining notes as of their due date.[66] By Polk's inauguration, 4 March 1845, the national debt had been reduced to $17,788,799 in various issues and types of obligations (see Table 1.3).[67]

Table 1.3: United States National Debt, 3 March 1845[68]

Debt	Amount ($)
Old funded and unfunded debt (prior to 1837)	176,451
Treasury Notes dating from the War of 1812	4,371
Certificates of the Mississippi Stock	4,320
Debts of the Corporate Cities of the District of Columbia	1,200,000
Treasury Notes Issued, 1837–43	1,244,779
Loan of 1841, 6%	210,815
Loan of 1842 (due 1862), 6%	8,343,886
Loan of 1843 (due 1853), 5%	6,604,231
	17,788,853

The federal government had scrupulously honoured its debt obligations since its inception; however, its credit standing abroad in 1845 was low. Efforts by an American commission to secure a European loan in 1842 were rebuffed by James Rothschild with the comment that 'you may tell your government that you have seen the man who is at the head of the finances of Europe, and that he has told you that you cannot borrow a dollar, not a dollar'.[69] Though Rothschild over-stated his importance, at least in American financing, most European capitalists and financiers shared his anger.[70]

The roots of European ire lay in the large debts incurred by the states, much of which were used to finance internal improvement projects started in the 1830s. Work on many of the projects ceased when the Panic of 1837 hit. The states, faced with the prospect of raising taxes to pay the interest or defaulting, reacted in different ways. Of the seventeen indebted states and the Territory of Florida (statehood 3 March 1845), nine continued to meet their obligations while eight – Pennsylvania, Maryland, Louisiana, Indiana, Illinois, Arkansas, Mississippi and Michigan – plus Florida ceased paying interest. Mississippi and Michigan repudiated part of their debt. Nine states were debt free. Polk's Tennessee was hard hit and had to repeal its internal improvement programme, but managed to stay solvent. As governor, Polk expressed a willingness to raise taxes, if necessary, to meet existing obligations.[71]

The Times of London reflected the bitterness of the British well-to-do. The blame for its deservedly low credit standing, *The Times* believed, lay in America's democratic principles and its lack of tradition. Governments at all levels were too beholden to the masses. The paper condemned the defaulting states, the failure to adequately tax the populace and the protective tariff that restricted British trade. The paper believed Americans must sink to the lowest depths before improvement could be expected.[72] The British public felt robbed and blamed all things American. It must be added, that the contempt of *The Times* for Mexican commercial honour was even greater. In respect to Mexico, it reasoned that any government that spent its limited resources on internal squabbling and failed to pay its just debts deserved the rough handling it was about to receive from the Americans. The main concern of *The Times* with any war between the United States and Mexico was the disruption of British–Mexican commerce.[73]

By 1 January 1843, state debts totalled $231,642,111, ten times the debt of the federal government. Influential individuals on both sides of the Atlantic demanded action by the national government. In 1842 and 1843 Congress considered the issue but refused to act. The most widely discussed plan envisioned the federal government issuing $200 million in its own debt obligations to the states. The distribution would be proportionate, without consideration of the actual state indebtedness. Proponents urged it as a means of giving credit to commerce, agriculture and manufacturing. During the third session of the Twenty-Seventh Congress both houses considered the measure and rejected it as too burdensome and a dangerous precedent.[74] Paying British creditors never received top priority from most Americans.

Nonetheless, on the eve of war the economic and financial outlook of the United States had considerably improved during the last four years. Government revenues comfortably exceeded ordinary expenses. The Treasury possessed a sufficient cash reserve to finance mobilization and the initial stages of the war.

Though American credit remained shaky abroad, at home United States 6 per cent bonds were selling well above par.

The outlook in Mexico was entirely different. In 1800, Mexico, or New Spain, was the crown jewel of the Spanish empire. The annual vice-regal administration's revenues for the first decade of the nineteenth century were sufficient to pay local administrative expenses and remit 2 or 3 million pesos a year to the royal Treasury in Spain. Its population of 6 million exceeded that of the newly independent republic to the north. Mining and agriculture were productive and commerce thrived. By 1845 the situation had reversed. The United States possessed one of the world's great merchant fleets, its foreign trade exceeded Mexico's by almost six times, its manufacturing sector produced ten times more goods and its population of 20 million surpassed Mexico's by 250 per cent. Only in the military officer corps did Mexico possess greater numbers.[75]

Mexico's War of Independence from Spain began in 1810 and continued, with varying levels of intensity, for eleven years. At its end, agriculture, mining and commerce lay in ruin. The new imperial government of General Agustin de Iturbide faced a bankrupt Treasury, high expectation on the part of its supporters and serious opposition from a large sector of the population demanding a republic. Raising sufficient funds to pay the army and maintain an efficient bureaucracy posed Iturbide's most serious challenge. The devastation of economic life limited tax revenues. Efforts to curry political favour by eliminating the most unpopular of the levies imposed by the old regime brought further reductions. Unable to support itself from the reduced revenues the government cut official salaries, imposed new taxes, resorted to forced loans and issued paper money. Popular discontent arising from these measures forced Emperor Iturbide's resignation on 19 March 1823.[76]

Political instability continuously racked Mexico and prevented economic and financial recovery. Between 1821 and 1856 fifty-three different administrations governed under four different constitutional arrangements. Twelve of these administrations attempted to deal with the crisis with the United States between 1844 and 1848. During the period leading up to the war Mexicans were fiercely and violently trying to decide whether they wanted a centralized republic (Centralists), a federal republic with extensive powers vested in the states (Federalists) or an empire (Royalists). Class conflict, regionalism, great distances and poor communication hindered Mexico's efforts to become a nation state. Numerous revolts and disturbances required all governments, of whatever stripe, to maintain a sizeable army for their own protection.

The economic elite contributed to the government's upkeep reluctantly, and with expenses consistently exceeding income, the only recourse seemed retrenchment or borrowing. Cutting back was unpopular with the military and civil bureaucracy and led to unrest and revolution. An inefficient tax administration and widespread corruption added to the government's woes. Smuggling, bribery of officials and diversion of receipts severely reduced income. The well-to-do had little faith in government promises and concentrated on individual and class well-being. At first the Mexican government believed the shortfall in revenue was temporary and that peace and independence would restore prosperity. It was simply a matter of covering temporary deficits with loans.[77]

The British money market was the infant Mexican republic's first recourse. During 1824 Mexico contracted two loans of £3.2 million (16 million pesos) each. The first loan agreement, 7 February 1824, stipulated that 16 million pesos of thirty-year 5 per cent bonds were to be issued to the underwriters, Goldschmidt and Company. The bonds were valued at 50 per cent of their face but Mexico did not receive this amount. From gross proceeds of 8 million pesos the underwriter deducted the first two years of interest, a sinking fund contribution, commissions and fees. Bonds with a face value of 16 million pesos yielded 5.7 million in cash to Mexico. Mexico pledged its general revenue and, additionally, assigned one-third of the customs receipts from its Gulf of Mexico ports. The process of pledging specific revenues for loans would keep the government starved for cash for most of its existence. Mexico obtained somewhat better terms from Barclay, Herring, Richardson and Company on the second loan. The banker sold the 16 million peso issue of 6 per cent bonds at 86.75 (86 pesos and 75 centavos per each 100 pesos in bonds), yielding 13,880,000 pesos. Commissions, prepaid interest, sinking fund contributions and a 1.5 million peso loss when the banking house failed reduced actual proceeds to less than 10 million. Three million of this went to pay off part of the prior loan.[78]

As the new funds, supplemented by foreign investment in mining and to a lesser extent commerce, filtered through the economy, trade and agriculture revived. In 1826 and 1827 increased tax revenues, coupled with a reduction of military expenditures, almost balanced the budget. By this time the proceeds of the two foreign loans had been spent on the most pressing domestic debts, military supplies and current administrative expenses including overdue salaries and pensions. Revolution dashed the growing hope of financial stability for the Mexican Treasury. In September 1827 the government defaulted on its foreign debt. Though the terms of the debt were renegotiated several times, the Mexican Treasury never consistently met its obligations. At the beginning of 1846 Mexico owed her British bondholders about 56 million pesos. With credit non-existent abroad, Mexico faced the prospects of relying on her own resources in waging war against the United States.[79]

Most of Mexico's twenty-five years of deficits were financed by internal borrowing. In 1846 these debts stood at 100 million pesos. Since propertied Mexicans were reluctant to advance funds, government financing passed into the hands of Mexican and foreign merchants called *Agiotistas*. Typically, they advanced short-term funds at high interest rates with pledges of specific government incomes or assets as security. Advances consisted of a mix of cash and depreciated government debt obligations. During the period 1838 to 1845 domestic loans of 47 million pesos produced less than half that amount in cash. Short-term relief only compounded long-term problems. In 1841, for example, 62 per cent of custom duties, the most important revenue source, were assigned to local capitalists, and one-sixth to foreign creditors, leaving only a little over 21 per cent for the Treasury. Important government assets such as the mint franchise and valuable mines also passed into the possession of the moneylenders. Lending carried considerable risk as the hard-pressed government often reneged on pledges and recaptured assets. Influence reduced the risk. By 1846 the government was unable to function without the *Agiotistas*.[80]

The Catholic Church possessed the one large block of wealth that might have provided the resources for a nation fighting for its territorial integrity. Precedent existed in both the vice-regency and republic for tapping this source. Bequests, gifts, purchases and mortgage foreclosures had made the Church the largest urban and rural landholder in the country. Its funds financed much of Mexico's commerce and underwrote many of the largest private landholdings. If the Church was required to suddenly call in these outstanding loans it might mean ruin for many well-to-do and influential Mexicans. In the past, when unable to avoid government levies, the church was often forced to sell property which then passed into the possession of the moneylenders. With little to show for its previous sacrifices the Church proved, in this crisis, a reluctant lender.[81]

Because Mexico lacked money, revenues and credit many doubted her ability and will to fight. The *Washington Union* believed Mexico could wage war only with British help. The paper concluded that both the Mexican army and Treasury were too disorganized to be effective.[82] *The Times* shared the *Union*'s appraisal of both the army and Treasury, holding out little prospect of a loan and reporting that a lack of funds had reduced Mexico's Army of the North to 'a state of absolute destitution'.[83] But, as historian Justin Smith points out, she did fight or at least found men willing to fight in her name.[84]

2 IDEOLOGY, REVENUE AND FINANCIAL SYSTEM

James K. Polk entered the White House determined to pass the Jacksonian financial agenda and to expand the nation's boundaries. He had devoted his career to furtherance of Jacksonian policies and refused to allow war, the threat of war or national divisions to detract from his mission. Besides the annexation of Texas, Polk set four major goals for his administration: settlement of the Oregon question, acquisition of California, passage of a revenue tariff and re-establishment of the Independent Treasury. By the late spring of 1846 the foreign agenda was well underway, thought not as Polk wished or expected. As unsatisfactory as many Americans found it, the division of the Oregon Territory along the 49th parallel did provide a clear title up to that point and allowed settlement to begin in earnest. Upon the outbreak of war with Mexico the administration took immediate steps to occupy California and New Mexico.[1] Political opposition and the war itself, however, placed the domestic measures in doubt. Polk, watching fretfully from the White House, pressed the Democrats in Congress for action. 'I considered the public good', he subsequently informed Senator Dixon Lewis, 'as well as my own power and the glory of my administration, depended in a great degree upon my success in carrying them through Congress'.[2] At the beginning of the summer few indications were present that the first session of the Twenty-Ninth Congress would, according to historian Charles Sellers, 'be the most remarkable congressional session of the nineteenth century'.[3] The financial and monetary issues that racked the Jacksonian era were nearing settlement.[4]

War financing introduced the one new element in the decade-long controversy over financial issues and the powers of the federal government. Otherwise, neither the administration's programme nor the political rhetoric offered anything different. Debates during the Jackson, Van Buren and Tyler presidencies had exhausted the ideas of supporters and opponents of tariff reform, the Independent Treasury, a warehousing system and the graduated sale of public land. Democrats pushed the measures and Whigs opposed them for ideological reasons, but it soon became clear to both that any new reforms must bear the stress of war. Change might affect the public perception and confidence. Lenders, in particular, would evaluate any new revenue bill's capacity to produce sufficient taxes to pay, in addition to ordinary expenses, the interest and principal on loans contracted. Additionally, changes in the Treasury Department's structure might improve or hinder its ability to collect the revenues and transfer funds to New Orleans and on to Mexico.

Charles Sellers, Polk's leading biographer, believes 'Polk's goals represented, on the one hand, a morally admirable agrarian social philosophy that was by his time so anachronistic as to be reactionary, and on the other, an arrogant though innocent racism and national chauvinism that have been the adverse of the finer tendencies of the American experience'.[5] Time may have passed Polk's ideas and beliefs by but rustic he was not. Polk descended from a southern gentry family that operated plantations and engaged in land speculation, first in Mecklenburg County (Charlotte), North Carolina, and later in Tennessee. He was educated at the University of North Carolina and in the law office of Felix Grundy (a future Attorney General of the United States). By the time of his inauguration his résumé included seven terms as a congressman, two as Speaker of the House of Representatives and one as governor of Tennessee. He had been widely exposed to national issues and all classes and occupations.[6]

For most of his public career, Polk represented the yeoman farmers, small plantation owners, country merchants and land speculators of middle Tennessee. He shared their beliefs in states' rights, an enduring federal union with limited powers and equal opportunity. Nothing in his career or the attitude of his constituents suggested a disdain for profit or commercial endeavours. Polk's brothers-in-law, and major supporters, engaged in merchandising, banking, mail contracting and newspaper publishing. Throughout his life, Polk attempted, by practising law, land speculation and planting, to achieve financial independence. He succeeded well enough to maintain his position in the slave-owning planter class, although he never attained great wealth. As late as 1842 he was attempting to stave off financial disaster by obtaining a loan from northern capitalists. Polk's financial problems of this period relate mostly to the expense of establishing a new cotton plantation in Mississippi. Though unsuccessful in borrowing, he managed to muddle through. Politics determined many of his attitudes. Small Tennessee towns such as Columbia, Fayetteville and Clarksville supported Polk. The larger cities – Nashville, Memphis and Knoxville – with their wholesale merchants and bankers, backed the enemy, the Whigs.[7]

Regardless of ideology or outlook, Polk was first and foremost a determined politician operating primarily on the national stage. Even his gubernatorial campaigns were waged on national issues, often to his detriment. His sudden emergence as the first dark horse presidential candidate in 1844 did not mean he lacked a political history. 'I have been too long in public life, and my opinions are too deeply rooted, for me now to change either my political associations or principles', he reminded the Tennessee electorate in 1839.[8] In the same address he reiterated his opposition to Henry Clay's American System, the Bank of the United States, high tariffs and federally financed internal improvements. He supported removal of the deposits, economical government, the Independent Treasury and a revenue tariff. In 1845 he retained the same views and remained a firm Jacksonian.[9]

Polk pledged in his inaugural address 'to assume no powers not expressly granted or clearly implied in its terms [Constitution]'.[10] He viewed himself as the head of a government of limited and delegated powers created by a federative compact binding together the states in a social union. To preserve this union the compromises, particularly in respect to slavery, must not be disturbed. Polk's theory of limited government did not prevent him from approaching the presidency in the manner of his mentor, Andrew Jackson. Polk proved to be a more involved and controlling chief magistrate than even Jackson himself.

Members of the cabinet first felt Polk's determination to impose his authority over the executive branch. In offering cabinet positions Polk extracted several promises from the six nominees – James Buchanan, Secretary of State; Robert J. Walker, Secretary of the Treasury; William Marcy, War Department; historian and politician George Bancroft, Secretary of the Navy; John Y. Mason, Attorney General; and Cave Johnson, Postmaster General. First, since he had committed himself to only one term, he demanded, in an effort to prevent dissension, that no cabinet member actively campaign for the 1848 presidential nomination. Second, their views on policy must correspond to his and the 1844 Democratic platform. Finally, he demanded they remain in Washington attending to government business and not be absent for long periods. Polk intended to work hard during his term and expected his chief subordinates to do likewise. Lower level government employees did not escape scrutiny. To ensure they discharged their duties faithfully and earnestly, Polk required bureau chiefs to maintain a log of employee absences and submit monthly reports. Further, the work must be fairly distributed and idleness, negligence and incompetency addressed by supervisors.[11]

Before Polk's presidency, the various departments and bureaus submitted their budget estimates directly to Congress for consideration. Polk was the first president to institute a policy of presidential review before the estimates were forwarded. He was not reluctant to demand revisions, usually downward.[12] Lack of military experience failed to deter Polk from exercising the duties of commander-in-chief and actively directing the war effort. Nor did he wait passively while Congress leisurely considered vital programmes. The Democratic congressional leadership was summoned to the White House for consultation and strategy sessions. At Polk's urging the administration's press organ, the *Wash-*

ington Union, turned up the heat on the party faithful in its columns. Much to the anger of the Whigs, cabinet members, at Polk's request, visited the Capitol during critical votes to rally the Democrats.[13]

Traditionally, the Treasury Department considered itself an independent fiefdom. Not surprising, in light of his views on presidential responsibility, Polk disagreed. As early as 1833 he affirmed that the secretary of the Treasury was not independent of the president. The secretary held office at the president's pleasure and subject to dismissal whenever the president felt it necessary.[14] The department's control over public monies and Secretary Walker's reputation further ensured Polk's vigilance. Almost with his last breath, Andrew Jackson had warned Polk against Walker. Jackson acknowledged Walker's talents and believed him personally honest, but advised Polk that Walker was 'surrounded by so many broken speculators, and being greatly himself encumbered with debt, that any of the other department would have been better, and I fear, you will find my forebodings turn out too true'.[15]

Walker and his subordinates retained considerable influence and authority in advocating and carrying out economic and financial policy. The administration's domestic programmes were, in fact, a joint collaboration between Polk and Walker. Fortunately, at this point in time, both held similar views. Whereas Polk's Jacksonian principles remained consistent, Walker's changed to meet his surroundings and times. Born in Pennsylvania, the son of a federal judge, and married into the prominent Bache family of Philadelphia, he migrated to Mississippi in 1826 to seek his fortune in the law and speculating in Native American (Choctaw) lands. Along the way he shed his protectionist heritage and became a forceful defender of slavery and southern rights. A credit contraction in the early 1830s almost bankrupted him and his speculator friends. In frustration he temporarily supported efforts to re-charter the Bank of the United States. By 1836, he had mended his fences with the Jacksonians and was elected to the Senate in that year as a firm supporter of Democratic orthodoxy. In the Senate, Walker championed southern rights, advocated a liberal land policy that favoured the common man (and land speculators) and pushed for the annexation of Texas. In furtherance of the Texas policy, he successfully opposed Martin Van Buren's bid for the presidential nomination at the Baltimore convention in 1844. Walker's machinations deadlocked the convention and allowed Polk's supporters to procure his nomination. By 1845 Walker's political creed embodied opposition to protectionism, federally financed internal improvements and a national bank. He supported rapid development of the public lands, hard money, expansionism and an Independent Treasury.[16]

Both Walker and Polk understood the divisiveness of the tariff in the country and their own party. Immediately after Polk unexpectedly received the nomination, Walker advised him that it was the one issue that might defeat the

Democrats. Walker believed the party's pledge to annex Texas would carry the South but not the manufacturing states, especially the critical state of Pennsylvania. He implored Polk to 'go as far as your principles will permit for incidental protection'.[17] Polk needed little advice on how critically his free trade history might be viewed in the north-east and Middle Atlantic states. No hope existed for carrying New England, but Pennsylvania and New York were vital. On 19 June 1844, he made a major effort to allay the fears of Pennsylvanians. He kept his comments short and ambiguous.[18] In the famous (or infamous) Kane Letter, Polk indicated he favoured

> a tariff for revenue, such as one as will yield a sufficient amount to the Treasury to defray the expenses of the government economically administered. In adjusting the details of a revenue tariff, I have heretofore sanctioned such moderate discriminating duties as would produce the amount of revenue needed, and at the same time afford reasonable incidental protection to our home industries. I am opposed to a tariff for protection merely, and not for revenue.[19]

The key issue of what constituted reasonable incidental protection went undefined.[20] In the South, Democratic stalwarts argued it meant a revenue tariff with low rates. Pennsylvania Democrats, on the other hand, assured their constituents that it provided adequate protection to the critical iron and coal industries.[21]

Once elected Polk made his views clear in his inaugural address and then gave his domestic programme substance in his first annual message to Congress the following December. He proposed a tariff based on a revenue standard with rates set at the lowest point that would produce the necessary revenue. Goods such as tea, coffee and salt used by poorer citizens would be free or taxed at a low rate. To Polk, the Tariff of 1842 provided protection only for the manufacturers. By raising prices it increase the cost of living, particularly for the poor and working classes. Under his proposal, Polk argued, all the great interests of the country, agriculture, commerce, shipping and manufacturing benefited. Manufacturers would receive sufficient protection under a revenue standard. Polk further recommended the rates be computed on the value of the item, the *ad valorem* principle, and not a specific amount based on ton, yard or other measurement.[22] Besides tariff reform, Polk recommended a return to the Independent Treasury system. In his view the Bank of the United States and the state banks had in turn proven faithless and untrustworthy. He believed the framers of the constitution and members of the first Congress had envisioned a public treasury under control of responsible government officials. This agency, and no other, should collect and disburse public funds. Further, Polk recommended that all transactions of this new institution be made in specie. To those who argued that the money was safer in the banks, Polk replied that a people capable of self-government were competent to look after their own funds.[23]

Walker immediately followed up on Polk's message in his Treasury Report of 3 December 1845. In connection with the revenues he recommended legislation based on six general principles.

> 1st. That no more money should be collected than is necessary for the wants of the government, economically administered.
>
> 2nd. That no duty be imposed on any article above the lowest rate which will yield the largest amount of revenue.
>
> 3rd. That below such rate discrimination may be made, descending in the scale of duties; Or, for imperative reasons, the article may be placed in the list of those free from all duties.
>
> 4th. That the maximum revenue duty should be imposed on luxuries.
>
> 5th. That all minimum, and all specific duties, should be abolished, and *Ad Valorem* duties substituted in their place – care being taken to guard against fraudulent invoices and under valuation, and to assess the duty upon the actual market value.
>
> 6th. That the duty should be so imposed as to operate as equally as possible through-out the Union, discriminating neither for nor against any class or section.[24]

At this time Walker neither suggested rates nor estimated the effects on revenues. He devoted his efforts to countering protectionists' arguments as to the benefits of a high tariff.

Walker pointed out that the manufacturing sector employed the small number of 400,000 workers and only 10 per cent received any benefit from a protective tariff. The main beneficiaries were a small number of wealthy capitalists. The worst consequence was the increased cost of domestic goods sheltered behind the tariff. Walker estimated the tariff cost American consumers $27 million in duties passed on and an additional $54 million from price increases by domestic producers.

The Whigs in the Senate did not allow these comments to go unchallenged. In response to the Senate's inquiry as to the source and accuracy of these figures, Treasury Department clerks analysed the impact of the tariff on the price of sixteen leading import items, including iron, manufactured tobacco and cotton goods. As a result, Walker revised his estimate of the impact on consumers. Walker estimated that $500 million worth of goods sold to American consumers received some protection. Domestic producers were able to raise their prices on the protected items. Based on the price enhancements found on the sixteen items, he concluded that the tariff increased the price of the $500 million of protected goods by $142 million. The government received $28 million of this sum in duties and domestic producers the rest. Walker argued that the major interest in the United States was agriculture and with its excellent soil the country could produce far more than it could consume. Since the small manufacturing population did not provide a sufficient market, exportation of the surplus seemed the only recourse. A policy of free trade, Walker believed, would greatly increase the sale of American produce.[25]

Walker portrayed the Independent Treasury as a currency reform measure. In addition to keeping the Treasury's funds safe, the use of specie in government transactions would increase its usage throughout the economy and make the nation's currency more stable, to the benefit of all classes. Walker expected the widespread use of specie and withdrawal of government deposits to restrict the banks' ability to over-expand, thereby halting the boom–bust cycle so detrimental to the country. The manufacturing section, Walker surmised, had the most to gain from a stable currency and orderly expansion.[26]

The old rhetoric concerning fairness, taxing one section or class for the benefit of another, free trade as a stimulus for exports and protecting the standard of living for American workers did not hide the new and vital question of war financing. Both parties acknowledged that ordinary income was insufficient and loans would be necessary to support an enlarged military. Adequate federal revenues would be vital in marketing the debt obligations at a reasonable price. The debate on the tariff began in earnest during the early summer of 1846 and the Whigs began to develop their central themes. They argued that the Tariff of 1842 had a proven record of revenue production and that wartime was not the moment for experimentation. Whigs believed that under Walker's plan tariff duties would fall $5 to $7 million unless imports increased. Their greatest fear was that a reduction in the rates would result in a great influx of foreign merchandise. If imports flooded in, the Whigs feared the export of specie to pay for the goods would cause tight credit and a financial panic with disastrous consequences for manufacturing and commerce. The Democrats defended the revenue qualities of the bill and argued that exports would rise to offset higher imports. They anticipated balancing trade at a higher level for both.[27]

James McKay (Democrat, North Carolina) brought the House debate to a close on 2 July 1846. He explained that the earlier bill, introduced in April, anticipated an income of $22 million in customs and $2.4 million from land sales and miscellaneous fees. This amount would have sufficed for peacetime since ordinary expenses were estimated at only $24 million a year. McKay acknowledged that circumstances had changed in the interim. Personally, McKay desired a short war, without territorial acquisitions, and no war taxes. However, a majority of the Ways and Means Committee did not agree, and as chairman, he felt an obligation to press for the amendments they favoured. Therefore, he proposed retaining tea and coffee on the free list, but rearranging the tax schedules to increase total revenue. In a series of amendments approved by the House acting as a Committee of the Whole, McKay secured changes increasing the uppermost rate on luxury items to 100 per cent, creating a new 40 per cent schedule for items such as expensive furniture and spices, and moving beer, ale and china to the 30 per cent schedule. Iron, coal and sugar remained at 30 per cent. After an effort to kill the bill by making salt tax free, to the detriment of New York salt manufacturers, it passed on 3 July 1846 by a vote of 114–95.[28]

The struggle in the more evenly divided Senate proved serious indeed. Senator Dixon Lewis (Democrat, Alabama), Chairman of the Finance Committee, introduced the House bill and urged passage. Lewis argued that the overall effective rate was 21.5 per cent and that such a rate would produce at least $28 million in customs revenue. He conceded that if imports remained the same as in fiscal year 1845 Treasury receipts from customs would total only $23.9 million. He anticipated, however, a sufficient increase in imports and population to produce an additional $4.47 million. In the long term, Lewis predicted, imports would average $154 million for the years 1847 through 1851, yielding duties in excess of $33 million annually. The effective rate varied according to the view of the advocate or opponent. Lewis believed it to be 21.5 per cent, Daniel Webster, 23.5 per cent, and the *New York Herald*, 22 per cent. In support of the Democrats, Walker provided his own estimates on 16 July. According to Walker, the United States imported $104 million of dutiable articles in fiscal year 1845 and under the House bill this amount would yield $24.5 million in duties. An additional $2.4 million could be anticipated from population growth likely to occur between June 1845 and November 1847. Finally, Walker believed increased imports would produce a further $4 million giving a final figure of slightly less than $31 million for the first full year, 1 December 1846 through 30 November 1847, of the law's operations.[29]

Whig senators immediately challenged the Democrats' projections. Senator George Evans of Maine argued that even if Lewis correctly estimated the effective rate, revenues would fall $3 million short of his total figure of $28.5 million. Further, if the Treasury obtained the $30 million in customs Walker estimated, the nation must import $140 million in goods. Evans doubted the country's ability to pay for so much. He also raised the spectre of large-scale fraud if the Treasury used foreign invoices to compute the *ad valorem* rates. Daniel Webster was equally pessimistic; he projected revenue, after expenses, of less than $20 million under the House bill. He increased Evan's estimates of required imports to $157 million and questioned whether sufficient specie existed in the country to pay the foreign sellers and the duties. The key moment proved to be a tie procedural vote that required Vice-President George Mifflin Dallas to cast the deciding vote. Political loyalty to the Polk administration came high to Dallas, a Pennsylvania patrician, deeply concerned about the reaction in his home state. Ironically, as a senator in 1832 he had introduced the bill extending the charter of the Second Bank of the United States that led to Jackson's veto. Further, his father, Alexander James Dallas, as Secretary of the Treasury (1814–16), had successfully manoeuvred the bill creating the bank through Congress. The Democrats eventually managed to pass the House bill with only slight modification on 28 July 1846, by a vote of 28–27.[30]

In its final form the Tariff Act of 1846 established eight tax schedules ranging from 5 per cent to 100 per cent and a large free list that included gold, silver, coffee, tea, copper, raw cotton, guano and fishery products. History provides the best gauge of the new law's revenue potential. As late as December 1846 Walker projected tariff revenues of $27.8 million for the fiscal year ending 30 June 1847. Much to his embarrassment, weak imports for the months preceding the effective date of 1 December 1846, caused duties to fall $4 million short of this figure. However, for fiscal year 1848 duties yielded $31,757,974, fell to $28,346,739 for fiscal year 1849, rebounded to $39,668,686 for 1850, soared to $49,017,567, for 1851, and dipped slightly to $47,339,326 in 1852. Increased trade after Britain's repeal of her Corn Laws and the California Gold Rush brought a prosperity that destroyed all revenue projections.[31]

Unlike the tariff, the Independent Treasury bill, a hotly contested and divisive issue throughout the Van Buren administration, moved through both houses of Congress with relative ease. The House of Representatives began consideration on 30 March 1846, and passed the bill on 2 April. The debate revolved around the effects on the economy of withdrawing the federal deposits from the banks and mandating the exclusive use of specie in government transactions. The Democrats believed such action a boon both to the government and public. Governmental use of specie would increase the metal in circulation, thereby improving the currency. At the same time the banks' inability to over-issue their own notes, because of an increased need for specie, would check the boom–bust cycles. The Whigs expected a credit crunch if $10 million in specie were withdrawn from circulation and locked in government vaults. Further, they feared the specie policy would lead to a loss of public confidence in bank notes, the most common medium of exchange. Whigs questioned the need to tinker with a system that kept Treasury funds secure and available for use by the public.[32] Doubts were also expressed as to the efficiency of Treasury operations under the new, untried system. Whig Congressman Garret Davis expressed the belief that the new organization's operations would be 'far less convenient, expeditious, and inferior in every respect'.[33] If the only criteria were collecting, paying and safekeeping of public funds, Davis had a valid point. Besides the safety provided by bank vaults, the convenience of both the public and government would be better served by paying out treasury drafts through bank tellers rather than federal officers.

Upon its arrival in the Senate the Independent Treasury bill disappeared for almost four months as Senator Lewis made good on his promise to give precedence to the tariff and warehousing bills. Even Daniel Webster's sarcasm failed to force the bill from the Finance Committee until Lewis and Senator John Dix of New York were ready. Finally, on 31 July 1846, shortly after passage of the tariff, the Whig stalwarts received their opportunity to denounce the measure. The tactics of condemning change and experimentation in the midst of war again failed. The debate did make the money market nervous and fulfilled the Whigs' prophecy of a tightening of credit. United States 6 per cent bonds ($100 par) fell from 115 to 105. Daniel Webster, the primary Whig spokesman, argued the new system would hinder government's effort to float the new loan authorized 22 July 1846. Borrowing $10 million in specie would be difficult, he predicted. Webster correctly anticipated the involvement of investment bankers in placing the securities. He believed it would prove impossible for the investment bankers to borrow sufficient specie from the banks to purchase bonds from the Treasury. An issue of treasury notes, however, Webster argued, would alleviate part of the damage caused by withdrawal of the deposits and provide a substitute circulating medium. Treasury notes could be issued to public creditors and not sold. The Democrats passed the measure on 1 August 1846, by a vote of 28–25.[34]

The new Independent Treasury was a unit of the Treasury Department, not its successor. As a percentage of personnel it was tiny. The major units of the Treasury were the customs service, land office (until 1849) and the administrative officers in Washington. The 1846 act only governed the manner in which government funds were controlled and disbursed. It did not affect the other functions of the department. The custom service and land offices continued to collect the duties, taxes and revenue from land sales. However, the Independent Treasury did collect the loan proceeds.[35]

The first Congress created the Treasury Department in 1789. The legislation provided for a Secretary of the Treasury, an Assistant Secretary, a Comptroller, an Auditor, a Treasurer and a Register. In 1830 Congress added a Solicitor to provide legal advice. During Walker's term the Washington office was divided into the Offices of the Secretary, Treasurer, Register, Solicitor, First and Second Comptrollers, First, Second, Third, Fourth and Fifth Auditors and the Post Office Auditor. In Washington 300 permanent clerks, 19 messengers and 14 watchmen/labourers were employed. The pay of the clerks ranged from $800 to $1,700 a year. Because of the workload the Treasury also employed a number of temporary clerks paid at a rate of $2 to $4 a day. Most Treasury employees were in the customhouses and land offices spread around the country. In New York City alone, 695 men were employed in the customhouse and another 315 on revenue cutters and barges. In financing the war the key officers were the secretary, who along with the president and cabinet set policy, and two of his subordinates, the treasurer and register, who supervised the actual work.

The treasurer's duties included receiving and keeping the government's money and disbursing it upon presentation of a valid warrant. During the first fifty-seven years of national life the treasurer used the services of the First and

Second Banks of the United States, deposit banks and the Independent Treasury. William Selden had occupied the position of treasurer since 1839. The register's duties included maintaining the records of debt obligations, issuing the certificates and computing interest payments. This officeholder, ex-congressman Ransom H. Gillet, was a Polk appointee. In 1847 he was appointed solicitor and was replaced by Daniel Graham, the Secretary of State of Tennessee.[36]

The Independent Treasury Act assigned the duty of accepting, safeguarding and disbursing public funds to seven major officers, and numerous minor officials in outlying areas. Responsibility fell mainly on the treasurer of the United States in Washington, the treasurer of the Mint in Philadelphia, the treasurer of the Branch Mint in New Orleans, and the assistant treasurers in Boston, Charleston, St Louis and New York. The last four were new and very desirable patronage positions. Clerks, quarters and fireproof safes were authorized, though Congress failed to appropriate sufficient monies to pay the first year's expenses. Numerous other officials such as receivers of public monies at land offices and collectors of custom outside the major cities received and maintained smaller sums. Keeping the funds safe until paid out or transferred proved particularly burdensome to this latter group. For practical reasons, funds in outlying offices were transferred to the seven major depositories as soon as possible. To ensure honesty, all depositories, regardless of size, were subject to periodic audits. The use of specie in government transactions was made effective on 1 January 1847.[37]

One aspect of the new law soon proved troublesome. To support the military operations along the Mexican border and coast, vast sums needed to be transferred from the east coast to New Orleans. Walker made the problem more severe with his Treasury Circular of 25 August 1846. The circular required treasury drafts to be made out to specific persons, not the bearer, and limited the assignee's ability to transfer the draft to another individual or firm. Further, the drafts specified the place of payment. Walker, a strict constructionist, sought to prevent the drafts from circulating within the commercial community as currency. The practical effect was to prevent the Treasury from moving specie by selling bills of exchange or treasury drafts in New York, payable in New Orleans. This forced the Treasury to employ less efficient means, such as the use of contractors (for a fee) and the actual shipment of coins, to get specie to New Orleans. In this instance, efficiency gave way to Jacksonian purity.[38]

The third domestic measure, the Warehousing bill, provided a counterweight to the tariff and Independent Treasury. By 1846, a consensus emerged favouring passage if the other two measures became law. Senator John Dix and the New York City Chamber of Commerce gave the effort real clout. Even John C. Calhoun responded favourably to calls from New York and New Orleans merchants. The existing British system impressed Calhoun and he was prepared to give an American equivalent a fair try. Under the proposal, bonded warehouses controlled by the collector of customs would store imported goods up to a year, for a fee, without payment of duties. Importers derived major advantages. First, the importer's money was not tied up in custom's duties until he withdrew the goods to fill an order. Second, if the goods were re-exported the complex draw-back procedures to receive a refund were avoided. The Democrats believed the Warehousing Act was a boon to small importers with limited capital, shippers and merchants in the re-export business. Its opponents, mostly advocates of protectionism, feared an increase in imports. Under Senator Dix's tutelage, the bill passed the Senate on 15 July 1846, and the House of Representatives on 1 August 1846.[39]

The remaining domestic measures set out in Polk's first annual message to Congress suffered a different fate. Polk and Walker favoured reducing the price of public land below the $1.25 an acre minimum if the land remained unsold for a specific number of years. They thought that reducing the price would bring lower quality land into production and give less prosperous farmers the opportunity to become landowners. After passage of the war resolution, the measure began to be promoted as a means of generating more revenue by quickening land sales.[40] In a bid for western support for the tariff, Calhoun proposed a bill reducing the sale price of public land to $1 an acre if unsold for ten years and further reductions of 25 cents an acre every three years thereafter until sold. The western and southern coalition held up in the Senate, but floundered in the House.[41]

Western aspirations suffered a series of blows in the waning days of the session. In addition to the defeat of the graduated land bill, Polk vetoed the Rivers and Harbors bill on constitutional grounds. Though he had expressed his intention of doing so earlier to his cabinet, Polk delayed the announcement until after the tariff and Independent Treasury bills passed with western support. The West lost on the issues most important to it: land, all of Oregon and internal improvements. Western politicians felt aggrieved and along with other Northern Democrats began to seek ways to express their dissatisfaction with what they perceived as Polk's devious conduct. The opportunity came in the form of one of the most deadly resolutions ever introduced in Congress, the Wilmot Proviso. The resolution sought to exclude slavery from any territory seized from Mexico. Since the South was providing a disproportionate share of the fighting men they took it as an insult. The debate over the expansion of slavery would be the bane of Polk's remaining term and, except for appropriations, war measures and establishment of the Interior Department in 1849, little significant legislation would be forthcoming. However, the revenue and financial system to be used to support the war had now been authorized. It remained to be seen whether they were up to the task.[42]

3 THE LOAN OF 1846

Since the American government lacked sufficient cash and current revenues to sustain a major war, loans were essential. Responsibility for authorizing the loans, determining their size and setting general parameters such as interest rates, length and terms of redemption lay with Congress. The administration supplied estimates of its financial needs and made recommendations. Neither Congress nor the administration had a master financial plan. The need for funds was evaluated yearly and depended chiefly on the resources needed to overcome Mexico's resistance. Before the war ended three loans, those of 1846, 1847 and 1848, were approved and sold. Both Congress and the administration drew upon the experiences of the War of 1812 and the financing of the 1837–42 deficits. However, each new loan was crafted to make the issue more saleable in light of current market conditions. After approval it was the Treasury's responsibility to dispose of the loan on the best available terms.

Secretary Walker's first effort, the $10 million loan of 1846, proved to be an embarrassing experience. The initial results were either mixed or outright failures. In August 1846, the Treasury began to issue treasury notes bearing a nominal interest rate of one mill to government creditors and suppliers. Neither these notes, nor subsequent ones bearing 5.4 per cent, served the government's purpose since they were used to pay public dues and rapidly returned to the Treasury. The failure of the treasury notes was followed by an unsuccessful attempt to negotiate a 5 per cent loan with New York bankers. Following this rebuff, Walker's problems were further compounded by his inability to sell $3 million in notes in a public offering. Finally, Walker realized that cooperation between the Treasury and financial community was essential. With the assistance of the leading investment bankers, a $5 million issue of 6 per cent ten-year bonds was successfully marketed in November and December of 1846. The money was needed to fund an enormous increase in the army and navy.

The American military was well trained, but small and underfunded in 1846. In spite of his belligerent attitude toward Mexico and Great Britain, President Polk showed little inclination to spend money on it. For fiscal year 1845 the army proper cost the country $3,155,027. In December 1845 Polk and Walker submitted their first full year's budget (fiscal year 1847), recommending a nominal increase to $3,364,459. In March 1846 the Oregon and Mexican crises elicited a reluctant request for increased funding, but only after a pointed Senate resolution inquiring whether some precautions needed to be taken. In response to the resolution Polk recommended Congress take action to improve the nation's defences, but left the actual measures to them. The House of Representatives passed a resolution on 25 March 1846 authorizing the recruitment of two new regiments to be composed of three-year volunteers. Additionally, the number of privates in the companies of the regular army was increased to eighty. Neither Polk nor the Senate foresaw any need to rush after the House acted. As late as 31 March 1846 Polk was urging Secretary of War William Marcy to cut the estimates of the army bureau chiefs for fiscal year 1847. The appropriations were still under congressional consideration. When Marcy encountered resistance, Polk personally met with the chiefs.[1]

Word of the clash on the Rio Grande brought quick Senate action on the House resolution. On 11 May the Senate voted to increase the size of the companies to 100 privates. The officer component of the companies and regiments was not increased. The Senate wanted more bayonets, not brass. The House concurred the same day. Assuming successful recruitment, this measure effectively doubled the size of the regular army. Before the increase the army consisted of eight infantry, two dragoon and four artillery regiments, in all about 7,200 officers and men. Each regiment consisted of ten companies. The authorized strength of the infantry and artillery companies was forty-two privates, ten non-commissioned officers and three officers. The regimental staffs consisted of four officers and a like number of non-commissioned officers. The Dragoons had fifty privates in each company. The units were somewhat understaffed. The troops were spread in small units along the frontier and coast.[2]

Concern with expenses had not prevented the administration from concentrating the military resources it possessed at Fort Jessup, near New Orleans, ready to move into Texas once annexation became official. The Texas legislature accepted the United States congressional resolution in July 1845 and General Zachary Taylor immediately began moving his forces to Corpus Christi, Texas. To this point reinforcements poured in from garrisons as far away as Florida and Detroit. These troops, plus a volunteer artillery battery from New Orleans, and a contingent of Texas Rangers, brought Taylor's army up to a respectable 3,900 men by mid-October. By the following March the army had advanced to the disputed ground near the Rio Grande River.[3]

The Treasury Department bore the responsibility of ensuring adequate funds were available at the point needed to purchase supplies and pay the troops. Difficulties were obvious even before the war began. Simply stated, the Treasury's resources were in the wrong place. New Orleans exported the produce of the Mississippi and Ohio River Valleys, but it imported from abroad only a modest amount. New York received two-thirds of the imports and then trans-shipped them throughout the country. As a result, two-thirds of the government's revenues were collected in that great port city. When customs receipts from Boston, Philadelphia, Baltimore and other eastern cities were added, that section's share approached 90 per cent. The Collectors of Customs deposited the proceeds in one of the local deposit banks to the credit of the Treasurer of the United States. To pay government expenses, the eastern banks transferred Treasury funds, without cost, to every corner of the nation. During the early part of the war the banks continued to transfer government funds. The huge increase in government expenditures in New Orleans and the southwestern United States disrupted normal trade patterns and complicated the task of the banks and Treasury. As early as 29 September 1845, John Cryder complained to George Peabody that profits in their New Orleans–New York–London exchange operation were down because of the government's need for funds in New Orleans. So much specie was required in New Orleans that any merchant who passed coins was able to purchase bills of exchange payable in New York for a premium of 0.5 per cent instead of the usual 1.5 per cent.[4]

Banks employed several methods to move specie to New Orleans. First, they tapped any deposits or funds they owned or could acquire in New Orleans. Second, they purchased or sold bills of exchange payable in New Orleans. Last, they assumed the expense and risk of shipping gold and silver coins by express. With the outbreak of fighting the Treasury increased the pressure on the banks to transfer ever greater sums. War, expectations of large transfers and the spectre of the Independent Treasury quickly brought tighter credit in both New York and New Orleans. The *New Orleans Weekly Picayune* felt the need to admonish the bankers for their over-reaction and war hysteria. In New York the situation began to ease when Walker pledged to limit withdrawals from the New York and Boston deposit banks to a combined $100,000 a week. Walker could be generous (temporarily) because by June 1846 he had built up Treasury reserves at the Canal and Banking Company in New Orleans to over $1 million.[5]

Initially, Walker relied on the services of the original deposit banks. Except in the capitol little of the government's money was transferred to other banks for political reasons.[6] Early on the most important movement was the increased accumulation of funds in the eastern money centres of New York, Boston and Philadelphia. Walker did take action against the District of Columbia banks whose re-charter the Democrats had opposed in the early 1840s. Even here, New York, not Walker's friend and adviser William W. Corcoran, benefited most. Two other changes, the withdrawal of deposits at the Bank of Baltimore and the Bank of Louisiana, were necessitated when the two banks declined to furnish the collateral security required by law. In Baltimore the Treasury began depositing all its receipts in the Chesapeake Bank instead of sharing them between the two local institutions. The Treasury replaced the Bank of Louisiana with the Canal and Banking Company of New Orleans early in 1846. This bank had strong Wall Street ties, through Matthew Morgan & Company and the Bank of the State of New York. Table 3.1 contains an analysis of deposit changes that Walker made during his first year.[7]

Table 3.1: United States Treasury Deposits, Location of Amounts Subject to Drafts[8]

Depositary	Location	24 March 1845 ($)	1 December 1845 ($)	30 March 1846 ($)
Bank of Mobile	Mobile, AL	165,893	46,161	57,257
Bank of Mobile	Mobile, AL	2,958	4,248	5,353
Farmers & Mechanics Bank	Hartford, CT	13,387	23,481	32,391
City Bank	New Haven, CT	9,996	0	0
Bank of Potomac	Alexandria, DC	19,347	9,993	9,493
Francis Dodge	Georgetown, DC	50,000	0	0
Bank of the Metropolis	Washington, DC	669,898	26,064	32,934
Bank of Washington	Washington, DC	122,825	16,005	13,655
Corcoran & Riggs	Washington, DC	382,734	472,288	458,807
Patriotic Bank	Washington, DC	128,718	15,632	14,761
Branch Mint	Dahlonega, GA	30,000	30,000	30,000
Planters Bank	Savannah, GA	59,257	50,975	57,257
Louisville Saving Bank	Louisville, KY	109,934	83,972	110,188
Bank of Louisiana	New Orleans, LA	247,343	391,896	10,553
Branch Mint	New Orleans, LA	123,238	153,238	203,208
Canal and Banking Co.	New Orleans, LA	0	0	408,396
Merchants Bank	Boston, MA	233,526	1,008,376	1,063,794
Bank of Missouri	St Louis, MO	331,984	203,931	347,316
Michigan Insurance Co.	Detroit, MI	145,812	122,623	48,301
Bank of Baltimore	Baltimore, MD	97,155	0	0
Chesapeake Bank	Baltimore, MD	103,069	125,818	176,324
Branch Bank	Cape Fear, NC	0	6,000	4,172
Branch Mint	Charlotte, NC	32,000	32,000	32,000
Commercial Bank	Portsmouth, NH	554	764	0
Mechanics & Traders Bank	Portsmouth, NH	0	0	7,326
State Bank of New Jersey	Morris, NJ	0	50,000	50,000
Albany City Bank	Albany, NY	20,965	139,957	165,236
Commercial Bank	Albany, NY	20,000	100,000	195,000
Mechanics & Farmers	Albany, NY	66,259	89,441	163,911
Brooklyn Bank	Brooklyn, NY	0	70,000	70,000
Oliver Lee & Co.	Buffalo, NY	0	50,000	51,710
American Exchange	NYC	225,162	243,043	322,343
Bank of America	NYC	228,377	626,279	1,254,254

Depositary	Location	24 March 1845 ($)	1 December 1845 ($)	30 March 1846 ($)
Bank of Commerce	NYC	240,580	620,758	495,993
Bank of State of New York	NYC	121,782	598,214	808,394
Mechanics Bank	NYC	140,373	453,887	655,494
Merchants Bank	NYC	246,834	510,253	396,990
North River Bank	NYC	144,000	226,094	730,814
Ohio Life & Trust	Cincinnati, OH	10,393	102,312	172,113
Firemen's Insurance Co.	Cleveland, OH	54,524	24,009	28,242
Clinton Bank	Columbus, OH	28,293	214,617	100,687
Bank of Sandusky	Sandusky, OH	35	0	0
Bank of Wooster	Wooster, OH	0	20,000	0
Bank of Erie	Erie, PA	100,000	76,752	30,566
Bank of Middleton	Middleton, PA	50,000	45,000	45,526
Bank of Commerce	Philadelphia, PA	56,946	215,675	291,680
Philadelphia Bank	Philadelphia, PA	144,569	198,463	262,718
Philadelphia Mint	Philadelphia, PA	204,961	784,761	644,762
Bank of Pittsburgh	Pittsburgh, PA	2,909	0	0
Exchange Bank	Pittsburgh, PA	225,549	152,190	207,076
Arcade Bank	Providence, RI	6,274	39,178	23,470
Southwestern Railroad Bank	Charleston, SC	97,829	257,645	158,796
Bank of Tennessee	Nashville, TN	0	0	9,327
Union Bank	Nashville, TN	53,143	50,989	57,808
Exchange Bank of Virginia	Norfolk, VA	50,798	72,528	92,615
Bank of Virginia	Richmond, VA	86,595	100,586	96,999
Farmers Bank of Virginia	Richmond, VA	52,000	54,175	56,490
Bank of Burlington	Burlington, VT	0	3,997	6,665
Wisconsin Marine & Fire	Milwaukee, WI	0	0	176,321
Total		5,758,778	9,014,268	10,945,486
Deduct: Suspense Account		10,014	90,983	5,782
Net Subject to Draft		5,748,764	8,923,285	10,939,704

The congressional resolution passed in May 1846 recognizing a state of war empowered the president to employ American regular military forces, the militia and up to 50,000 twelve-month volunteers to 'prosecute said war to a speedy and successful termination.'[9] Congress also earmarked 'ten millions of dollars out of any money in the Treasury, or to come into the Treasury, not otherwise appropriated' to pay and supply the new recruits.[10] Congress apparently saw no need to impose new taxes, make provisions for a loan or otherwise identify the source of the $10 million. For a war of any length, the appropriation was clearly a stopgap measure, even if the Treasury could collect the $10 million or take it out of reserves. The *New York Morning News* aptly observed that there are 'too many men, or there is far too little money'.[11] Which is it, the paper demanded? If the administration planned a defensive war, the *Morning News* believed the 50,000 volunteers excessive, while an offensive war required much more money.[12] The Senate also expressed curiosity as to the administration's objectives and the likely cost. In a resolution passed on 3 June 1846, the senators called upon the president to make recommendations on ways to raise the necessary funds to prosecute the war.[13]

The president's response to the resolution incorporated the increased army and navy estimates prepared by those two departments and the secretary of the Treasury's proposals for obtaining the money. The always frugal and hopeful Polk expressed to Congress his opinion that the estimates were too high. The army projected increased cost of $2,805,000 for the period 13 May 1846–30 June 1846, and $17,166,472 for the following fiscal year. This latter figure increased army estimates to six times that proposed the preceding December. The additional funding was necessary in order to double the strength of the regular army to a total of 15,500 officers and men, and to recruit, train and equip 25,000 of the authorized 50,000 volunteers. Since the Mexican government possessed few warships the navy's expansion was less drastic. Secretary Bancroft proposed an increase of $4,296,823 for fiscal year 1847, to bring the total to $10,320,000.[14]

After a slight reduction, Walker estimated he needed an additional $23,952,904 to carry the country through the first thirteen-and-a-half months of fighting. Economic growth and the administration's fiscal policies would, he believed, supply half of the deficit. The remainder must be found elsewhere (see Table 3.2).[15]

Table 3.2: Walker's Estimates of Military Needs, 15 May 1846–30 June 1847[16]

	Expenses ($)	Total ($)
Increased Army and Navy expenditures due to the war:		23,952,904
Sources:		
Reduction of cash reserves	332,441	
Increased revenues from economic growth	4,000,000	
Increased revenue by amending tariff bill	5,534,057	
Increased revenue from warehouse system	1,000,000	
Increased revenue from the graduated sale of land	500,000	
Total Sources:		11,366,498
Remaining Deficit:		12,586,406

Excise levies on items such as whiskey were rejected because of the difficulty of rapidly setting up a collection system and the administration's desire to avoid internal taxes. Democrats had been forced to resort to these measures in 1813 and the results were not encouraging. Walker recommended the deficit be covered by a loan or an issue of treasury notes. He preferred a combination of the two. Any credit instruments, in his judgement, should be sold at par or above and carry an interest rate no higher than 6 per cent. Polk gave the recommendations his approval and reiterated the objections to internal taxes.[17]

Serious deliberation by Congress on the loan proposals began in July. On 14 July, James McKay introduced a bill prepared by the Ways and Means Committee based on Walker's recommendation. The legislation provided for the issuance of up to $10 million of one-year treasury notes. New notes could be issued in place of those redeemed but outstanding notes must not exceed the $10 million limit. The bill further provided that, at the president's option, part or all of the $10 million might be obtained by selling ten-year United States bonds. Restrictions against selling the bonds or notes at less than par or paying more than 6 per cent interest were incorporated in the bill. Additionally, the Treasury Department was forbidden to pay any commissions for the negotiation or sale of the loan.[18]

Congressman Garrett Davis, a Whig of Kentucky, immediately gave notice of his intention to amend the bill by striking out the treasury note provision and leaving it a simple loan bill. He viewed the issuance of short-term notes as dishonest and urged acceptance of the need to increase the nation's long-term debt. To Davis, the notes represented an effort by the Democrats to humbug the people. His real target was the administration's economic and financial measures – tariff, Independent Treasury and graduated land sales – still under congressional consideration. He deemed these measures unwise, inefficient and unlikely to produce sufficient revenue to meet the war's needs. In his view, a more honest approach would be to obtain the means through increased taxation and if this proved insufficient, then openly borrow. Even better, Congress could leave the old Whig programme in place.[19]

McKay sped up deliberation by obtaining a resolution cutting off debate as of noon on 15 July. In his defence of the bill, McKay acknowledged it incorporated Walker's views on increased revenues. However, he pointed out, even if the projections proved to be inaccurate, $10 million should suffice until Congress met again the following December. Additional means could be found at that time if the war continued. A speedy conclusion might eliminate the need for further borrowing. The treasury notes, McKay explained, would be issued in denominations of $50 and up and be signed by two officials, the treasurer and register of the Treasury Department. The interest rate would be fixed by the secretary of the Treasury, with the concurrence of the president. The buyer could use the notes to pay customs duties or purchase public land. McKay observed that the government's use of treasury notes during the War of 1812 and the period 1837 through 1843 provided adequate constitutional precedent.[20]

To the Democrats, the advantage of short-term treasury notes lay in the ability to redeem them, all or in part, whenever funds became available. McKay pointed out that the long-term bonds sold in 1842 now commanded such a high premium in the market that it was not in the government's interest to redeem them before maturity. As a result, over $1 million in interest a year continued to be paid while large surpluses accumulated in the Treasury. If the war was short an increase in the government's long-term debt could be avoided. Finally, McKay denied any inconsistency between the loan bill and that of the Independent Treasury. He envisioned the Treasury Department selling the notes for specie or issuing them in payment for supplies. After one year the notes would be redeemed for specie. The bill passed on 15 July by a vote of 118–47. Accepting the inevitable, the House Whigs, except Davis, used their debate time opposing the expansion of slavery (Joshua Giddings) or criticizing the administration's Oregon and pre-war Mexican policies.[21]

The Senate acted as speedily as the House. That body referred the bill to its Finance Committee the afternoon of House passage. The next morning, 16 July, the Committee reported the bill back to the full Senate without amendment. Following the printing of the bill and one night to review it, debate began. As in the House, the vocal minority proved ineffective. The Whigs, with sound reasoning, expressed doubt as to the government's ability to redeem the notes after one year. Senator George Evans chided the administration for not anticipating the needs earlier and predicted unnecessary strain on the money market if a loan was floated. Unlike Davis in the House, Evans preferred an issue of treasury notes, which he considered a perfectly safe and much needed currency. Senator Jacob Miller of New Jersey criticized the Democrats for not showing the same zeal for taxes as they had in pushing the war resolution though Congress. He pointed out that they refused to tax the people's tea and coffee to pay for it, but showed no reluctance to borrow.[22]

The hard money Democrats, led by Senator Thomas Hart Benton, raised a further objection. Benton was such a strong advocate of the use of specie that he was known as 'old bullion'. A native of Tennessee, his efforts to achieve military glory during the War of 1812 ended in conflict with Andrew Jackson. A dispute between Benton's brother and members of Jackson's military coterie led to ill-feelings and, eventually, to a gun battle in a Nashville tavern. Benton and his brother escaped with their lives, but Jackson lay on the floor badly wounded. This effectively ended Benton's military career and two years after the war ended he left Tennessee to the 'old hero' and migrated to the Territory of Missouri. In 1821, upon the admission of Missouri to statehood, he was elected United States senator and served thirty years. After making peace with Jackson he proved a staunch Democrat.

Benton viewed the provision to issue new notes in place of those redeemed as a dangerous departure from previous legislation. He believed this provision gave the notes the status of currency to which he, unlike Evans, objected. Benton also feared the provision destroyed the dollar limitation. He argued, erroneously, that the government could incur a debt far in excess of $10 million by continuously re-issuing notes.[23] Benton recommended 'taxes first, loans next (and) treasury paper last'.[24] On the final day of debate, 18 July, the Senate refused to consider an amendment to tax tea and coffee and then passed the House bill intact by a voice vote. With the Treasury's needs obvious, objections by the Whigs and hard money Democrats proved futile. Polk signed the bill into law on 22 July.[25]

Even before completion of congressional action, the press and financial community began to speculate and offer advice on the best means to raise the $10 million. At the end of May, George Newbold, the influential president of the Bank of America in New York, expressed his hope for a treasury note issue instead of a loan. Newbold possessed a long history and considerable influence in the area of federal finance. In the War of 1812, as cashier of the Bank of America, he was a leading member of the New York associates that participated in the Parish, Astor and Girard syndicate. Though a political opponent of the Jacksonians, Newbold enthusiastically supported withdrawal of the federal deposits from the Second Bank of the United States. His bank profited handsomely as one of the leading 'pet' institutions. During the second administration of Andrew Jackson and, subsequently, that of Martin Van Buren, he functioned as a leading advisor to the secretary of the Treasury. In the depression years of 1837–42 his bank served as a leading contractor of treasury notes. In this endeavour he used a small firm, Corcoran & Riggs, as the bank's agent in Washington. Newbold was influenced in this selection by the fact that Elisha Riggs, a business associate and member of the Board of Directors of the Bank of America, was George Riggs's father.[26]

Newbold believed $5 to $10 million through the sale of treasury notes could be raised without difficulty. Above that amount a loan would be required. In the parlance of the day, a loan meant selling long-term bonds. Newbold foresaw no difficult in raising $15, $20 or $25 million by selling 6 per cent long-term government bonds, assuming final settlement of the Oregon question. A week later Newbold began to hedge when it appeared that the first issue would be treasury notes and at a nominal interest rate. Such notes, he believed, would benefit commerce by serving as a circulating medium, but would not be held for investment. The Treasury should not count on them remaining in circulation. If the intent was to keep the notes outstanding until their maturity date, he recommended they bear at least a 5.4 per cent rate.[27]

William W. Corcoran, with better access to Treasury officials than Newbold, reached the same conclusion and on 13 June advised Elisha Riggs of the Treasury's need to raise money soon and predicted the most likely method would be treasury notes. Nine days later, after Polk and Walker's response to the Senate's resolution, he confidentially predicted congressional approval of a treasury note bill. The secretary, in Corcoran's judgement would offer the first notes at a low interest rate, but afterward the rate would slowly advance to 5.4 per cent as more notes were issued.[28]

After reviewing the president and secretary's response to the Senate in June, the *Washington National Intelligencer* labelled the proposals inadequate. In the paper's opinion, Walker's estimates of the benefits of the economic programme would not be realized. The Democrats' economic package would decrease, not increase revenues. Ignore reform and just contract a loan, the paper advised. The New York papers worried about the effect of a loan and the Independent Treasury on the ability of that city's merchants to secure adequate financing. The use of treasury notes to finance the war, the *New York Tribune* believed, would inflate the currency and counteract any credit crunch.[29]

Until August 1846 the Treasury Department met increased military needs by drawing down its deposits at the banks. By the end of July these deposit balances had fallen from a high of $12,035,559, after deducting outstanding treasury drafts (similar to cheques), on 27 April 1846, to $7,725,797. A further decrease of $2,313,000 occurred in August. Falling revenues compounded Walker's dilemma as merchants reduced their imports in anticipation of the decrease in tariff rates effective from 1 December. Custom duties fell by $2.7 million for the quarter ending 30 September 1846 over the same quarter of the previous year. Worst, expenditures exceeded revenues by $7.2 million for the same period.[30]

In the midst of drawing down deposits at the state banks, Walker began to implement part of the Independent Treasury Act. On 25 August he instructed all collectors of customs and receivers of public money to hold the funds collected or deposit them with one of the seven major Independent Treasury offices. Issuing directives proved easier than creating a functioning system. The Treasurers in Washington and at the Philadelphia and New Orleans mints were in place and could be assigned additional duties. The other four officials must be selected and appointed, with due consideration to patronage aspects, and their offices and staffs created from scratch. It was November before the Independent Treasury began to accept government funds in large amounts. In St Louis the delay was even longer because the newly appointed assistant treasurer did not return from the New Mexico campaign to open the office until April 1847.[31]

Even with the new Treasury system only partially in place, Walker began the process of moving government funds from the banks to the new depositories. Expenses continued to be paid by treasury drafts or transfer orders drawn on the banks, but receipts were diverted to the Independent Treasury's new vaults. The Boston and Philadelphia banks felt the effects first. Deposits at the Merchants

Bank in Boston dropped from $806,511 on 27 July to $71,109 on 26 October. In Philadelphia, funds in the two deposit banks fell from $343,830 to $97,483 during the same period. The seven deposit banks in New York City received gentler treatment. Their deposits fell from $2,943,417 to $1,845,983. However, in November the process accelerated as ex-governor William C. Bouck assumed his duties as assistant treasurer and the Independent Treasury's New York office became fully functional. By the end of November more of the government's money was in its own strong boxes than on deposit with the banks.[32]

With a deficit averaging $2.4 million a month and the bank balance melting away, the time seemed right to make use of the new borrowing authority. In late August, Walker elected to start issuing treasury notes bearing the nominal interest rate of 0.1 per cent (one mill) to public creditors. The Treasury distributed the notes to military officers and procurement officials who, after purchasing supplies, endorsed the notes over to the seller. Colonel Thomas Hunt received the first batch of $50 and $100 notes on 21 August 1846. On 26 August he received more. On the last day of the month Captain George Waggaman and Lieutenant Colonel J. P. Taylor were provided with similar notes. In the last ten days of August, $660,000 of the new notes was distributed. The public received the news on 28 August when the *Washington Union* announced the Treasury was issuing $500,000 of treasury notes.[33]

A set of books to record information on the new securities (Treasury Notes of 1846) was established in the office of the register. The Treasury Note Register captured each note's number, the date issued, and to whom issued. Additional columns provided space to collect redemption information. Eventually five separate journals were used – one each for the $50 one mill notes, the $100 one mill notes, the $50 5.4 per cent notes, the $100 5.4 per cent notes, and a fifth that included the larger, $500 and $1,000 notes.[34]

The distribution increased in September as $1,293,950 of the one mill certificates were issued to army officers and quartermaster agents including Major Robert E. Lee and Lieutenant Winfield Scott Hancock. A further $320,000, including the first of the $1,000 denomination, was distributed in early October. By 22 October it was obvious that the one mill notes were returning to the Treasury too rapidly to be an effective means of borrowing. As of that date, a total of $2,282,500 of the one mill notes had been placed in circulation.[35]

Throughout the conflict New Orleans served as the major assembly point for troops, supplies and equipment. The quartermasters, paymasters and purchasing agents brought their newly minted treasury notes to this point. The influx of government paper increased existing problems. With the low interest rate the one mill notes held little attraction as an investment. Suppliers and merchants who received the notes immediately sought to convert them into cash. The use of the notes to pay customs duties was the most effective way to obtain full value.

However, demand in New Orleans was limited since the port functioned primarily as an exporter, not importer of goods. Though issued to the suppliers at par ($100) in payment of their invoices, the notes quickly fell to $97.5. With the notes selling in the local market at less than par, the New Orleans banks refused to accept them for deposit or redeem them for specie at face value. The collector of customs in New Orleans compounded the problem by temporarily refusing to accept the notes. New York, the import centre, provided a much better market. Brokers soon began to buy up the notes in the South and forward them to that city. The New York City banks with government deposits accepted the notes at par from their customers for deposit. Additionally, city merchants willingly purchased them at small discounts to pay custom duties. The demand from New York caused prices in the delta city to rise to the $99.25 to $99.75 range, but it was April 1847 before the notes reached par. By then the very nature of the notes had changed.[36]

The actions by the New Orleans banks and collector caused concern in New York and Washington. George Newbold asked William Corcoran to investigate and advise him whether the banks and collector were outright refusing or only declining temporarily because they lacked instructions from Washington. If the former was true, Newbold feared a great influx of notes into New York for redemption. With the Independent Treasury becoming a reality, Newbold now wanted the notes to circulate like currency, at least in the mercantile community. He feared the flow of specie into the vaults of the Independent Treasury or to New Orleans to purchase treasury notes would decrease the supply in New York and cause that city's banks to restrict credit. Circulation of the notes like a paper currency would offset the loss of specie.[37]

Walker had already taken action. On 1 September 1846, he sent each of the deposit banks a letter. 'It is expected', he wrote, 'that you will not refuse treasury notes in payment from your customers or depositing of such notes made by them to the extent of the public monies in your keeping. If an objection exists to your adopting this course you will please forthwith inform this department.'[38] To help the banks, Walker informed them on 15 September that they might pay back out any treasury notes they received to customers willing to accept them and not forward the notes to the Treasury for cancellation. In New Orleans Walker lacked leverage because government deposits were exhausted. At the end of August the Treasury was technically overdrawn by $800,000 at the Canal and Banking Company. Transfers amounting to $827,000 had been ordered but not yet received. The reserves of the early summer were exhausted and the Treasury was encountering difficultly transferring funds fast enough to meet the pace of military expenditures. It was the end of December before the government managed to get a positive balance in the New Orleans bank. Government resources were decreasing everywhere. In August, in spite of the treasury note issue, available funds fell by $2.1 million, another $800,000 in September and a further $1.35 million in October.[39]

During the cabinet meeting of 29 September, Walker informed Polk and his fellow secretaries that only a fraction over $4 million dollars remained in the Treasury and in his opinion a loan or another issue of treasury notes was essential. Polk, supported by Secretary of State James Buchanan, recommended an issue of twelve-month treasury notes bearing interest at 6 per cent, but was prepared to leave the final decision to the secretary of the Treasury. Walker decided to test the waters in Wall Street. On 1 October Polk received a note from Walker advising the president of his intention to go to the North immediately to negotiate a twelve-month treasury note loan. Upon further inquiry the unhappy president learned the secretary hoped to keep the mission secret. Walker intended to meet with Cornelius Lawrence, the highly respected collector of customs in New York, and George Newbold, the New York bankers' representative, in Princeton, New Jersey.[40]

The time to probe the nation's premier financial market seemed promising in early October. The money market was recovering from the psychological scare caused by passage of the Tariff and Independent Treasury Acts and the banks were coping with the steady drain of federal deposits. The *Philadelphia Public Ledger* believed money (credit) to be easy in both New York and Boston. The *New York Tribune* reported capital abundant with loans secured by the best stock securities being made at 5 per cent and on the best commercial paper at 6 per cent. The price of United States bonds fell with the coming of war, but rallied and on 30 September the 6 per cent bonds due in 1862 were being quoted at 106 asked and 105.5 bid. New York State 5.5 per cent bonds were selling at par.[41]

Walker's mission surprised Polk but not the press. Even before his departure *Niles' National Register* reported that the secretary was daily expected in New York to negotiate a loan on part of the $10 million authorized by the Act of 22 July 1846. The *Washington National Intelligencer* dismissed the rumours that Walker planned to visit New York to arrange practical details of the Warehousing Act and to recruit competent custom house appraisers. The paper correctly divined the purpose of the visit. Walker left Washington on 30 September and after an unsuccessful conference with Lawrence and Newbold in Princeton, came on to New York City. The *New York Tribune* announced his arrival in its 6 October edition.[42]

The secretary, now joined by William W. Corcoran, spent a week in New York attempting to convince the bankers to lend the government $4 or $5 million at 5 per cent. As security he offered to deposit a like amount of treasury notes with the banks. Though the notes would be redeemable any time in payment of public dues, Walker express his hope they would be held, at least for a while, as an investment. The bankers were willing to advance the money but demanded 6 per cent interest. While negotiations continued, Corcoran made a trip to Boston to evaluate prospects there. He found them unpromising. The difference in opinion over the interest rate proved irreconcilable and after a futile trip to Philadelphia, Walker returned to Washington to explain his fifteen-day absence to an anxious president.[43]

The press, naturally, placed differing interpretations on the mission. The art of spinning is not a phenomena limited to the latter part of the twentieth century. Labelling it a total failure, the opposition press ridiculed the administration for its need to approach those institutions from which it was actively seeking to divorce the government. Such an approach represented a total failure of the administration's domestic policies. The administration's friends portrayed the trip as a fact-finding expedition to learn the interest rate necessary to float a loan. Even Horace Greeley's *New York Tribune*, early on, defined it as an effort to feel the bankers' pulse. The *Washington Union* applauded the secretary's refusal to compromise.[44]

Walker's severest press critic during the negotiations came from the ranks of the Democratic Party. The idea of the secretary of the Treasury running around Wall Street soliciting a loan appalled the *Philadelphia Public Ledger*. In its view an administration that had fought so hard to separate the banks and government should be 'ashamed to [again] seek the connection and is justly punished by the failure, for its want of pride'.[45] A mutual dependency between the banks and government, the *Public Ledger* feared, would corrupt both. The safety of the people demanded separation of the political and monetary interest of the nation. The paper preferred that the government borrow from individual capitalists and predicted as much as $10 million of 6 per cent notes could be sold at a 5 per cent premium. The *Ledger* deemed the difference between 5 and 6 per cent interest a small price to pay to keep the government out of the clutches of the banks. Even if the notes failed to sell, the secretary retained the option of paying them out to public creditors. Anything was preferable to allowing the banks control of the notes. The papers feared that bank control of the treasury notes would fuel an increase in the banks' own paper money and cheapen the currency.[46] The more neutral *New York Herald* shared the *Ledger's* concern about the secretary 'coming into Wall Street and putting himself in the hands of the shylocks of that place'.[47] The *Herald* also believed it safer to increase the interest rate and sell the notes to small investors. It optimistically predicted that 5 per cent notes would disappear into investment portfolios and not be seen again for years.[48]

In public, Walker lambasted the bankers and announced his intention of getting along without them. In private, he admitted to Polk that his mission to New York to arrange a loan had failed. On 17 October a subdued secretary reported on his efforts to the full cabinet. As a group, the cabinet considered the steps necessary to alleviate the government's financial problems. If 5 per cent was inadequate then what rate would suffice? Walker recommended issuing 5.4 per cent notes and paying them out to public creditors. James Buchanan proposed 6 per cent one-year notes not redeemable until the maturity date. He feared a quick return of the notes to the Treasury without this restriction and an adequate rate of interest. Walker predicted such notes would sell well to New York capitalists and banks, but made no commitment. After considering his cabinet members' comments for several days, Polk gave his own advice on 20 October. He now favoured an issue of 5.4 per cent notes to be sold for specie or paid out to creditors. However, as Polk again reminded Walker, the final decision was his. Two days later, not unexpectedly, Walker advised the president of his intentions to sell not more than $4 million of 5.4 per cent treasury notes. The interest rate computed to 1.5¢ a day on each $100 note. Polk gave his approval at once.[49]

Walker lost little time. The official notice appeared in the *Washington Union* on 22 October. The Treasury Department offered to sell up to $3 million (not $4 million) of 5.4 per cent one-year notes bearing interest from the date the purchaser deposited specie with one of the seven major Independent Treasury offices. Sales were limited to lots of $1,000 and upward. The notes were acceptable, before and after their maturity dates, at the custom houses and land offices.[50] In an editorial accompanying the official announcement, the *Union* predicted a large demand for the notes that it described as 'specie bearing an interest'.[51] The Whig papers adopted a more critical attitude. The *New York Tribune* carried the official announcement but expressed the opinion that success was by no means certain. In the days following, the *Tribune*'s pessimism became more pronounced. On 29 October its inquiries in Wall Street found little interest in the issue and it gleefully announced that the hard-pressed Treasury even had to draw down deposits at its pet bank, Corcoran & Riggs. The *Washington National Intelligencer* pronounced the issue's failure even earlier. Walker's position was less desperate than his opponents portrayed, but as the Treasury balance fell $1.5 million below the $4 million deemed safe, even he conceded other means must be found.[52]

Walker informed Polk of the treasury notes' failure on 30 October and advised him of the necessity of a long-term bond issue. After Buchanan and John Y. Mason, now secretary of the Navy, concurred, Polk gave the necessary presidential authorization. That same day the official notice appeared in the *Washington Union*. The Treasury announced its intention to accept bids on a new $5 million loan. It proposed to issue ten-year government bonds paying 6 per cent semi-annually. The bonds were not redeemable before 12 November 1856. Parties interested in bidding were instructed to submit a written proposal to the secretary by 12 November. Bidders must indicate the price they were prepared to pay and the Independent Treasury office they wished to deposit the money. To secure the bonds successful bidders must deposit funds with the Independent Treasury, obtain a certificate of deposit and forward it to the register in Washington, who would record the transaction and issue the certificate.[53]

The new advertisement did not cancel the offer to sell the $3 million in notes. The *Washington Union* still believed the notes would be taken and noted that the Bank of the Metropolis purchased $50,000 and offered to buy $50,000 more if the Treasury would leave the money on deposit with the bank until needed. Walker rejected the second offer. Richard Smith, cashier of the bank, was credited with the $50,000 in notes on the Treasury's books on 29 October. Corcoran & Riggs was also a major purchaser, taking $27,000 in the $500 and $1,000 denominations on 24 October and a further $52,000 early in November. Corcoran & Riggs attempted to resell the notes to individuals who would hold them for investment. Few other brokers showed any interest in buying the notes for specie. This became more pronounced after the announcement of the 6 per cent bond issue. The slowness of sales convinced Walker that the holders of the one mill notes and public creditors might be a more viable market. On 2 November the Treasury announced its willingness to exchange the 5.4 per cent notes for the outstanding one mill notes. The Treasury ceased issuing the old notes on 24 October 1846, the date of the official announcement of the 5.4 per cent notes. Besides selling and exchanging the new 5.4 percent notes, the Treasury began distributing them to military officers and purchasing agents to buy supplies and pay the soldiers and sailors.[54]

During late October and November the Treasury succeeded in paying out (primarily) and selling $2,084,150 of the new notes, bringing the amount of the 1846 notes issued to $4,366,700. A total of $513,600 was redeemed through customs, land sales or repurchase in the same period. As of 1 December 1846, $3,853,100 of treasury notes was outstanding. After mid-November, the Treasury's focus changed to the $5 million bond issue. However, it continued to market the notes authorized by the Act of 22 July 1846, until July 1847. Between 21 August 1846 and July 1847, $7,687,800 of the notes were issued, reissued or sold. Use of the notes allowed the Treasury to stay liquid during a critical period, but the public's unwillingness to treat the one mill notes as currency or the 5.4 per cent notes as an investment limited their usefulness. Up to this point the government's ability to raise the money in an orderly and businesslike manner remained in doubt. The emphasis now turned to bonds.[55]

The announcement of the sale of $5 million in government bonds sent the press into a frenzy of speculation. Initially the reaction was positive, with the *New York Tribune* predicting that the whole issue would sell at 0.5 to 1 per cent premium. Two days later, on 5 November, the paper's faith began to erode and doubt filtered into its financial columns. The arrival of William W. Corcoran in New York on 7 November to stir up interest in the issue seems to have overcome the *Tribune*'s doubts and by 12 November it was again predicting success. The *Washington National Intelligencer*'s New York correspondent consulted his Wall Street sources and concluded that if the loan was taken it would be in small lots for speculation. By 9 November the *Intelligencer* was reporting the issue's likely failure because most capitalists planned to bypass this loan in order to participate in a larger one expected later. The *New York Journal of Commerce* also detected a reluctance to bid in Boston and New York because of anticipated future loans. The papers disagreed on the method of payment to be used by the purchasers. The impression in Washington was that deposits of specie would be required, while New York financiers were convinced current funds, the notes of specie-paying banks, would suffice. Slowly the reluctance to bid was overcome. The *New York Journal of Commerce* reported that Wall Street really wanted the government to succeed and over $1 million in bids would be submitted from New York. Failure would signal a dangerous lack of confidence.[56] However, the *Journal of Commerce* expected the bankers and capitalists to 'all and each take care of themselves according to their own views'.[57]

The financial community took the more practical steps of forming bidding groups and estimating the price the bonds would command. The New York financiers quickly aligned themselves into two groups headed by officers of the Bank of the State of New York and the investment banking firm of John Ward & Company. The capitalists, being in a better position to evaluate the situation and motivated by profit, placed more faith in the issue. George Newbold informed William Corcoran that the stock would be taken but believed the Treasury could have made a better bargain, a premium of 3 or 4 per cent, if Walker had accepted the offer the bankers' made during his New York visit the previous October. Though Newbold was encouraging his friends to join the State Bank list, he committed $50,000 to the group organized by John Ward & Company. James J. Palmer, president of New York's Merchants Bank, informed Corcoran that he and fellow banker W. R. Hallet were committing $150,000 to the State Bank group. Palmer and Hallet, if successful, wanted to pay in one half immediately and the remainder the following month. They requested that Corcoran arrange this at the Treasury though he was part of a competing group.[58]

Speculation and controversy did not end with the opening of the bids on 13 November. The failure of the New York and Boston mail to arrive on time had delayed the ceremony a day. A Mr Kershaw of New York appeared to be the successful bidder. According to the *Washington Union*, Kershaw's name was Alfred L., the *New York Journal of Commerce* referred to him as E. H. Kershaw, *Niles' National Register* simply called him Mr Kershaw. Since Treasury officials did not know the bidder, Walker sent McClintock Young, chief clerk of the Treasury Department, to New York with the bonds and a demand for immediate payment. Kershaw was unable to produce the money. Later investigation revealed that he was the promoter of a defunct insurance company and without standing in the New York financial community. Walker explained to the cabinet that he felt obliged to offer the loan to Kershaw because he was the highest bidder if he produced the money. Since he failed to do so the entire $5 million was allocated to other bidders.[59]

Walker accepted offers in the amount of $5,146,000 ranging from par to 105. Commander Charles Garnett of Philadelphia was the highest bidder, offering 105 for $1,000 of the new bonds ($105 for each $100 bond or a total of $1,050). The total included bids for $4,699,000 at par, $412,000 between par and 101, and $35,000 at 101 and above. Thirteen bidders obtained $50,000 or more (see Table 3.3). Corcoran & Riggs, John Ward & Company, Cammann & Whitehouse, Henry Roland & Associates and DeRhann & Moore were investment bankers who purchased the bonds for resale to the investing public. Richard Withers served as the agent for the group of officers, directors and investors assembled by the Bank of the State of New York. The other bank officers represented their institutions that purchased both for investment and resale to clients. Most of the purchasers were speculators who hoped to realize a quick profit. Corcoran & Riggs's bid included $300,000 for the firm and $50,000 for Elisha Riggs.[60]

Table 3.3: $5m Bond Issue of 1846, Bidders over $50,000[61]

Name	Residence	Bid	Amount ($)
Corcoran & Riggs	Washington, DC	par	350,000
Joseph E. Nousse	Washington, DC	100.10	100,000
James White, Treasurer (State of Maine)	Belfast, ME	par	150,000
Cammann & Whitehouse	NYC	par	115,000
C. O. Halstead, President (Bank of Savings)	NYC	par	50,000
DeRhann & Moore	NYC	100.20	100,000
Henry Roland & Assoc.	NYC	par	350,000
John Ward & Co.	NYC	par	1,450,000
Richard Withers, Cashier (Bank of the State of New York)	NYC	par	1,173,000
Wayne McMullen	NYC	100.25	80,000
John D. Sheaff	Philadelphia, PA	100.50	50,000
J. Sparks, President (Southwark Bank)	Philadelphia, PA	par	125,000
H. W. Connors, President (Bank of Charleston)	Charleston, SC	par	285,000
H. Hutchinson, President (Bank of Hamburg)	Hamburg, SC	par	100,000

John Ward & Company bid for $3,550,000 at par, but after allocating bonds to the other par bidders their share was reduced to $1,450,000. However, the secretary informed the firm that further allocations might be made if other bidders failed to take up their share. Henry Roland's bid was inadvertently listed by Treasury Department clerks at par, though the firm actually submitted a bid at 100.75. Upon discovering the error Walker demanded Roland and his associates pay an additional $2,625, though official notification of the par bid had been sent. Subsequently, Walker reversed himself and advised Roland that the stock would be issued at par if the entire $350,000 was deposited with the assistant treasurer in New York within ten days.[62]

Individual letters sent to successful bidders on 17 and 18 November specified that the bonds would be issued upon presentation of evidence that the necessary funds had been deposited. No deadline for making the deposits was specified. Bidders notified on 19 November were required by the secretary to make the deposit within thirty days. All the major bidders, naturally, were notified within the first two days, thereby avoiding the deposit time limit.[63]

Only registered stock, not coupon, was to be issued. With registered stock, clerks in the Register of the Treasury's office recorded each certificate on the Treasury's books and if subsequently sold or transferred cancelled the original certificate and issued a new one. The owner of record received the semi-annual interest payments. Transfer books were closed on 31 May and 30 November to give the department sufficient time to bring its books up to date and prepare the schedule of interest payments due on 1 July and 1 January. If the bond had been of the coupon variety, twenty coupons, one for each semi-annual interest payment, would have been attached to each certificate. Such bonds need not be transferred on the department's books. The bearer simply presented the appropriate coupon and received the interest.[64]

The Treasury made use of existing record-keeping procedures to record the transactions and ownership of the new bond issue. Similar procedures were being used to control the bond issues of 1842 and 1843. A stock (bond) register, a journal and a ledger were set up. Volume three, the ledger, was later expanded to volumes four and five. The system can be envisioned as a double-entry set of books. The journal captured the information from the transactions, the register served as a subsidiary journal to identify outstanding certificates and the ledger sheets identified creditors and what obligations each owned.

The bond register consisted of a numerical listing of the certificates issued, both on the original and later transfers. Information collected included the owner's name, certificate number, date, the certificate's face value and the documentation used to issue the certificate. A certificate of deposit provided documentation for the original issue and the old bond certificate on subsequent transfers. The date the certificate was surrendered or transferred was also recorded. On subsequent

sales the old certificate was cancelled and a new one issued. Information similar
to the above was recorded on a new line for the buyer. The bond register provided a way of accounting for the bond certificates issued in numerical order and
a ready means of determining whether a certificate was outstanding or cancelled.
Each denomination of bonds started with certificate number one, complicat-
ing the task. Bonds were sold in denominations of $100, $500, $1,000, $3,000,
$5,000 and $10,000. The clerks kept the numbers straight by developing a code
consisting of dashes, semicircles, circles and rectangles open at the top. The certificate number for the $100 bonds was circled, the $500 certificate received a
semi-circle in front of the number, the $1,000 a rectangle open at the top, the
$3,000 a semi-circle behind the number, the $5,000 a dash in front, and the
$10,000 a check mark behind. The last transfer was recorded on 13 September
1856, shortly before the maturity date.[65]

The journal accumulated, in chronological order, the raw data to be posted
to the individual ledger accounts. Information such as name, date, folio number
(account number), certificate number issued or cancelled and the amount of the
certificate was captured for both the buyer and seller. For the new owner, information on the place of interest payment, the date interest commenced, and the
type of documentation submitted to facilitate the transfer was collected. Transactions continued until 3 April 1861, as the last of the matured bonds straggled
in.[66]

Treasury clerks periodically posted the information from the journal to the
ledger, the most critical of the records. As transactions took place, clerks posted
the date, the certificate number(s), the par value of the certificate, the interest payment site and the total value of the transaction to the individual ledger
account of both the buyer and the seller. Every six months the ledgers were balanced and closed. The balances of the individual accounts provided the means
to prepare a transcript of the interest due each bondholder. A separate transcript
for each outstanding bond issue (1842, 1843 and 1846) was sent to the seven
cities where interest was paid – New York, Boston, Philadelphia, Washington,
Charleston, New Orleans and St Louis. The transcript specified the payee, the
amount of bonds owned and the interest due. Until well into 1848, the Treasury
deposited the necessary funds in one of the city banks and the investors or their
agents presented themselves at the bank. Owners residing outside the major cities usually furnished an agent with a power of attorney to do the collecting. For
a small fee, the agent, usually a broker or private banker, forwarded the money
to the owner's place of residence or deposited it with a city bank according to
instructions. Most of the interest was paid in New York because of its large ownership in the loan, its foreign connections and because many owners needed
funds or deposits in that money centre. The Bank of America grudgingly paid
the interest in New York.[67]

The Treasury made the first entry in its new set of books before the official notification to the successful bidders. Corcoran & Riggs deposited $15,000 on 14 November and received certificate numbers one to three for $5,000 each. John Ward & Company began its operation with deposits of $250,000 on 16 November, $100,000 on 17 November and another $100,000 on 18 November. The Treasury issued the entire $450,000 in bonds on 20 November. The firm took $265,000 in its own name, $50,000 for John Jacob Astor, $25,000 for brokers Nevins, Townsend & company, $50,000 for wealthy China merchant William S. Wetmore, $5,000 for the Nautilus Insurance Company, $25,000 for George Newbold (half of his commitment) and the remainder in small lots to investors and speculators. Richard Withers, agent for the Bank of the State of New York, deposited $594,000 within the first three days and was issued the bonds on 23 November. All but $22,000 was issued in his name. John J. Palmer, in spite of his request to Corcoran, deposited the entire $150,000 on 28 November and the Register of the Treasury issued his and Hallet's bonds on 30 November. Cammann & Whitehouse deposited $115,000 on 20 November and received their entire allotment. Already $20,000 had been sold to the Brooklyn Savings Bank and another $25,000 to Cornelius Vanderbilt. DeRhann & Moore also received quick distribution of their entire allocation.[68]

Investors and institutional bidders who sought the bonds for investment purposes joined the brokers in the initial surge. The Albany Savings Bank obtained its $40,000 of bonds on 18 November, the Southwark Bank of Philadelphia received $100,000 for itself and another $25,000 for customers on 21 November, the Bank of Charleston obtained $100,000 for its own account and $35,000 for clients on 30 November, and the Bank of Hamburg, South Carolina received its $100,000 allocation on the same day. The Bank of Charleston was issued its final portion on 8 December, receiving $130,000 in its own name and $20,000 for customers.[69]

During November purchasers of the 6 per cent loan deposited $3,461,600 with the treasurer, assistant treasurers and treasurers of the mints. In December another $959,000 went into government coffers, bringing the total to $4,420,000. Receipts totalled only $395,000 in the January–March quarter, $73,149 from April to June and a final $111,000 in July 1847. At the end of the operation $4,999,149 of the bonds were sold.[70]

For purposes of its public quarterly reports, the Treasury Department considered deposits to be revenue. A delay of several days usually occurred between the date of deposit and the issuance of the stock certificates, partly because of the mail and partly because of administrative delays. In the case of the South Carolina banks the delay ranged from seven to fourteen days. As a result, the books of the treasurer, who received the deposits, and the register, who issued the certificates, did not balance until the entire issue was sold (see Table 3.4).[71]

The Treasury treated its public reports for 31 December, 31 March and 30 June as interim, to be adjusted as its far-flung agents and depositories provided more current information. The quarterly reports, especially in respect to land sales and miscellaneous income, do not add up to the official yearly totals. Since the fiscal year ended on 30 June and the official report did not go to Congress until the following December, sufficient time was available to make needed adjustments. The reports for the July through September quarters were incorporated in the secretary of the Treasury's annual report in order to inform Congress of the results of the first quarter of the ongoing fiscal year. As a result it tended to be highly accurate.[72]

Table 3.4: $5m Issue of 1846, Deposits versus Issuance of Certificates[73]

Treasurer's Public Statement of Revenue (Avails) from the Loan of 1846

Deposits	Amount ($)
November–December 1846	4,420,000
January–March 1847	395,000
April–June 1847	73,149
July 1847	111,000
Total	4,999,149

Certificates of Loan of 1846 Issued

	Monthly ($)	Total ($)
1846		
November	3,233,300	3,233,300
December	972,400	4,205,700
1847		
January	96,949	4,302,649
February	389,900	4,692,549
March	90,100	4,782,649
April	16,000	4,798,649
May	89,500	4,888,149
June	0	4,888,149
July	111,000	4,999,149

The investment bankers and speculators expected to profit by reselling the bonds to the public. The *New York Journal of Commerce* speculated that 'Wall Street will make a pretty thing of it, say $200,000, or so'.[74] Both the *Washington National Intelligencer* and the *Washington Union* considered the *Journal* wildly optimistic. The market seemed to share the more conservative opinion. If the brokers made anything of the issue the market price must rise and they needed to work hard at selling it. Immediately after the close of bidding, brokers offered the new bonds for sale in New York at 101, but attracted few buyers. During the first week sales on the New York Stock Exchange ranged from 100 to 100.75, well below the 104, plus a margin for expenses, needed to earn the predicted $200,000. In

December the brokers struggled to keep the price above par as it became obvious another larger loan would be needed early in 1847. Table 3.5 contains a listing of the prices in the New York market of the Mexican–American War debt obligations for the period 1 January 1847 to 30 June 1849.[75]

Table 3.5: Prices of Mexican–American War Securities in the New York Market, January 1847–June 1849[76]

Date	6% Treasury Notes	6% Bonds Due 1856	6% Bonds Due 1867	6% Bonds Due 1868
1847				
January		99.000 (1st)*		
February		101.000 (1st)		
March	101.750 (2nd)	101.500 (5th)		
April	101.750 (1st)	101.750 (2nd)		
May	103.875 (1st)	105.000 (3rd)		
June	105.375 (1st)	105.000 (14th)	104.500 (1st)**	
July	107.500 (1st)	106.500 (3rd)	108.000 (3rd)	
August	106.000 (3rd)	105.500 (7th)	106.500 (2nd)	
September	103.250 (1st)	104.000 (13th)	104.000 (2nd)	
October	103.125 (1st)	102.000 (28th)	104.500 (1st)	
November	101.000 (1st)	101.500 (2nd)	103.000 (2nd)	
December	100.000 (1st)	102.000 (14th)**	102.000 (1st)**	
1848				
January	98.750 (3rd)	97.000 (3rd)	99.000 (3rd)	
February	99.625 (1st)	96.500 (1st)	99.500 (1st)	
March	101.375(1st)	101.000 (3rd)	102.500 (2nd)	
April	101.625 (1st)	103.000 (13th)	103.000 (3rd)	
May	102.500 (1st)	102.750 (3rd)	104.500 (1st)	
June	102.500 (1st)	101.000 (3rd)**	102.500 (2nd)**	
July	104.250 (1st)	103.750 (10th)	104.625 (5th)	104.750 (8th)
August	102.750 (1st)	102.000 (5th)	103.375 (1st)	103.625 (1st)
September	103.375 (1st)	103.000 (18th)	104.250 (4th)	104.000 (1st)
October	103.250 (2nd)	103.000 (11th)	104.000 (6th)	104.250 (3rd)
November	103.000 (1st)	103.250 (2nd)	104.875 (1st)	105.000 (1st)
December	105.625 (1st)	103.000 (7th)**	105.500 (2nd)**	106.250 (1st)**
1849				
January	108.000 (3rd)	107.000 (4th)	108.000 (2nd)	108.500 (2nd)
February	107.500 (1st)	104.000 (1st)	108.000 (1st)	109.000 (1st)
March	111.000 (1st)	104.750 (12th)	111.625 (1st)	113.000 (1st)
April	108.000 (2nd)	104.000 (2nd)	109.000 (2nd)	110.000 (2nd)
May	110.000 (1st)	106.500 (3rd)	112.500 (1st)	113.000 (1st)
June	111.625 (1st)	106.000 (6th)**	111.500 (1st)**	112.500 (2nd)

*First Day of Month with Transaction
**ex-dividend

Since few purchasers wished to physically cart gold and silver coins to the Independent Treasury offices, much less any bankers wishing to part with their specie reserve, one of the first chores was to convince the secretary to accept another mode of payment. Elisha Riggs suggested that Corcoran ask Walker to accept certified cheques issued by the deposit banks in lieu of specie.[77] Encouraged by his initial conversation with the secretary, Corcoran requested Riggs's assistance. It would be helpful, Corcoran advised, 'if some interested party, Mr. Ward for instance, would write him [Walker], he will do what he can to facilitate the operations of the Sub-Treasury'.[78] Corcoran was able to advise Riggs on 27 November that orders had gone out to the assistant treasurer in New York to accept certified cheques. Having failed once, Walker decided to cooperate with the bankers. The Specie Clause of the Independent Treasury Act did not become operational until 1 January 1847.[79]

Contractors for the $5 million loan used similar methods to market it. First, fellow participants in their bid took all or part of their share. Next, the contractors resold as much as possible to their own clients. John Ward & Company sold large amounts to the Astors and Boston Brahmins. Finally, the major firms used local brokers to sell bonds at the market or a specific price. The brokers' commissions ranged from 0.125 to 0.75 per cent.[80]

John Ward & Company, the largest dealer in government securities for half a decade, possessed an initial advantage. The connections and network built up over the period, combined with a willingness to sell at low margins, allowed the firm to dispose of its allotment rapidly. In mid-December Ward bragged to Corcoran that he had already paid in to the Treasury $1.25 million on the loan. Despite some initial sales, Corcoran was not having the same success. Corcoran & Riggs established a broker network that included Charnley & Whelen in Philadelphia, Sam Harris & Sons in Baltimore and Gilbert & Sons in Boston. Since no investment banker controlled the loan considerable competition emerged. In this environment brokers made the best arrangement possible. Charnley & Whelen entered into a pooling agreement with their Philadelphia competitors. The firm, acting secretly for Corcoran & Riggs, received a one-third share of the Philadelphia group's sales. During November they were able to dispose of $13,800 of Corcoran & Riggs's bonds by this means. Sales were at 101 less a 0.125 per cent commission. Charnley and Whelen's commission was $17.25. Sam Harris & Sons managed to sell $13,000 worth to a family friend in Baltimore.[81]

William W. Corcoran's junior partner, George Riggs, believed the safest way to dispose of the firm's bonds was through an allegiance with John Ward & Company. By 23 November he had entered into negotiations with Ward in New York. Ward refused any additional commitment until he evaluated his critical Boston market. Two days later George proposed a profit-sharing arrangement by which each firm would receive half the proceeds above par. Corcoran did not entirely share his partner's concern and advised Elisha that sales were reasonably good and he did not care if George sold $150,000 to $200,000 of bonds to Ward or not. He expected government trust funds to take any of his bonds remaining unsold. George succeeded in arranging a profit-sharing agreement. Ward agreed to participate to the extent of $200,000 with an option for another $100,000. The option was not exercised. This arrangement, persistent efforts by Corcoran & Riggs's brokers, especially Charnley & Whelen, and a final sale to the government for its trust funds, allowed the firm to dispose of its bonds before bids were due on the next big issue.[82]

The experience gained by the Treasury in selling the loan of 1846 proved invaluable. Walker learned that government debt obligations must meet the demands of market conditions and he could not simply set his own terms. From now on the Treasury cooperated with the bankers. Treasury notes proved to be a stopgap measure and without additional incentives unlikely to be a viable financial resource. On the other hand, the interest rate and terms of the bond issue were acceptable and its sale was a success. Likewise, the investment bankers proved capable of reselling an issue of this size. However, the larger loans on the horizon would need more control and coordination if the bankers were to reap much profit.

4 THE LOAN OF 1847

The year 1847 opened with the United States still at war and the administration and Congress grappling with the best way to finance the ongoing conflict. Despite the administration's urging, Congress dismissed tax increases and elected to cover the deficit by borrowing. The Loan Act of 28 January 1847 authorized the Treasury to borrow an additional $23 million. The sale of the loan in three instalments (contracts) assured the military sufficient resources for the conquest of Mexico. The successful sale resulted from several factors. Secretary Walker was now willing to give serious consideration to the bankers' views. Their cooperation resulted in a series of treasury notes and bonds suitable for market conditions. The most prominent feature was the convertibility of the short-term treasury notes into long-term twenty-year bonds. The issues were also sold during a period of high prosperity. Finally, the marketing of the treasury notes and bonds brought a new, highly capable investment firm, Corcoran & Riggs, to the forefront of government finance.

The need for the loan arose from the inability of the American government to force the Mexicans to the peace table. A series of victories in the spring and summer of 1846, and the occupation of north-east Mexico, California and New Mexico failed to have the desired effect of ending Mexican resistance. Although the territories demanded by Polk as an indemnity were occupied, legal title remained elusive. The administration needed a peace treaty recognizing its gains. Failing this, an expensive and bloody campaign from Vera Cruz into Mexico's heartland would be required.[1]

Despite the defeats, the Mexican government and people were determined to resist. General Mariano Paredes's government fell in late July 1846, but was replaced by one even more anti-American. The new government, dominated by a coalition of supporters of Santa Anna and radical democrats led by Valentin Gomez Farias, promised the country a vigorous defence and vowed not to yield any territory. On 17 September the new government appointed Santa Anna commander-in-chief of the Mexican army and a few days later he left for the north to oppose Taylor. Clearly any peace acceptable to the Americans had to be won by conquest.[2]

In early December 1846 members of the Twenty-Ninth Congress arrived in Washington for their second session. The administration was ready with a series of proposals as to the ways and means necessary to sustain the war effort. Congress, however, retained the ultimate authority. The Democrats enjoyed a 143–77 advantage in the House and a 31–25 majority in the Senate. Though outnumbered, the Whigs were greatly encouraged by the results of the congressional and state elections of the preceding autumn. Whig prediction of disaster arising from the Democrats' economic plans had fallen on a receptive electorate. These predictions later proved false, but in the meantime fear brought the Whig's significant gains including the important governorships of New York and Pennsylvania. Some states elected their congressional delegation in the autumn of even numbered years; others did so the following year. With control of Congress resting on the results of the remaining elections, politics dominated the debate over war financing. The Democrats accused the Whigs of being Mexico's best allies. The Whigs questioned the conduct of the war and its objectives, but lacked the courage to deny the soldiers in the field the supplies needed.[3]

The state of the Treasury necessitated quick action. The heavy sale of the 6 per cent ten-year bonds in November only temporarily restored government finances. As sale of the bonds slackened, available funds fell to $2,947,162 as of 31 December and further to $2,684,984 on 25 January 1847. In the last quarter of calendar year 1846 expenditures exceeded ordinary income by $7.85 million. The Treasury covered the deficit by increasing indebtedness by $6.3 million and drawing down cash.[4]

In its preceding session, Congress, for the fiscal year ending 30 June 1847, appropriated $10 million to prosecute the war and $11,957,359 to equip and pay the volunteers. These sums were in addition to the normal army and navy appropriations. The Act of 22 July 1846 provided a means of raising $10 million of the extraordinary appropriations for fiscal year 1847, but not the balance. Additionally, if the war continued, army and navy expenditures for the next fiscal year (1848: 1 July 1847–30 June 1848) were expected to exceed peacetime requirements by $21 million. Even after applying all current revenue and exhausting the cash reserves, as well as the remaining borrowing authority, a shortfall of $19 million was projected for the remainder of fiscal year 1847 and all of fiscal year 1848 (1 December 1846–30 June 1848). The need to maintain a cash balance of $4 million raised the requirement to $23 million.[5]

President Polk and Secretary Walker proposed to meet the financial needs by increasing revenue and further borrowing. In his second annual message Polk requested that Congress consider taxing items on the free list and implementing a graduated land policy. He estimated these measures would produce an additional $4 million to $5 million between the implementation date and 30 June 1848. Increased revenues would reduce the need to borrow to $17 million or $18 million. If Congress disagreed with his revenue proposals then Polk wanted the authority to borrow the entire $23 million. Further, Polk requested the power to repurchase government bonds at the market price once peace and the surplus returned. Polk called upon Congress to limit non-military expenditures in light of the war's cost. Finally, he asked the representatives and senators to give the new tariff a chance and not make any changes other than those he suggested.[6]

In his report accompanying the president's message, Secretary Walker clarified the administration's position on taxes and borrowing. The major proposal was a 25 per cent duty on tea and coffee. Walker projected the measure would raise an additional $2.5 million a year. He urged passage early in the session to prevent a loss of revenue from heavy imports before the effective date. Borrowing could be safely limited to $17 million if the additional duties and the graduated sale of land were passed. More important than the revenue itself was the psychological effect on the Treasury's ability to borrow in the money market. The measures would assure lenders that the government possessed the means to repay.[7] Without the additional resources, Walker informed Congress, 'the government may be subjected to a serious loss in negotiating the loan, or involved in embarrassments alike injurious to the credit and honour of the country'.[8] In private, Walker informed the cabinet that it would be very difficult to float a large loan without increasing taxes.[9]

Unlike the Treasury, the American economy was experiencing a period of great prosperity in the winter and spring of 1847. The Irish famine, crop failures in Europe and repeal of the Corn Laws in Great Britain created a strong demand, at good prices, for American products, particularly breadstuffs. Grain exports and war expenditures brought prosperity to farmers, manufacturers, merchants and shippers. *Merchants' Magazine* reported that all the elements of great prosperity were present, money was abundant and exports were strong. The one drawback was the caution exhibited by some of the leading traders. The magazine attributed this to uneasiness over the new Independent Treasury. The *Washington Union* denied that the Independent Treasury was producing any adverse effects and noted that in 1846 the banks acted quite regularly and there was little effect on their specie reserves.[10] To the *Union* 'all these things show that, neither the war, the change in the tariff nor the Constitutional Treasury, has sensibly diminished the power of the banks to afford facilities to regular traders or even speculators'.[11]

Because of the increased exports specie poured into the country and became available for investment. The *Union* reported that $10 million of specie was imported in the first three months of calendar year 1847 and another $7 million was on the way. By the end of June the nation had gained $22,276,170 in specie. In April the *Economist* concluded that the United States was probably the most prosperous country on earth and attributed this happy state to free trade.

The British magazine believed the only obstacles to continued prosperity were avarice and political dishonesty by talented leaders who wished to re-instigate economic privilege (read protective tariff).[12]

As 1847 progressed the prosperity began to confound Whig politicians and proved a boon to the administration. To the surprise of the Whigs, the government, through war expenditures, pumped money into the economy instead of drawing it out. Henry Clay could only advise the faithful to keep criticizing the tariff and wait for prosperity to slow.[13] Elisha Riggs summarized the upturn as a 'fortunate turn of events for the United States at this time when it had the Mexican War to finance'.[14] War expenditures, tariff reduction and the warehouse system prevented surpluses from accumulating in the Independent Treasury and increased the pace of economic activity. With their expectation of economic disaster dashed, the Whigs adopted the tactics of continued criticism of the administration's efforts to achieve victory and opposition to territorial expansion.[15]

The beneficial effect of prosperity on war financing and the new financial system's longevity was not immediately apparent on Wall Street. Government bond prices fell during December 1846 as the prospect of a large new loan became a certainty. The new ten-year bonds closed the year below par, at 98.875 bid and 99 asked. The *New York Herald* doubted the government's ability to float a loan of the size advocated by Polk and Walker. The *Herald* feared that in its rush to make a loan the government would place itself in the power of the financiers. The paper favoured temporarily suspending the Independent Treasury Act and emitting a massive issue of treasury notes to increase the money supply.[16] The 'financial measures admirably calculated for periods of peace, are not so favourable in their operation for time of war', the paper concluded.[17] The *New York Evening Express* wondered at the source of the specie needed to take up the loan and doubted the government's ability to sell new bonds above 90 per cent.[18]

The administration quickly reminded Congress of the need for immediate action on the war measures. Walker wrote to James McKay, Chairman of the House Ways and Means Committee, on 21 December 1846, requesting early consideration of the tea and coffee duty. The *Washington Union* added its exhortation and demanded that the Democrats unite and provide the means vigorously to prosecute the war. Even the Whiggish *Washington National Intelligencer* questioned the delay in light of the urgency conveyed by Walker. The *Intelligencer* observed that one of three factors must account for the month-long delay. The Democrats in Congress were either more divided than the *Union* believed, or they felt Walker mistaken in the need for additional revenue, or, finally, they had already decided not to pass the administration's tax bill. Not one, but all three of the *Intelligencer's* propositions proved correct.[19]

The House made its sentiments known in early January. On 2 January 1847, John Wentworth, a Democrat of Illinois, introduced a resolution declaring 'that it is inexpedient to levy a duty on tea and coffee'.[20] Wentworth wanted to ensure that the secretary of the Treasury was aware of the attitude of the House. The resolution passed 115–48. Moments later another member offered a second resolution declaring 'that the people of the United States were too patriotic to refuse taxes required by the exigencies of war'.[21] It seemed the people were patriotic enough to pay for the war but their representatives lacked the will to test them. The second resolution passed to the accompaniment of Whig laughter and Democratic sniggers. *The Times* of London, tongue in cheek, surmised that a tax on tea must be unconstitutional in light of the nation's history. The tax affected too many of the congressmen's constituents. Polk blamed the defeat on a small number of dissident Democrats. Presidential politics, disappointments over patronage and western mistrust had alienated part of the Democratic Party and gone far towards eliminating Polk's working majority in Congress.[22]

With or without additional revenue, a new loan bill was clearly necessary. The bill, prepared by the Ways and Means Committee under the guidance of the Treasury, proposed an issue of one- or two-year treasury notes in the amount of $23 million. In lieu of treasury notes the president might elect to issue twenty-year bonds paying 6 per cent or less for all or part of the $23 million. As an added incentive the treasury notes were convertible into the 6 per cent bonds at the purchaser's election. In the event bonds were issued, the public lands were pledged as additional security for the principal and interest. This pledge did not extend to the treasury notes. Their security remained the good faith and credit of the federal government.[23]

The bill also extended the conversion privilege to the treasury notes issued under the Act of 22 July 1846 and to any note still outstanding under legislation prior to 1846. Potentially, $28,370,000 in twenty-year bonds could be issued. The secretary, with the president's concurrence, might also sell the bonds for specie. The bill distinguished between bonds sold for specie and those used for conversion in two aspects. Bonds issued to convert treasury notes were required to bear an interest rate of 6 per cent, while those sold for specie might bear 6 per cent or less depending on market conditions. Bonds issued in a conversion had a maturity date of 1 December 1867. Those sold were redeemable after 31 December 1867. In order to assist with the increased workload the register and the treasurer were authorized to hire a total of five new temporary clerks at an annual salary of not more than $1,250 each.[24]

In the House debate the Whigs renewed their attack on the tariff and Independent Treasury and questioned specific provisions of the loan bill. They argued that administration measures had destroyed the confidence of capitalists and placed the loan's success in doubt. The war was squandering national resources and the cost was being passed on to future generations. Two sections of the bill came in for specific criticism: Section 4, which allowed the secretary to use the notes as collateral for bank loans, and Section 19, pledging the public lands. Congressman William S. Miller (Whig, New York), demanded the elimination of Section 4 because he feared it allowed the secretary to violate the provision against selling the notes below par. He argued that under the proposed bill the secretary might pledge a larger sum in notes than the amount borrowed. His real objective was to force the sale of the notes in the market for whatever they would bring. If they sold for less than par the administration would be embarrassed. Miller dismissed the land pledge as valueless because it failed to increase the government's ability to raise funds.[25]

The *Washington Union* carried the burden of defending the administration's financial strategy. The paper accused the Whigs of being Mexico's allies, obstructionists and subverters of the government. As January began to lengthen without congressional action the *Union* lashed out at both parties. In the paper's view, congressmen were wasting too much time on inconsequential matters such as slavery, the Oregon Question and the original cause(s) of the war. Congress, not the administration, had to meet the ongoing financial crisis. Democrats who drew Congress's attention away from the crucial measures played into the hands of the Whigs and embarrassed the administration.[26]

During the House debate a further effort was made to tax tea and coffee. Representative William F. Giles (Democrat, Maryland) introduced an amendment placing a duty of 20 per cent on the two items. To make the levy more palatable he suggested limiting its life from 1 March 1847 to 1 March 1849. If Congress felt this inappropriate, Giles suggested raising the rates on selected dutiable items. He preferred this to a rumoured 5 per cent general increase. The tea and coffee amendment failed 75–71. Efforts to increase revenues by other means also failed but the loan bill itself with minor changes passed the House easily. The representatives did add an amendment preventing the Treasury from borrowing against the notes for less than par. The entire debate lasted less than a day.[27]

Four days after House passage, the Senate leadership brought the bill up for consideration. Senator Dixon Lewis urged immediate passage and stated that 'he was authorized by the Secretary of the Treasury to make as strong an appeal as could be made' for speedy action.[28] The bill passed the Senate on 26 January and was signed into law by Polk on 28 January 1847. The opposition was prepared to embarrass the administration but not withhold necessary supplies from the military.[29] Senator William Magnum of North Carolina summed the position up best when responding to the question of how the Whigs could support a war they deemed unjust. 'When the country was engaged in war', Magnum replied, 'whatever the cause – whatever the blunder – whatever the want of foresight

– whatever the lack of wisdom which had placed the country in that position – it was still the country's war and they must stand or fall by the country'.[30]

The people's representatives in their debate paid little attention to the section that drastically increased the loan's marketability. Section 13 allowed the holder to convert the short-term treasury notes into twenty-year bonds. In recommending the provision to Walker, William Corcoran estimated it would increase the value of the notes by 2 or 3 per cent. George Newbold agreed and asked Corcoran to use his influence to have the conversion period extended to six months after ratification of a peace treaty with Mexico. The final bill placed no time limit at all. In Newbold's judgement the conversion privilege would allow $8 to $10 million to be absorbed. He believed the sale of the entire $23 million possible only at a 5 per cent discount. Elisha Riggs was more optimistic and advised that a large loan was possible if government expenditures remained high enough to prevent accumulations of large amounts of specie in the Independent Treasury. The government needed to pay the money out as quickly as it received it and not reduce the currency in circulation by locking up the gold and silver coins.[31]

After passage of the loan bill, the search for additional revenue continued. On 6 February, at the urging of Congress, Walker made recommendations that would raise the tariff on selective items including a 10 per cent increase of the iron and steel duty. The proposed increases would yield $1,418,000 a year. Walker again requested a duty on tea and coffee but scaled the rate back to 15 per cent. The efforts to increase taxes in whatever guise did not receive a warm reception and all such attempts failed. The final compromise bill was voted down in the House 136–68. Patriotic Americans were not to be further burdened by their representatives this session.[32]

The last financial measure considered by the Twenty-Ninth Congress was an effort to improve the ability of the Independent Treasury to transfer funds from one depository to another. Under the proposal, public creditors could accept treasury drafts in lieu of specie if they desired. More importantly, it allowed representatives (officers and employees) of the Departments of War, the Navy and the Treasury to exchange treasury notes or drafts for coins at the market value of the notes or drafts, even if below par. A final provision allowed the secretary of the Treasury to pay the cost of physically transferring specie from one depository to another. This last point later became moot when the solicitor of the Treasury ruled that the secretary already possessed this authority. The objective of the legislation was to give the Treasury the authority to sell its own bills of exchange. Such authority would facilitate the movement of funds from the North to New Orleans. The measure passed the House too late in the session to receive Senate consideration.[33]

Walker quickly exercised his new borrowing authority by advertising for a loan on 9 February 1847. The public announcement stated the Treasury's intention of accepting sealed proposals for $18 million of 6 per cent two-year treasury notes. The bids, due on 10 April, must clearly indicate the premium the bidder was prepared to pay. Bids for less than par were unacceptable. To be more democratic and provide an opportunity for all economic classes to participate, bids for amounts as low as $50 were acceptable. Importantly, the Treasury retained the right to fix the schedule for the funds to be paid in. Both the Treasury and the financial community wanted the funds paid in instalments over many months. Balancing deposits against the Treasury's need would prevent unnecessary interest and allow the specie to return to circulation quickly. Funds were to be deposited with one of the seven major Independent Treasury officers: the treasurer in Washington, and the assistant treasurers in Boston, New York, Philadelphia (mint), Charleston, New Orleans (mint) and St Louis.[34]

Walker took advantage of the authority granted him under both the Loan Acts of 1846 and 1847 to raise additional funds during the two-month interim between the announcement of the $18 million loan on 8 February and 10 April. A group of investment bankers and individual investors agreed to take $4 million of the new 1847 treasury notes and almost $1 million of the 1846 5.4 per cent notes. The buyers purchased at par, without competitive bidding and paid in specie. Under this contract the Treasury sold $965,750 of the 1846 notes at 5.4 per cent and all $4 million of the new 1847 notes. Of the latter, a total of $471,000 bore 5.4 per cent and the remainder 6 per cent. Matthew Morgan & Company of New York and Corcoran & Riggs of Washington purchased the bulk of the 1847 notes. Their contract required $2 million to be deposited with the treasurer at the mint in New Orleans and the remainder in New York. Morgan, an ex-New Orleans druggist, maintained strong personal and business ties with the delta city. His wife was the daughter of the president of the Canal and Banking Company of New Orleans and Morgan served as its New York agent. Marriage ties also linked him to the Bank of the State of New York through his son-in-law Dudley Selden, one of the bank's principal officers.[35]

The 5.4 per cent 1846 notes went to a number of speculators. The buyers expected to convert their purchases into the new 6 per cent bonds. Corcoran & Riggs and their allies, John Thompson and James J. Palmer, took $195,000, Beebe, Ludlow & Company, $200,000, Congressman Washington Hunt (Whig, New York), $200,000 and a variety of brokers and investors, $120,750. Between 5 January and 1 March 1847, the Treasury sold or reissued $715,750 of the notes at par. In one last questionable transaction on 31 May 1847, Congressman William W. Woodworth (Democrat, New York), obtained $250,000, bringing the final total to $965,750. In addition to the 1846 notes, Hunt obtained $71,000 and Woodworth $50,000 of the 1847 5.4 per cent notes at par. At the time Walker was rejecting offers from others. Both Hunt and Woodworth were influential bankers in addition to being congressmen. Other congressmen and senators were accommodated to a lesser extent. Over thirty members obtained allocations from $1,000 to $5,000 of the new 6 per cent notes. Most received $2,500.[36]

The two largest purchasers of the 1847 notes under the February contract, Corcoran & Riggs and Morgan & Company, agreed, as part of the marketing campaign, to a joint venture for $2.4 million. The $2.4 million commitment called for the sale of $1.4 million on joint account. Each firm was responsible for marketing half of the remaining $1 million. Additionally, each firm and its principals bought more notes that were not part of the $2.4 million agreement. Corcoran & Riggs's total commitment approached $1.7 million. Together, the two firms bought almost 80 per cent of the $4 million issue. They began their operation in February 1847, when Morgan, as assignee for the group, deposited $1.5 million with the mint treasurer in New Orleans and secured a like amount of 6 per cent notes in $1,000 denominations. During the remainder of February a further $1 million went in the coffers of the assistant treasurer in New York. In March an additional $351,500 was deposited. By March 31 the venturers' share of the $3,251,350 in the new 6 per cent notes issued by the Treasury up to that time was $2,851,500.[37]

In the operation's beginning, Corcoran, expecting a price rise, advised his personal allies to delay their deposits or hold the notes once received. Moreover, under the joint agreement he allowed Morgan a free hand in the sale of the jointly-owned notes. Both the delay in selling and trusting Morgan to look after everyone's interest proved mistakes. Morgan disposed of his group's holdings and those of the joint account at an average price of 102. Free of his inventory he then attempted to force the price down in order to keep the bids low on the upcoming $18 million dollar issue. With the 10 April deadline approaching, Corcoran & Riggs, Corcoran personally and the firm's friends still had almost $1 million to sell.[38]

In mid-March both Corcoran & Riggs and Elisha Riggs instructed their broker network to start selling in earnest. By this time the market was saturated and they did well to net 1 per cent profit on their remaining notes. Elisha authorized Charnley & Whelen in Philadelphia to sell $20,000 of his personal holdings at 101.75 or above on 18 March. Between that date and 31 March the firm managed to sell this $20,000 plus another $4,000 at prices ranging from 102 to 101.125 less their 0.125 per cent brokerage commission. Charnley & Whelen blamed their inability to sell more on a fully supplied market. They believed if the notes had been released earlier they could have sold as much as $200,000 in Philadelphia at prices ranging from 101.125 to 102.[39]

Corcoran & Riggs also used the services of Charnley & Whelen and others to market the firm's share of the notes. The brokers did slightly better for Corcoran & Riggs than for Elisha. By 22 March they had deposed of $47,700 of a $50,000 allotment at prices between 102 and 103. A reconciliation of their account with Corcoran & Riggs on 22 April indicated Charnley & Whelen's sales of the new notes and 6 per cent bonds had reached $155,000. Samuel Harris & Son sold an additional $80,000 of Corcoran & Riggs's notes between 2 March and 14 April. In an effort to expand their market further, Corcoran & Riggs entered into a profit-sharing agreement with John Ward & Company. The joint operation commenced on 22 February and continued through 22 March. The firms sold $220,000 of the 6 per cent notes at prices from 101.5 to 101.75. The proceeds of $223,277.80 less carrying charges of $2,169.64 yielded a profit of $556.00 for each firm. Elisha's profits were also small. In a profit-sharing venture with his youngest son, Elisha, Jr, the two bought $154,500 in 6 per cent notes at par and resold them between 15 March and 8 April at between 101.5 and 102. The pair divided $1,480.50 after deducting carrying charges and commissions. To this point participation by Corcoran & Riggs and Elisha in the sale of the 1846 6 per cent ten-year bonds and the first $4 million of the 1847 6 per cent treasury notes had provided much experience but little profit.[40]

The ability of the government to prosecute the war vigorously without undue financial strain for the next year depended on the success of the $18 million flotation. The early sales under the February contracts only provided interim financing. During March and early April the speculators and investment bankers debated the bid price sufficient to secure a large part of the new loan. The heavy exports had made money plentiful and more specie was arriving by each packet boat.[41] 'If money is scarce this spring', the *New York Journal of Commerce* observed, 'it will never be plenty while the world stands'.[42] The *Journal* acknowledged the loan's likely success and attributed the government's good fortune to the prosperous agricultural sector. The drop in custom revenues for the quarter ending 31 December 1846 caused the paper some concern. These concerns faded with the approach of spring and a leap in duties from $3,645,965 (October–December 1846) to $6.3 million (January–March 1847).[43]

As 10 April approached, the bidders anxiously watched the market price of the outstanding notes and bonds on the exchanges. During March the price of the new 6 per cent notes fluctuated between 101 and 102. On 10 April, the day bidding closed, the notes on sale in New York sold at 101. The heavy upcoming sale served as a drag on the market. Another factor entering into the bidders' consideration was the rate at which the money must be paid in to the Treasury. Instalments due over several months would allow the bankers to sell one month's allocation and use the funds for the next month's deposits. Serious bidders attempted to obtain the information from the Treasury. In mid-February Corcoran informed Elisha that the secretary had not yet decided on the amount of the monthly instalments, but in Corcoran's opinion the payments would be less than $3 million a month. After receiving a direct inquiry from James G.

King, Walker informed the investment banker that payments depended on the government's needs. Walker believed immediate requirements to be $5 million or less. Matthew Morgan was informed that monthly payments would not exceed $3 million. Walker qualified his statements and warned all parties that no agreement would restrict the government's right to demand the money if need arose. Rumours circulated in Wall Street that the government's real needs would not exceed $2 million a month.[44]

Greed and ambition doomed efforts by the major New York and Washington bidders to combine. Matthew Morgan initially refused to cooperate with Corcoran & Riggs and John Ward & Company. He formed his own group with the support of the officers of the Bank of the State of New York. Subsequently, Morgan and Ward did reach an agreement to take a third each. Corcoran refused their offer to join and bid for the last third. Instead, waiting until the afternoon of 10 April and probably benefiting from knowledge of his competitors' bids, Corcoran in the name of Corcoran & Riggs submitted a bid for the entire $18 million at 100.125 ($100 and 12.5¢ for each $100 in bonds). The bid came as a shock and unpleasant surprise to his junior partner, George Riggs, and to George's father, Elisha. In addition to this bid, Elisha had already submitted one for $1,650,000 at 100.15 ($100 and 15¢ for each $100 in bonds). Half of this latter bid was for the account of Corcoran & Riggs and $100,000 for Elisha's nephew Samuel Riggs in Baltimore. The Corcoran & Riggs bid joined others from New York and Boston. Before the bids were opened the *Philadelphia Public Ledger* predicted total bids of $40 million with $20 million coming from New York.[45]

On Monday, 12 April, Walker, joined by McClintock Young, chief clerk, and two loan clerks, opened the envelopes containing the bids. The ceremony accorded with Treasury Department procedures and precedents. Each bidder submitted a sealed bid specifying the amount of notes they were prepared to take and the price to be paid.[46]

Four major groups, two from New York, and one each from Washington and Boston, bid for large percentages of the entire loan. Winslow & Perkins led one of the New York groups and bid for $12,333,333 at 100.05. The second New York group, John Ward & Company and Morgan & Company, bid for $12 million at the same price. A Boston group headed by David Henshaw, banker and Jacksonian political leader, bid for $7 million at 100.0625. Corcoran & Riggs's bid at 100.125 secured the lion's share of the loan. Elisha's bid for $1,650,000 at 100.15 was also successful. Altogether, $21,291,350 was bid at 100.125 or above and $36,431,633, unsuccessfully, below that point. Individuals or firms that equalled or exceeded Corcoran & Riggs's bid received the entire amount of their bid. In the end Corcoran & Riggs was allocated $14.7 million. When added to Elisha's bid, the total under contract exceeded 90 per cent of the issue. The other major successful bidders included John Thompson, $500,000, a friend of Corcoran, and two banks, the Bank of North America (Philadelphia), $200,000, and the Bank of the Metropolis (Washington), $100,000. The remaining 5 per cent was spread among small investors and speculators. The large New York, Boston and Philadelphia investment houses were shut out and angry about it. They and median-sized dealers such as Chubb & Schenck of Washington, E. W. Clark & Company of Philadelphia and Cammann & Whitehouse of New York had to go to Corcoran & Riggs if they wished to participate in the marketing of the notes to the public.[47]

Congratulations and a sense of relief greeted news of the Treasury's successful sale of the loan above par. The *Washington Union* believed bids nearing $58 million at par or above demonstrated public confidence in the administration, its policies and the resources of the nation. To the *United States Magazine* success reflected the faith of the people and served as a rebuke to those critics predicting the country's ruin. The *Philadelphia Public Ledger* stretched the point by stating that no European nation was capable at borrowing above par. It stated, incorrectly, that the American loan was taken by a broad group of men with modest means, not a small group of money dealers as in Europe. William Corcoran's current means might be modest, but his ambitions equalled those of any European banker. He was on his way to becoming a money dealer of the first class. Still, in light of the terms extracted from most countries, the loan must be rated a success, especially since the contractors were dependent on the American market to absorb the notes. Indirectly, much of the capital did come from Europe. Exports and war profits created a large pool of unemployed capital available for investment in government debt obligations.[48]

The unsuccessful bidders and their supporters in the press quickly began to charge Walker with dishonesty and favouritism. They accused him of assuring Corcoran that not more than $2 million a month would be needed and of informing him of his competitors' bids. The *New York Courier* believed bids would have been higher if the monthly needs had been known. *Merchants' Magazine* questioned the secrecy of the bidding process. Both allegations came to naught, mainly because of a strong defence of Walker by the *New York Journal of Commerce*. The *Journal* pointed out that the size of the instalments was generally known in Wall Street. The paper attributed the New Yorkers' and Bostonians' lack of success to their desire to drive too hard a bargain. The close relationship between Corcoran and Walker does provide a basis for speculation. Robert Shenton in his biography of Walker concludes that Corcoran was allowed access to competing bids. Henry Cohen, in his study of Corcoran's business career, equivocates. Cohen believes Corcoran's information may have come directly from his competitors, with whom he was negotiating almost to the deadline. The size of the bid certainly surprised the Riggs family. Later events indicating favouritism by Walker towards Corcoran clearly support Shenton's allegation of insider information. Corcoran bid just high enough to control the marketing of the loan. This control was cheap at 7.5¢ on each $100 note. On the entire $14.7 million the extra price was slightly over $11,000.[49]

The successful bid made Corcoran the most influential factor in government financing. He held this position well into the 1850s. Corcoran, the son of a moderately prosperous Washington merchant, real estate investor and local politician, was born in Georgetown, Maryland, in 1798. He worked in his older brothers' mercantile business until he was able to convince them to open a branch store under his management in 1817. The business failed in 1823 and Corcoran turned to managing the District of Columbia real estate of his father and that of two banks, the Columbia Bank of Washington and the Washington branch of the Second Bank of the United States. Between 1823 and 1837 he built up a small supply of capital and made useful friends. In 1837 he opened a stock brokerage business in Washington. Three years later he joined George Washington Riggs to form Corcoran & Riggs.[50]

George brought much needed capital and, more importantly, access to the resources and contacts of the far-flung and influential Riggs family. This extended family, originally from Maryland, had prospered as merchants and private bankers during the first half of the nineteenth century. By 1845 they were managing mercantile and private banking firms in Baltimore, Philadelphia, St Louis and New York. Elisha Riggs, George's father, had engaged in an importing business with a younger partner, George Peabody, until 1829. At that time he moved to New York to engage in banking and continued to prosper.[51]

Corcoran & Riggs moved successfully into the vacuum created by the Panic of 1837. Its original capital consisted of $5,000 supplemented by $20,000 deposited by the two partners. Short-term loans from Elisha provided much of the capital for the firm's extensive dealing in treasury notes during the period 1837–43. Because of Elisha's influence the firm was able to become the Washington agent of such New York interests as the Bank of America and Merchants Bank. The firm dealt in exchange, bank notes and treasury notes and acted as a broker. Corcoran cultivated government patronage and expanded his contacts to include such influential bankers as the Baring Brothers, George Peabody in London and George Newbold.[52]

Much of the firm's success resulted from its political connections and Corcoran's commitment to the Democratic Party. The Van Buren administration, surrounded by District of Columbia chartered banks that were dominated by Whigs, welcomed the upstart and made as much use of its facilities as possible. The firm's influence continued to grow after Van Buren's defeat. The Tyler administration needed friends wherever they could be found. In August 1844, it designated the private banking firm of Corcoran & Riggs a government depository and proceeded to build this account up to one of the largest in the nation. The growing influence was carefully noted in financial circles.[53]

Corcoran personally proclaimed his intimacy with the government in quarters where such influence was deemed useful. In the last year of the Tyler administration, he assured George Peabody 'our position and standing with the Executive and heads of departments gives us advantages in transactions with the government not enjoyed by others'.[54] The Democrats' victory in 1844 enhanced his position. In September 1845 Corcoran informed Peabody that 'our position here gives us many advantages, having the earliest information in relations to matters and things'.[55] Corcoran solidified his position by hosting lavish dinner parties attended by the capitol's political elite and actively participating in civic affairs such as serving as financial advisor to the Smithsonian's executive committee. The museum's trust fund also provided a ready market for securities. Astute observers quickly recognized Corcoran & Riggs's position as the government's de facto banker.[56]

As a private bank the firm provided discreet financial services to political leaders badly in need of such assistance. James K. Polk, James Buchanan, Daniel Webster, Henry Clay, Stephen Douglas and freshman congressman Abraham Lincoln were among the many availing themselves of the firm's assistance. Upon arriving in Washington, Polk established an account where he regularly deposited his salary and drew drafts paying such expenses as his private secretary's salary and the cost of building his Nashville retirement home.[57]

Polk also used Corcoran's investing and purchasing services. On 12 March 1847, Corcoran & Riggs sold Polk three $1,000 6 per cent bond certificates, numbered 60, 61 and 62, at the market price, 101. The certificates were part of a $14,000 lot obtained by Corcoran & Riggs by converting treasury notes. By May, Polk's conscience was bothering him and he began to doubt the ethics of the president owning such securities. He demanded Corcoran buy the bonds back at Polk's cost. Corcoran resold the stock at 105 and donated the profit to charity. Apparently Polk later overcame his scruples because documents in the Polk Papers indicate he possessed nine $500 treasury notes in December 1847. An additional $6,500 in treasury notes and bonds were issued to him between 29 February and 3 June 1848.[58] Besides financial services to Polk, Corcoran assisted in the refurbishing of the White House. For these services he was reimbursed $11,816.20 for furniture and furnishings ordered and paid for by him.[59]

Though a partisan Democrat, Corcoran did not limit his largesse to that party. Daniel Webster received loans and outright gifts. Henry Clay used Corcoran's services to collect drafts, send money to his children and as a source of loans for speculative investments. Clay also sent solicitors from his favourite charities to the banker. Lincoln availed himself of Corcoran & Riggs's services to collect drafts and transfer money. The firm's successor, Riggs & Company, served as Lincoln's personal banker during his presidency.[60]

Once it became clear that Corcoran & Riggs controlled the loan, investment bankers, brokers and speculators approached them with offers to assist in its distribution. First in line were the unsuccessful bidders and the large purchasers on their lists. The Bank of America requested $500,000. Corcoran & Riggs accepted an offer from Henshaw in Boston to buy $300,000 at 102.5 with an option for $200,000 more. Matthew Morgan & Company agreed to purchase $250,000 remaining from Corcoran & Riggs's February contract at par and $500,000 of the April contract at 101.25. As part of this arrangement Morgan agreed to deposit $500,000 of this amount in specie with the assistant treasurer at the New Orleans mint. In association with Morgan, John Ward took an additional $500,000 of the April notes. Beebe, Ludlow of New York took $100,000 at 103.5. Smaller brokers such as Gilbert & Son of Boston, Gundy & Dawes of Charleston, Jacob Little & Company of New York, Josiah Lee of Baltimore and Asa Clapp of Portland, Maine, agreed to take small amounts.[61]

After negotiating agreements with the large purchasers, Corcoran & Riggs began to market the notes to the public. The circumstances were favourable with money easy and a prosperous country. Once it was known the new issue was controlled by strong hands, the 6 per cent treasury notes immediately rose from 101.5 to 103 on the New York market. The notes began a steady upward climb on the open market, reaching 104 in early May, 105 by mid-May, 106 by mid-June and a high of 108 on 3 July. At this point the notes began to decline, falling to 106 on 3 August, 103.25 on 2 September, 103 on 1 October, 101 on 1 November and descending to par on 1 December. The market price of the notes in New Orleans was consistently 1 to 4 per cent lower than in New York.[62]

The pricing structure in selling the 6 per cent treasury notes and the new 6 per cent twenty-year bonds was different. The interest on the treasury notes accumulated from the date the purchase price was deposited and was paid every six months *from* that date. Individuals who purchased notes from Corcoran & Riggs, or anyone else, paid a specific quoted price, plus the accumulated interest up to that date. Interest on the 6 per cent bonds was paid on 1 January and 1 July. The price of the bonds quoted in the newspapers and on the stock exchanges included accrued interest. The price of the bonds, but not notes, naturally increased during the period between interest dates to reflect the value of the accrued interest. For example, as of 1 April the price of the bonds included 1.5 per cent for three months of interest. As of the ex-dividend dates (1 June and 1 December) the price usually fell 3 points to reflect the loss of six months' interest. The 6 per cent bonds dropped from 107.5 at the end of May to 104.25 on 1 June. The treasury notes were not affected and retained their value at 105.375 bid and 105.625 asked.[63]

To obtain the actual treasury notes, Corcoran & Riggs first had to obtain the permission of the secretary of the Treasury to make a deposit at one of the Independent Treasury offices. Unless the assistant treasurers or depository had obtained authority from Washington, they consistently refused to accept the money. On 14 April 1847, Walker authorized Corcoran & Riggs to make the first deposit towards the $18 million April contract. The authorization totalled $1.6 million, broken down between New York, $1 million, Washington, $100,000, Baltimore, $100,000, Philadelphia, $200,000 and Boston $200,000. Elisha received permission to deposit $200,000, equally divided between Boston and New York. On 20 April Walker issued permission for another $980,000 plus the balance of the premium of $14,386 to be deposited. On 26 April Corcoran & Riggs was authorized to deposit $250,000 in New Orleans and Matthew Morgan & Company a further $250,000 there as Corcoran & Riggs's agent. Permission to make the first St Louis deposit was given 27 April.[64]

The firm's customers made most of the $4,637,100 deposited to the credit of Corcoran & Riggs during April and May. In dealing with the major subcontractors and brokers, Corcoran & Riggs successfully instituted a policy of having the purchasers make the deposits for them. The major subcontractors used their own resources to make deposits, secure the notes from the government and then resale them. Brokers working on commissions made agreements to sell, obtained the money from the buyer and deposited it with the Independent Treasury or in one of the banks where Corcoran & Riggs maintained an account. In the latter event the bank deposits were pooled and then a large deposit made by Corcoran & Riggs with the Independent Treasury. Not every broker or customer was enamoured with using their own funds. Samuel Harris & Sons of Baltimore refused to make deposits. The 0.125 per cent commission was not sufficient to put up money on the front end. They informed Corcoran that if they were disposed to do this they would have bid on the notes themselves.[65]

Despite isolated complaints, Corcoran & Riggs disposed of the first $4 to $5 million of the notes with limited use of the firm's funds. Most of the money came from the large subcontractors. Henshaw & Sons deposited $500,000 in Boston in accordance with their agreement. Matthew Morgan deposited $500,000 in New Orleans and together with John Ward another $750,000 in New York to complete their initial agreement with Corcoran & Riggs. After completion of this subcontract Morgan and Corcoran alternated between hostility and cooperation. Money and ambition drove them apart and then brought them back together.[66]

With the large subcontracts completed, Corcoran & Riggs turned to its broker network to market directly to the public. Institutions and large individual customers might receive a discount but not the general public. The firm started selling on the open market at 104 and refused any offers below that price. A series of victories in Mexico, including Scott's storming of Cerro Gordo, and periodic rumours of peace helped the price of the notes rise. Peace, the *New York Tribune* speculated, would increase the price of the notes by 5 per cent. Additionally, by 1 June the other successful bidders were almost out of the market, leaving it to Corcoran & Riggs, Elisha and John Thompson.[67]

In an effort to market the notes in an orderly fashion Corcoran urged restraint on his allies. Control of the loan allowed the firm to match sales to demand. In April Corcoran asked Elisha to hold his earliest purchases for forty days and predicted a rise to 110. The psychological effect, not the volume, of any sales by Elisha was the real concern. Both Elisha and John Thompson deposited steadily and by 30 November Elisha had honoured $1 million of his $1,650,000 commitment and Thompson $415,000 of his $500,000. Additionally, between 13 April and 30 November a total of $11,661,850 was deposited and credited to the account of Corcoran & Riggs. Most of this was applicable to the $14.7 million April contract.[68]

The first few months were the most profitable period and Corcoran & Riggs, their subcontractors and brokers worked hard at marketing the notes. The territorial arrangements occasionally led to strife. In the middle of June Corcoran requested Elisha to assure their New York associates that Corcoran & Riggs had not used outside brokers to sell notes in that city for two weeks. He did admit to selling $100,000 to William B. Astor at the bargain price of 101.5 in a private transaction. Advances were also made to August Belmont, the New York representative of the Rothschilds, with a view to selling that firm treasury notes. Care needed to be taken against giving offence because finally both Corcoran & Riggs and Elisha were profiting mightily from their venture in government securities.[69]

The fiscal year beginning 1 July 1847 opened auspiciously with treasury notes selling at 107.5 and the Treasury's balance at a healthy $6.1 million. The situation began to deteriorate as the summer advanced and as Scott demanded more resources for his march on Mexico City. On 20 July, Walker called upon Corcoran & Riggs and Elisha for a deposit of $2 million. This was in addition to the $1,598,700 that they were in the process of depositing for the month. Corcoran managed to get the demand put off until after 1 August when he expected the New York money market to be easier. The Treasury's needs were great because heavy military and semi-annual interest, pension and Indian Department payments reduced the cash reserves to $2.4 million during July. The $2 million demand was met, but just. Corcoran & Riggs and Elisha's deposits totalled $2,070,000 for August. In September, their deposits fell to $367,100.[70]

During the summer it finally became necessary for Corcoran & Riggs to borrow money in order to carry their inventory of unsold notes. In the beginning arrangements were made to borrow $1 million at 4 per cent. A profit could be made on treasury notes paying 6 per cent at this rate. The money was provided by the Merchants Bank, $700,000, and the Bank of America, $300,000, both of New York. Elisha secured an additional $50,000 from the Mutual Atlantic Insurance Company. Treasury notes were used as collateral. The strong financial backing and a buoyant market helped Corcoran & Riggs withstand a July bear raid on the notes by their erstwhile friends, Matthew Morgan and the officers of the Bank of the State of New York. As summer approached its end without peace, the interest rate rose. In September Corcoran was in Albany negotiating a $300,000 loan at 6 per cent.[71]

Fortunately the Treasury's need for money decreased as the July–September 1847 quarter progressed. Walker could be considerate of his friends. General prosperity and anticipation of large autumn sales dramatically increased imports. Customs revenues were the largest of any quarter during the Polk administration. The $11,106,257 in duties and $955,417 in land and miscellaneous income came within $2 million of paying the military and ordinary expenses for the quarter. The Treasury's balance rebounded to $4.3 million and remained in the $4.2 to $4.5 million range for the rest of the calendar year.[72]

The increasing tariff duties, however, made the stock market uneasy. Nervous bankers feared the huge imports would trigger a massive export of specie to pay for the goods. A reasonable harvest in Europe would reduce the export of foodstuffs and adversely affect the favourable exchange rate New York enjoyed with London. In August, Charnley & Whelen reported a softening in the demand for treasury notes. In its September issue *Bankers' Magazine* gave the financial situation a mixed review. On the negative side the magazine foresaw a tightening American money market, a British financial crisis, heavy military expenditures and an expected drain of specie. On a positive note, *Bankers'* concluded the currency was sound, adequate credit available for good borrowers; the commercial community was in good shape and the entire nation wealthier. The more pessimistic *New York Herald* feared expenditures of $1 million a week would exhaust government resources before Congress met again.[73]

The favourable market enjoyed by Corcoran & Riggs did, as Charnley & Whelen surmised, begin to deteriorate in August when treasury notes fell from 106 to 103.5. During September the price in New York stabilized in the 103–4 range, but in October the downward spiral resumed and the notes dropped to par on 1 December. There was a considerable specie drain, but not as yet directly to Europe. The *Washington Union* reported the export of $12 million into Mexico during 1847 to pay the troops and purchase supplies locally. By autumn many observers were also predicting large exports of specie to Europe. The *Economist* of London feared competition between the American government and merchants for a dwindling supply of coins would disrupt the American money market. The magazine foresaw higher American interest rates, an unfavourable exchange rate for the Americans and a slackening of trade. Though the situation proved less dire than predicted, specie did finally begin to move to Europe. In the first twenty days of November, *Niles' National Register* reported shipments of $1.5 million and estimated a monthly total of $2 million. The same day, the paper reported the sale of treasury notes at 99.875.[74]

Government revenue fell precipitously in the quarter beginning in October. The end of the import season cut custom duties by almost half. Fortunately, expenses dropped by 40 per cent. During this era the Treasury made its semi-annual interest, pension and Indian Bureau payments in January and July. Unless something highly unusual occurred payments in these two quarters were significantly higher than the other two. Military activity also slowed after Scott's army stormed the outlying defences of Mexico City and occupied the capital on 14 September 1847. This lessening of activity in no way accounted for a drop of almost two-thirds in military expenditures between the July–September and October–December quarters. In comparing the October–December quarter with the preceding and following quarters it becomes obvious the Treasury was rolling some expenses over into January 1848 and beyond.[75]

Corcoran & Riggs responded to the falling market for treasury notes by restricting American sales whenever possible, seeking foreign markets and finding new ways to profit. Fortunately for the firm, the reduction in federal expenditures limited the need for instalment payments on the $18 million contract. Deposits during the October–December quarter of 1847 by Corcoran & Riggs, Elisha Riggs and John Thompson totalled only $1,567,500. In September Corcoran attempted again, without success, to interest August Belmont in making large purchases for the account of the Rothschilds. They were not quite ready. George Peabody in London also expressed little interest in marketing the 6 per cent treasury notes though Elisha did send him $20,000 worth, unsolicited, on consignment. Both the Rothschilds and Peabody blamed the chaotic British money market. Specie exports and the bursting of a railroad-building bubble had brought recession and bank failures to Great Britain. American commercial banks provided a potential market that Corcoran attempted to exploit. To further this goal Corcoran and his associates attempted to have the New York Free Banking Act of 1838 amended. Corcoran's proposal was reasonable. It allowed New York banks to use federal treasury notes and bonds, in addition to those of New York State, as collateral for the bank notes being issued. It was hoped the plan would open up a new market and increase the price of the treasury notes and bonds. The law was amended in 1849 and had the desired effect.[76]

The effort to limit sales did not always prove successful. In November Corcoran & Riggs pleaded with Elisha not to sell notes below par. The firm feared the banks would call its loans if the price broke further. Corcoran & Riggs offered to buy Elisha's current inventory of $200,000 at 100.25 to hold them off the market. The firm had a $3 million commitment of its own to work off in the next four months. In their rush to accomplish this task they did not always follow their own advice and made sales at a loss. By 21 January 1848 they were able to report success. They expected to make their final deposit before the end of the month and had only $350,000 in notes to sell. The effort was completed by the end of February. The firm earned $250,000 on its portion of the April contract, 80 per cent of which was made on the sale of the first $5 million. William Corcoran and the Riggs family earned additional profits by trading on their individual accounts.[77]

Means other than sales were found to profit from the marketing of the notes. Part of Elisha's mercantile operations included the firm of Riggs and Levering of St Louis. The managing partner, Lawrason Riggs, was Elisha's son. The partnership engaged in a mercantile business and used Elisha's facilities to sell exchange to St Louis wholesalers who needed to pay creditors in New York. In August 1847 Corcoran & Riggs began to make extensive use of the St Louis firm. They authorized Lawrason Riggs to sell exchange on them or Elisha whenever a premium could be obtained. The specie collected in St Louis was deposited with the assistant treasurer in that city and used to obtain treasury notes. Elisha or the Bank of America, acting for Corcoran & Riggs, redeemed the bills in New York. Corcoran & Riggs earned a tidy profit from the sale of the bills (Jay Cooke estimates 2–3.5 per cent). The operation started in September with the deposit of the proceeds from the sale of two $50,000 bills of exchange. By 21 January 1848, Riggs & Levering were reporting exchange sales of $419,916. Before the operation ceased it totalled $800,000. During the marketing of the next large loan this source of profit became a small gold mine operated by Corcoran & Riggs and its competitors.[78]

With the $18 million contract approaching completion and new loan legislation still under congressional consideration, Secretary Walker decided to announce a third contract, in the amount of $5 million, under the authority of the Act of 28 January 1847. A drop in the Treasury balance from $4.2 million on 27 December 1847 to $2,331,268 on 24 January 1848 necessitated the effort. The source of the notes was the $1 million remaining from the original $23 million authorization and $4 million of notes previously sold and returned to the Treasury in payment of public dues. Once the notes fell below par it became profitable for importers to buy them up and use the notes to pay custom duties. The collector of customs accepted the notes at 100 regardless of their market price. In New York alone, $3,072,525 was received between 1 January and 31 March 1848. Additional notes were redeemed for specie by the Treasury or paid in at the land offices. After March rising prices reduced the flow to a trickle. During the fiscal year ending 30 June 1848, a total of $5,912,200 in previously issued notes was redeemed by the Treasury. Those issued under the authority of the Act of 28 January 1847 accounted for $4,584,250 of the total.[79]

The *Washington Union* announced the upcoming sale of an additional $5 million in treasury notes on 26 February 1848. The instructions for bidding, except for two items, were similar to those of the $18 million contract. Two-year 6 per cent treasury notes convertible into 6 per cent twenty-year bonds were again being offered. This time specific rules on instalment payments were included. Three equal payments due in March, April and May would be required. Additionally, the bidders must deposit the premium in advance.[80]

Corcoran & Riggs's repeated approaches to the Rothschilds finally bore fruit and the two agreed to submit a joint bid for the entire amount. Their agreement apportioned 60 per cent of the notes to N. M. Rothschild & Sons of London and 40 per cent to Corcoran & Riggs. When the bids were opened their offer of 101.26 appeared to capture 85 per cent of the issue. However, Walker had already disposed of $1,920,000 of the total in prior sales at par.[81] The prior sales, according to *Bankers' Magazine*, were 'made by the Secretary of the Treasury some thirty or forty days ago [before 8 March 1848] while treasury notes and United State sixes were yet below par'.[82] The private buyers included the State of Alabama Sinking Fund, $1 million, John Thompson, $500,000, Matthew Morgan & Company, $170,000, Corning & Company, $50,000, and, surprisingly, August Belmont for the Rothschilds, $200,000. Of the $3,280,000 remaining, the joint venturers, Corcoran & Riggs and the Rothschilds, obtained $2,350,000. The remainder went to John S. Riddle of Philadelphia, $500,000, Charles Macalester and E. W. Clark & Company, both of Philadelphia, $350,000 jointly, and others in the amount of $80,000. Walker accepted $200,000 in bids beyond the $5 million announced.[83]

In the weeks before the 8 March closing date the prospects for peace brightened and drove up the price of notes. News arrived in Washington on 19 February of the treaty negotiated by Nicholas Trist and representatives of the Mexican government. Despite personal reservations and politically-motivated opposition from James Buchanan and Robert Walker, Polk submitted the treaty to the Senate for consideration on 23 February. Strong peace prospects increased confidence in American investments on both sides of the Atlantic.[84]

The return of foreign capital to the American market received a favourable reception from the press. *Bankers' Magazine* labelled it the most agreeable financial development of the month. The *Washington Union* believed it displayed rising confidence by European bankers in American stocks and should bring relief to a tightening domestic money market. The *New York Courier and Inquirer* disputed these benefits. It surmised that the specie to buy the notes would come from the United States, not Europe. The paper believed the Rothschilds would obtain the specie by selling exchange in New York, not by shipping coins across the Atlantic. The *New York Tribune* anticipated that the Rothschilds would use Mexican funds and speculated that an agreement to provide the American military with funds in Mexico had already been reached. The *Tribune's* speculation held much truth.[85]

The successful bid for $350,000 by E. W. Clark & Company in combination with broker Charles Macalester introduced an aggressive new competitor into the field of federal finance. E. W. Clark & Company entered the private banking business in Philadelphia in 1837 just as the Panic of that year got under way. The principal partner, E. W. Clark, had gained considerable experience and made many business acquaintances as an employee of S. H. Allen & Company. This latter firm began as a distributor of lottery tickets and expanded into the sale of exchange and stock brokerage. E. W. Clark & Company possessed little capital when it began business, but neither was it encumbered with debts or other obligations. The firm managed to ride out the Panic of 1837 as many of its more established competitors failed. E. W. Clark & Company began by selling exchange and dealing in out-of-town bank notes and expanded into stock brokerage. Between 1837 and 1847 the private banker built up a network of allied firms and family partnerships located in most of the major cities. The important related firm of E. W. Clark & Brothers was established in St Louis in 1842. E. W. Clark & Company's most valuable asset was its aggressive young partner, Jay Cooke. Marketing Mexican War loans provided Cooke the experience needed to become the dominant factor in financing the Civil War.[86]

Jay Cooke began to market his firm's share of the third contract on 17 March. In the next two-and-a-half months Cooke made $432,450 in deposits. In addition to marketing its own notes, the firm was selling for Corcoran & Riggs. After May, E. W. Clark & Company turned its attention to the loan of 1848. Corcoran & Riggs also seems to have lost interest and allowed Corning & Company and the Morgans the major role in disposing of its remaining 6 per cent treasury notes.[87]

The Treasury Department closed its books and ceased issuing the treasury notes authorized under the Act of 28 January 1847 on 30 November 1848. Under the three contracts a total of 40,050 treasury note certificates were issued. The face value totalled $26,122,100. All but $471,000 were at 6 per cent.[88]

The certificates were printed for the Treasury by the firm of Rawdon, Wright, Hatch & Company of New York. The firm supplied both the note and bond certificates for the loans of 1846 and 1847. Two certificates were printed on each sheet and forwarded to the Register of the Treasury in lots varying from 200 to 2,500 sheets. Each denomination was printed separately. As a means of control Walker required the register to advise him in writing of the number and denomination of the certificates received.[89]

In addition to the treasury notes, the Act of 28 January 1847 authorized the issuance of $28 million in twenty-year 6 per cent bonds to be used to redeem the 1846 and 1847 treasury notes. Inclusion of notes issued prior to 1846 potentially increased the total by another $370,000. Early on, Walker ruled that a bidder who deposited specie might take bonds instead of treasury notes, thereby avoiding the conversion procedure. This ruling led to the sale of $3,542,372 in bonds for specie.[90]

In spite of direct sales, funding of treasury notes was the bonds' major function. Funding prevented a drain on the Treasury's immediate resources. Without funding the Treasury would have been forced to pay off the matured notes or accept them in payment of public dues. The 6 per cent bonds served their conversion function admirably. Through 1891 a total of $24,691,178 in bonds was issued to redeem treasury notes. When added to cash sales the total of the bonds issued rises to $28,233,550.[91]

The successful funding of the treasury notes allowed the federal government to wait until 1867 before it faced the task of paying back the money used to wage war during 1847 and the first half of 1848. By that time, the unpaid portion of the loan was a minor part of its financial problems. Several factors contributed to the successful sale of the loan. Closer coordination between the Treasury and financial community produced notes and bonds readily saleable. The first two sales took place during a period of great prosperity. The third occurred as international markets were improving and signalled a return of foreign capital to the United States. This latter event held great portents for the future. Control of the issue by Corcoran & Riggs allowed the investment bankers to increase profits by implementing a plan of orderly selling. War demands also kept specie from piling up in the Independent Treasury.

5 MEXICO'S FINANCES

The failure of Mexico to find a way adequately to finance the war seriously undermined the country's ability to resist the American onslaught. She entered the war with an empty Treasury, inadequate revenues and weak credit. The lack of money left the government disorganized and the army poorly equipped, seldom paid and badly trained and supplied. Class, geographical and political divisions compounded the problems. The economic elite were prepared passionately to praise the idea of Mexico but not to contribute to its support. Individual and class interest, not national community, were paramount. None of the governments that attempted to deal with the crisis were able to collect sufficient revenues or provide political stability. The story of Mexico's war financing is one of a continuous search for loans.[1]

The lack of records and Treasury reports greatly complicate the task of understanding Mexico's finances during the period 1846–8. Historians attempting to reconstruct Mexico's war effort have relied on known transactions, which provide an understanding of the methods but in no way give a complete picture. The government and army survived on what ordinary revenue flowed into the Treasury, forced loans, requisitions, donations, sale of government property and franchises and loans secured by Church property. The Mexican army supplemented its meagre allowances by drawing supplies from nearby communities or the surrounding countryside and paid by issuing treasury paper that might or might not be honoured.[2]

When the conflict opened much of Mexico's future revenues were pledged to repay existing loans. Barbara Tenenbaum estimates that 4,780,560 pesos of the 1845 income was pledged to foreign and domestic lenders. She places 1845 revenues at 11.7 million pesos. Tenenbaum provides no figures for 1846 but believes tax collections dropped to 8.8 million pesos in 1847 under the pressure of the American blockade and the disruption of domestic economic activity. Wilfred Hardy Callcott reckons Mexico's federal government's revenues at 10,680,000 pesos in 1845 and 10,250,000 in 1846. The ordinary revenues, from 700,000 to 900,000 pesos a month, in no way sufficed to maintain large armies.[3]

Mexico possessed a rudimentary financial system dominated by a small group of domestic and foreign-born merchants who also provided financial services. No formal chartered banks existed in the country and the entrenched merchant bankers opposed every effort to establish one. Merchants, with ready cash, moved money around the country and to foreign destinations by bills of exchange and made short-term loans to the commercial community. The Church provided much of the long-term financing needed by landowners, manufacturers and businessmen. A special group of the wealthier merchants, the *Agiotistas*, dominated the high-risk business of government finance. In spite of the traditionally shaky condition of the Mexican Treasury, the peso remained a sound currency. Coinage of new silver pesos during the period 1846 to 1850 averaged 18.2 million a year. Most of the newly minted coins were exported to pay for foreign goods. Britain supplied Mexico with 10 million pesos a year in goods and took half of the silver in payment. Other European countries and the United States took most of the rest.[4]

A new government headed by General Mariano Paredes y Allellaga seized control in January 1846 with the avowed aim of resisting the United States and upholding Mexico's honour. Resources were needed to back up the brave words. A failed attempt to borrow from the Church in March convinced the Paredes government of the need for stringent measures. On 2 and 7 May, shortly after the initial clashes along the Texas–Mexico border, decrees were issued mandating a decrease in expenditures and recapturing pledged government revenue. The 2 May decree reduced non-military salaries by 25 per cent. On 7 May all payments on the public debt were suspended. Suspension of debt payments allowed the government to ignore the pledge placed on much of its income, especially that on the all-important Vera Cruz customs house. The minister of finance followed up the decree with an appeal to the clergy for a 2 million peso loan to be paid into the Treasury in twelve monthly instalments commencing on 30 June. After appointing a commission to study the request, the Archbishop of Mexico City informed the minister that the Church lacked the means to make such a commitment. [5]

Military defeats along the Rio Grande increased both the government's unpopularity and its financial needs. To reverse the earlier defeats, Paredes proposed to lead reinforcements north, assume command and drive Zachary Taylor and his army from Mexican territory. The clergy was expected to supply the funds for the counter-attack. However, revolution ended the endeavour. Widespread dissatisfaction with the Paredes government convinced the liberals and supporters of General Antonio López de Santa Anna of the government's vulnerability. The revolt began in Vera Cruz and spread rapidly. By the end of July much of the country had risen. Paredes turned the government over to Vice President Nicholas Bravos on 28 July, and Bravos's resignation on 6 August ended the Paredes administration. An interim government headed by General J. M. Salas, the commandant of Mexico City, assumed power.[6]

The new government depended on the supporters of Santa Anna and the radical liberals (*Puros*) led by Valentin Gomez Farias. Santa Anna returned from exile in Cuba and landed at Vera Cruz on 16 August. Passage through the American blockade had been authorized by Polk on the assumption that he was likely to enter into peace negotiations. Whatever Santa Anna's original intent, he found the people belligerent and committed to war. Obtaining and retaining power required leading the war movement, not becoming a peace advocate. Control of the army and victory in the field would solidify his position.[7]

Santa Anna arrived in the capital on 14 September 1846 to negotiate a power-sharing arrangement and to discuss the financial problems. On 17 September he accepted the office of commander-in-chief of the Mexican army. Gomez Farias resigned the ministry of finance and became head of the new Council of Government. Salas remained as acting president. New financial means were required if Santa Anna and Farias were to keep their promise of prosecuting the war vigorously. During his short stint as minister of finance, on 7 September, Farias had already unsuccessfully appealed to the state governments to make up the national government's shortfall in revenue. Santa Anna spent two weeks making direct appeals to businessmen, the clergy and anyone else who might lend or donate money for his campaign. He finally left Mexico City on 28 September for San Luis Potsi in order to reinforce the northern army. Instead of the 2 million pesos sought, he possessed 27,000 pesos and had supplies for little over a week.[8]

In addition to Santa Anna's efforts the Mexican Congress sought to replenish the Treasury and regularize the tax laws. It was about time, since the Treasury contained the grand total of 1,839 pesos on 6 September. Congress, on 17 September, decreed the national government's right to all port taxes, the revenue from the sale of land, a 4 per cent tax on coinage, the proceeds of the lottery, the taxes on official papers (stamp) and the revenues from salt and mint taxes. All taxes collected from the federal district (Greater Mexico City), the territories and the income from previously confiscated Church properties were also allocated to the national government. Additionally, the states were required to contribute a total of 1,011,000 pesos a year. The decree abolished the sales tax but imposed new taxes on property and a 50 per cent surcharge on existing income, luxury and business taxes. Congress's efforts proved futile as a new minister of finance quickly secured repeal of the unpopular law.[9]

News of Monterrey's fall caused the government to try another tack. On 2 October a special war contribution was imposed on the entire citizenry. The decree required owners of houses and land to pay over one month's rent. Owners living on their own premises were to pay an amount equivalent to rent. Tenants were assessed an amount equal to a quarter of a month's rent unless the monthly charge was less than 1 peso. To assure the populace that the funds would be properly spent, they were to be locked in a special safe. The three keys needed to remove the money were to be given to the president, the minister of finance and the mayor of Mexico City. The public was not impressed, and, since the government lacked the means to enforce the decree, few paid.[10]

With Santa Anna in San Luis Potsi incessantly demanding money for his growing army, the government turned again to the Church. On 19 November it demanded 2 million pesos. Since the Church lacked liquid funds and the need was immediate, the government proposed to issue two-year treasury drafts paying 5 per cent interest. The clergy was expected to redeem the drafts on their due dates. The government decree also required specific wealthy individuals to purchase the drafts from the government. Individuals and business firms in the federal district were assessed 800,000 pesos. Seventeen Mexico City individuals and firms were assessed 20,000 pesos each, twenty-seven, 9,000, and twenty-one, 5,000. The remainder was parcelled out in lots ranging from 200 to 2,000 pesos. Church resistance to the plan led to a temporary compromise on 5 December. The clergy agreed to two loans, 850,000 and 1 million pesos, and the politicians promised to abandon plans to seize ecclesiastical property. Such measures provided some immediate relief but failed to supply the funds for a long war.[11]

A newly elected Mexican Congress assembled in Mexico City in December 1846 and reluctantly began to consider long-term solutions to the financial crises. Another new minister of finance, J. N. Almonte, recommended an immediate 600,000 peso forced loan to be levied in the federal district and a monthly contribution from the states and territories equal to 3,000 pesos a month for each congressional representative. Congress appointed a special commission to consider the proposal. In its report of 23 December the commission rejected the idea of levying taxes on the states as too burdensome. It also dismissed the idea being put forward of contracting a 20 million peso loan secured by the Church's property as unjust and indecent.[12]

The commission acknowledged Congress's responsibility to support the army and make arrangements to satisfy domestic creditors. The interest on the foreign debt must wait. The commission devised a plan to support the war for the next six months. It advocated a reduction of 25 per cent on the salaries of federal and state office holders and 75 per cent on the pensions of retired civil and military officers. The sacrifice would reduce non-military expenses to 264,000 pesos a month. The war effort was to receive first call on national resources. Military expenses were estimated at 600,000 pesos a month. The commission's six month budget consisted of 5,185,000 pesos in expenses, revenues of 4.3 million and a deficit of 885,000. An advance of 1,111,000 pesos from the states should cover the deficit and produce a small surplus. Those called upon to sacrifice were to be reimbursed after the war. Appropriation of 600,000 pesos a month in cash, supplemented by the requisitioning of supplies, might suffice for the army, but the sums allocated to the civil officers were wholly inadequate if a viable, functioning government was to be maintained (Table 5.1 gives the commission's financial projections).[13]

Table 5.1: Mexican Congressional Committee Projections for Income and Expenses, 1 January–30 June 1847[14]

Income	Amount (pesos)
Tobacco Revenues	1,613,307
Tax on consumption of Foreign Products	1,566,047
4% Tax on Coins Exported	981,652
Export Duties	666,762
Duties on Mining	410,938
Stamped Paper	216,067
Post Office	154,171
Direct Contributions	109,286
Lotteries	108,300
State Contributions	1,011,000
Retrenchment of salaries, fees, pensions	960,286
All Other Sources	803,160
	8,600,976
One-Half Year's Income	4,300,488
Add: Advance Contributions by States	1,111,000
Income anticipated for Six Months	5,411,488
Expenditure	
Department of Foreign Affairs	79,620
Justice and Ecclesiastical Offices	95,840
Treasury Department	227,183
War and Marine – Ordinary	1,182,335
War and Marine – Extraordinary	3,600,000
	5,184,978
Surplus	226,504

In addition to considering financial measures Congress took steps to reorganize the executive department. On the same day the commission issued its report, Congress elected Santa Anna president and Gomez Farias vice-president. With Santa Anna at San Luis Potsi, executive authority fell on Farias. Santa Anna restricted his efforts to a continuous clamour for money needed for his offensive against Taylor.[15]

Both financial need and ideology made an onslaught against the Church's wealth attractive to Farias and the *Puros*. Since the 1830s they had attempted, unsuccessfully, to reduce the Church's financial and political power by nationalizing its property. Farias began the new campaign with an article published in the official journal on 31 December. He stressed the need for large sums to protect the nation's territorial integrity and the necessity for the Church to contribute heavily for this purpose. Santa Anna concurred with the need for a forced loan from the clergy. Farias proposed legislation authorizing a 15 million peso loan secured by Church property.[16]

Necessity alone caused the Mexican Congress seriously to consider dispossessing the clergy. On 4 January 1847, it rejected legislation confiscating Church property outright. However, a day later the minister of finance reported the impossibility of borrowing on the credit of the republic alone. In response, Congress ordered the Commission on Finance to prepare a bill for its consideration that provided sufficient monies to finance the war for the next six months. The administration pointed out the bankrupt status of the Treasury and the great wealth of the Church but did not recommend confiscation. It wanted to leave that unpopular act to Congress. The Commission proposed that the government be authorized to borrow 15 million pesos by any convenient means. The means included selling or mortgaging church property.[17]

Congress began the debate on 7 January and continued deliberating for three days. The *Puros* argued that Mexico faced defeat and the loss of national sovereignty unless money was found. In their view the Church, as custodian of the nation's wealth, not private individuals, should bear the greatest burden. The dire financial strait demanded this sacrifice to prevent the country's dismemberment. The moderates, led by Mariano Otero, accused the government of seeking a dangerous increase in its powers. Such action would further divide Mexican society and bring economic ruin. Further, the moderates accused the government of seeking to close the churches, suspend worship and starve priests and nuns. The bill passed on 10 January and the next day Farias issued the decree declaring it law.[18]

The Chapter of the Cathedral of Mexico immediately protested and threatened to excommunicate anyone despoiling the Church of its property. The governor of the federal district refused to publish the decree and it became necessary to replace him with Juan Jose Baz, a younger, more aggressive, *Puro* supporter. Baz published the decree on 14 January along with an edict restricting the right of assembly. The next day the churches closed their doors and a priest harangued a crowd in front of the cathedral. On 16 January the government demanded the churches be reopened and reminded Church leaders of the Circular Letter of 31 October 1833, restricting political comments from the pulpits.

The churches did reopen but denunciation of the law continued. States with strong Church influence refused to enforce it.[19]

Despite strong resistance, Farias attempted to turn the legislation into cash. The government decided to seize 10 million pesos in Church property immediately and apportioned the sum among the richer dioceses in Mexico's central valley – the Archbishopric of Mexico City, 5 million pesos; the Bishoprics of Puebla, 2 million; Guadalajara, 1.25 million; and Michoacan, 1.75 million. The remaining 5 million was to be collected later from the rest of the country. The clergy refused to cooperate by producing title deeds and lists of the properties. Further, government officials were reluctant to seize properties because of public outrage and the threat of excommunication. Even when properties were seized few buyers were found.[20]

Farias reported the lack of success to Congress on 25 January and requested a modification of the law. His proposals included limiting the use of any funds collected to the war effort, developing better ways to regulate the mode of payment for confiscated property that was sold and holding the minister of finance personally and exclusively responsible for negotiating all sales. *El Republicano Monitor* found the suggested mode of payment the most objectionable feature. The government now sought authority to sell the properties at 40 per cent of their value. The law of 11 January set a minimum of 77 per cent. Under Farias's proposal half of the sales price must be paid in cash, but government securities would be accepted for the remainder. Since Mexican government debt obligations were heavily depreciated, the actual cash yield would be less than 25 per cent of the properties' value. The low sales price raised serious doubts whether the sale of ecclesiastical property would produce 15 million pesos.[21]

In the face of massive resistance Santa Anna wavered and sought to remove himself from the centre of the controversy. He censured the government for using his private letters as support for passing and enforcing the new law. He now proposed modifying the law if any other means could be found. The legislation had produced hostility, not money. Santa Anna was using more direct methods. In San Luis Potsi, he seized silver from the mines owned by foreigners and requisitioned heavily from the surrounding territory. Santa Anna also borrowed on his personal credit and generally sought money wherever it could be found.

Congress responded to the hostility and need for funds with a new law passed on 4 February 1847. This legislation gave the government extraordinary authority to raise 5 million pesos. However, it made this difficult by prohibiting forced loans, the seizing of private property or alienating land belonging to the nation. The latter prohibited any peace treaty acceptable to the United States. The law partially repealed that of 11 January, but did not specifically prohibit seizure of ecclesiastical property. The government continued its campaign against Church assets with a series of raids against its institutions that produced little results. Adequately warned, Church officials hid their funds. The government harvested mostly ill-will from a religious population resentful of troops entering churches.[22]

Farias and the *Puros* compounded their problems by ordering unreliable National Guard units garrisoning the capital to march to the defence of Vera Cruz. This move sparked a revolt beginning on the night of 26 February 1847. Most National Guard units declared for the rebels. The insurgents made thirteen demands; the most important were the repeal of the laws of 11 January and 4 February and the resignations of Santa Anna and Farias. Santa Anna would be allowed to retain the position of commander-in-chief, but not the presidency. Church officials provided the government's opponents with money and moral support. Farias refused to yield, however, and rallied loyalist troops. Both sides fortified their positions in the capital and waited.[23]

Negotiations, not fighting, marked the revolt. The populace went about their business as usual and attempted to stay out of the line of fire. On 8 March the rebels reduced their thirteen demands to one, the resignation of Farias. Dismissal was sought on the grounds that Farias was irreligious. Throughout the rebellion, Farias remained in his office discharging his duty. Though public opinion turned against the insurgents, Farias was unable to end the conflict. Both sides appealed to Santa Anna for support.[24]

The revolt occurred at a time of great danger to Mexico and Santa Anna resolved to end it. Defeat at Buena Vista in northern Mexico shattered his army and an attack on Vera Cruz by a new American army was expected daily. Because of disorder in the capital few supplies or troops were being sent to the threatened coastal city. The Americans landed on 9 March 1847 and forced the surrender of Vera Cruz's citadel on 27 March. The way lay open for an advance into Mexico's heartland. On 13 March Santa Anna informed both sides in the revolt of his intention to return to Mexico City and demanded hostilities cease. When he arrived on the outskirts of the city, the two opposing military commanders hastily came to an agreement. Hostilities were declared at an end and prisoners exchanged. Farias remained in office and the laws of 11 January and 4 February in force.[25]

The new threat posed by General Winfield Scott's landing at Vera Cruz made a compromise essential. Santa Anna abandoned the *Puros* and came to an understanding with the moderates and the Church's supporters. On 28 March Congress passed a new law giving the executive the power to bargain with the corporations and individuals affected by the prior laws. The law of 28 March also empowered the executive to raise 20 million pesos instead of 15 million. However, the law's major purpose was to allow a settlement to be negotiated. Santa Anna quickly reached an agreement with the Church. In return for annulling the laws of 11 January and 4 February 1847, the Church and its institutions agreed to assume responsibility for redeeming 1.5 million pesos of short-term bonds to be issued by the government. The *Agiotistas* purchased the bonds based on this security. Santa Anna revoked the prior laws on 29 March. The unpopular Farias was disposed of by abolishing the office of vice-president.[26]

Though the clergy was able to reduce the liability, great sacrifices were still required. The Church's assets consisted mainly of urban and rural real estate, mortgages and loans. The wealth was spread among numerous institutions, charities and dioceses. Cash resources were limited. Payment of the obligations the Church assumed for the government often required the calling of loans or sale of property at a loss. The demand for payment of mortgages and loans created a hardship on the borrowers, many of whom were influential. Congress, more sensitive to the property rights of private persons than of institutions, responded with a new law on 17 May 1847, restricting the Church's ability to demand payment. The new law went further and annulled or reduced the mortgages on properties destroyed or damaged during the war. These measures greatly handicapped the Church's ability to supply money and forced the government to ease its restrictions. The Church agreed to limit sales of property and foreclosures unless in extreme need of funds to meet payments on the government's debt obligations. In spite of an easing of the restrictions, sale of property was often necessary. Sixteen properties in Mexico City alone were sold and passed into the possession of moneylenders.[27]

Santa Anna left Mexico City on 2 April with the army and the money borrowed on the security of Church property. Both the army and the money disappeared in the disaster at Cerro Gordo on 18 April. With the way open to Mexico City, Santa Anna and Congress were forced to take steps to defend the capital. On 17 June a special tax amounting to 1 million pesos assessed against the entire population was decreed. The assessment was mostly ignored. On 27 June it was announced that those paying overdue taxes would receive a rebate of from one-third to two-thirds depending on the type of tax. The clergy guaranteed another 0.5 million but made arrangements to redeem the pledge from the moneylenders at a discount of 40 per cent. Individual citizens provided most of the ordinance used in the capital's defence. Canvassing for funds door-to-door brought in small sums.[28]

In July 1847 additional funds were raised by ratifying the agreement reached with the British bondholders. This agreement, know as the Convention of 1846, reduced the foreign debt to 51,208,250 pesos. Of this sum, 40,531,475 in new bonds went to the British creditors in lieu of old bonds in the amount of 56,013,875 pesos. The remaining 10,676,775 in new bonds was at the disposal of the Mexican government. Ewen MacKintosh, *Agiotista*, merchant and British consul, bought the bonds, paying 200,000 pesos in cash and the remainder in depreciated domestic debt certificates.[29]

Mexico's efforts to finance the war in any formal way ended with Scott's capture of Mexico City on 14 September. After one final attempt to strike at the Americans' lines of communication at Puebla, Santa Anna resigned his command on 11 October. Faced with anarchy, the moderates and those with an economic stake in the country sought peace. Negotiations began with the American envoy, Nicholas Trist, on 20 October. Congress made one last effort to collect the funds due the government. In November 1847 it offered to accept half of unpaid taxes levied before 1 May 1846, provided the remaining half was paid by 1 February 1848. Like previous efforts, this came to naught.[30]

In spite of the physical barriers that made the conquest of Mexico difficult, her fate was foretold by the superior material and financial resources, organizational skills and political stability of the United States. Lack of a sense of nationhood and the economic elites' past experience with corrupt regimes made the task of supplying the military impossible. The various governments holding power in Mexico City lacked the moral authority, force or administrative skills to enforce their laws and decrees. Without a viable financial plan the army and government subsisted day-to-day. The army consistently went into battle ill-trained, ill-supplied, ill-paid, ill-equipped and ill-led. The peasant conscripts fought harder than the generals had a right to expect. The war ended with Mexico's credit non-existent and her financial system in disarray. The one hope was the $15 million treaty payment due from the United States. Used properly it might provide a new opportunity for financial stability.

6 MAKING WAR PAY: THE MEXICAN ASSESSMENTS

Mexico's rejection of the July 1846 peace overtures made by Secretary of State James Buchanan dashed all hopes of a quick and inexpensive war. Faced with growing military expenses and heavy borrowing, Polk and his cabinet began to consider ways to pass part of this burden on to the stubborn Mexican people. The measures held the promise of weakening Mexico's resistance and reducing the financial demands on the American people. Polk adopted the idea enthusiastically and pressed the concept on his hesitant generals. The administration attempted to tax the enemy through requisitioning of supplies, collection of duties at occupied Mexican ports and direct assessments against Mexico's civil governments. The difficulty of forcibly collecting revenue in a large, rural country such as Mexico and the good sense of his generals limited success despite Polk's continued exhortations. The generals, operating with relatively small armies deep in enemy territory, consistently displayed a reluctance to aggravate the local inhabitants.[1]

Until September 1846 the American army operating in Mexico bought supplies at a liberal price from those Mexicans willing to sell. The rejection of the peace initiative caused Polk to abandon what he deemed a conciliatory policy. Anger, along with a desire to reduce financial demands, provided the motivation. The Treasury's cash reserves were fast disappearing and its success in borrowing was not yet established. On 19 September, immediately after learning of the Mexican government's reply to Buchanan's proposal, Polk met with the secretaries of war and the navy and suggested quartering American troops on the population and seizing supplies where possible. Mexicans friendly to the United States would continue to be reimbursed. The cabinet agreed to the policy change the next day.[2]

Secretary of War William Marcy immediately informed General Zachary Taylor of the decision and instructed him to start demanding contributions of supplies from Mexican authorities in occupied territory. Marcy conveyed Polk's hope that Taylor would 'be able to derive from the enemy's country, without expense to the United States, the supplies you may need, or a considerable part of them'.[3] Property owned by non-Mexican nationals was exempt from the levy. Taylor might disregard the order if in his opinion such action endangered his army and limited its ability to secure adequate supplies. Continued purchases, if necessary, must be at an economical price and profiteering was not to be tolerated. Taylor elected to take advantage of the leeway in his instructions and advised Marcy of his decision on 26 October. Taylor believed it impossible to sustain his army by forcible seizures. The land the army currently occupied was poor and produced only corn and beef in quantity. Taylor also feared arousing a now inert people. He assured Marcy that prices were moderate and promised to implement the government's policy when it could be safely done.[4]

In March 1847 the administration began consideration of a plan to collect duties at occupied Mexican ports. This was at variance with the initial policy of allowing the free entry of American but not foreign goods into northern Mexico. Walker's Treasury Circular of 30 June 1846 limited the trade to American vessels carrying products of the United States or foreign goods on which the American duty had been paid. No further duties were to be collected at the occupied ports. Military commanders possessed authority under the circular to exclude spirits and contraband of war. A second circular in December clarified the original regulations and required American vessels outbound from a foreign port to land in the United States, pay the duty and secure a clearance from the local collector of customs before proceeding to Mexico. The policy aided Americans desiring to trade with Mexico, but produced little income.[5]

The seizure of the major ports around the Gulf of Mexico made it feasible to levy a tribute on Mexico's foreign trade. Opening Mexican ports to the commerce of all nations held certain advantages in addition to any revenue it produced. It might moderate complaints about the blockade from foreign merchants who normally traded with Mexico. More importantly, to Walker, it held the promise of obtaining specie in Mexico without having to export it from the United States. America was still reaping the benefit from the export of its foodstuffs, but the length of this good fortune was unknown. Reduction of specie exports to Mexico would keep the American money market liquid and assist in the marketing of the $23 million loan of 1847.[6]

Polk based his authority to levy tribute on international law and his position as commander-in-chief. In March he began to build support for a Mexican tariff during discussions with Democratic congressional leaders including Senator Benton and Congressman Stephen Douglas. Both agreed he possessed such authority. On 13 March 1847, after the attorney general researched the issue, the cabinet reached a similar conclusion. Polk recommended a 25 per cent duty on all goods, both American and foreign-owned. Walker preferred the much higher Mexican rates. In the end the cabinet asked the secretary of the Treasury to prepare a rate schedule for their consideration. Throughout the discussion Polk insisted the issue was a military, not civil, matter and that the revenue must be collected by army and navy officers. With some difficulty he convinced Walker that the Treasury's responsibility lay in drawing up and publishing the rate schedule, not its enforcement.[7]

Walker responded to the cabinet's request by proposing a schedule consisting mainly of specific duties. He believed the lack of experienced appraisers in the military or Mexico made an *ad valorem* system unmanageable. Walker wanted rates high enough to be onerous on the Mexican people, but low enough to produce revenue. To promote the sale of American goods and increase receipts, he proposed to allow the importation of goods prohibited by Mexican law for protective reasons. Walker's proposed rates were half existing Mexican duties. Additionally, a tonnage tax equal to $1 per ton was to be levied on vessels entering the ports. Duties were to be paid exclusively in gold or silver coins. Walker envisioned a windfall of up to $9 million in specie. After some modification, Polk accepted the report. Polk then prepared an order to the secretaries of war and the navy directing them to issue the necessary instructions to the military officers to put the new Mexican tariff into effect.[8]

The Tariff Regulations for Mexican Ports, dated 30 March, established duties based on weight, measurements and, to a limited extent, *ad valorem*. The rate on cotton cloth was 5¢ a yard; coffee, 3¢ a pound; tea, 40¢ a pound; sugar candy, 10¢ a pound; unbottled beer, 25¢ a gallon; boots, $1 a pair; and gold watches, $10 each. Carriages, hosiery, lace and unenumerated items were to be taxed at 30 to 40 per cent of their market value. Gunpowder and weapons were declared contraband and subject to seizure along with the vessel transporting them. Steel was prohibited on penalty of forfeiture of the goods (but not the ship). To foster the production of gold and silver, mining machinery and quicksilver were exempt. For security reasons, only American vessels could carry cargo between two occupied ports. The regulations empowered the American commandant of the port to designate officers to inspect the ships and cargo and prepare an estimate of taxes due. After payment, the ship's captain received a receipt and was allowed to land the goods. Finally, the regulations forbade the collection of Mexican revenues, taxes or monopoly proceeds in American-controlled areas.[9]

Scott seized the port of Vera Cruz before he received news of the administration's Mexican tariff policy. Aware of his government's wishes to impose duties, Scott acted and imposed his own levies. On 28 March, he designated Brigadier General William J. Worth governor of Vera Cruz with the authority to maintain order and to 'establish a temporary and moderate tariff of duties ... on all articles imported by sea from countries other than the United States, the proceeds of said tariff to be applied to the benefit of the sick and wounded of the army, the squadron, and the indigent inhabitants of Vera Cruz'.[10] Based on this authority

Worth decreed an *ad valorem* tariff of 5 per cent on provisions, 15 per cent on wine, 75 per cent on liquor, and 10 per cent on all other merchandise except raw cotton, which was taxed at 4¢ a pound. Commissary supplies for soldiers and sailors were duty free. Additionally, foreign ships must either have paid the American tariff or do so now. Cargoes arriving before publication of Worth's regulation owed the Vera Cruz duty, but not the American duties.[11]

Scott supplemented Worth's decree with General Order 103, prohibiting the export of gold or silver without the permission of the port's collector and payment of a 6 per cent export duty. Francis M. Dimond, previously American consul in Vera Cruz and accompanying the army as an adviser, was appointed to the lucrative position as collector. Two days after issuing his directive taxing the export of gold and silver, Scott suspended the order. The order had served its purpose of bringing the foreign merchants in Vera Cruz to heel. The suspension was to last as long as the army's disbursement officers were able to sell short-term drafts on the principal American cities at par. Faced with an export tax on specie the Vera Cruz merchants became more accommodating in the matter of purchasing the army's drafts.[12]

Scott's tariff was short-lived and was quickly superseded by formal orders from the secretaries of war and the navy to implement the tariff regulations prepared by the Treasury. Marcy even denied Francis Dimond's request to remain as collector at Vera Cruz. The application was refused because Dimond was not a military officer, and only they were to be allowed to collect the revenues. Polk wanted there to be no doubt he was acting in his capacity as commander-in-chief, not as chief magistrate. In Dimond's case the problem was eventually resolved by appointing him a captain in the army, thereby allowing him to retain his position.[13]

Polk showed good instinct in basing his authority on his military capacity. In the newspaper and political debate following implementation of the Mexican tariff it provided his strongest defence. Initially, the press reacted favourably to the idea of placing part of the war's burden on the Mexican people. The *Washington National Intelligencer* reminded the public that a similar proposal had been put forward in their columns by Waddy Thompson, formerly American minister to Mexico. The *New York Herald* believed it a brilliant scheme, providing revenue ($8 to $10 million) and weakening the enemy.[14] 'There is not a Yankee in all New England', the *Herald* crowed, 'but that would consider himself immortalized by being the originator of such a measure'.[15] The optimistic *Washington Union* predicted revenues of $6.5 million assuming a liberal tariff rate and good management. The *Union* argued that a moderate tariff would prove beneficial to both American and Mexican commerce. The *Philadelphia Public Ledger* also supported the measure and in defence of its legality pointed out that the British had opened captured American ports during the War of 1812.[16]

Despite initial praise the tariff quickly became a partisan issue. It faced attack from two directions. Americans trading or wishing to trade with Mexico complained that it placed foreign competitors on an equal footing. They argued that they were mostly men of small means and unable to pay the tariff within the required thirty days. The *New York Journal of Commerce* gave the traders a public forum, but rejected their arguments. To the *Journal* the benefits to individual Americans from discrimination was not worth offending those nations who up to now had maintained strict neutrality. The administration shared this view.[17]

Whig politicians and papers took another tack and accused Polk of assuming dictatorial powers. The *Albany Statesman* argued that jurisdiction over captured territory lay with the sovereign people of the United States, not the president. Only Congress, acting for the people, possessed the authority to establish a civil government in occupied lands and raise revenue from a defeated people. Within two weeks of its first comments the *Washington National Intelligencer* began to refer to the Mexican tariff regulations as the hated British 'Orders in Council'. The *Intelligencer* now viewed Polk's actions as high-handed and a dangerous usurpation of congressional power. The paper denied that Polk was acting within his capacity as commander-in-chief, but instead was assuming the powers of a European monarch. The war might swallow up the liberties of the country. Fortunately for Polk, Congress had adjourned and left Washington before publication of the tariff regulations. He was spared a concerted attack by the Whig politicians until December 1848.[18]

Before advancing into the interior, General Scott issued a proclamation to the Mexican people pledging to protect the Catholic Church, its property and the property of private individuals. Additionally, he assured them that supplies would be purchased, not seized. The citizenry was urged to remain at home and act peacefully. Scott's proclamation was at odds with the wishes of his government. At the time the proclamation was issued, 11 April 1847, a message was en route from the secretary of war repeating the instructions previously given to General Taylor. The administration expected Scott to draw supplies from the enemy whenever possible. Like Taylor, Scott was very reluctant to enflame the civil population and used his discretional authority to ignore the request.[19] He informed Marcy on 20 May that if the army attempted 'to support itself by forced contributions levied upon the country we may ruin and exasperate the inhabitants and starve ourselves'.[20] As Scott advanced further into Mexico the administration repeated its request. In addition to confiscating supplies, Scott was urged to extract contributions from city and state governments and from wealthy individuals. Scott continued to ignore the request until he captured Mexico City.[21]

With the confiscation or levying of supplies proving impossible the administration concentrated on making the Mexican tariff profitable. First results were not encouraging. In June 1847 Walker obtained Polk's permission to modify the regulations issued on 30 March. Cotton manufactures were now to be taxed at 30 per cent *ad valorem* instead of 5¢ a yard and the payment period lengthened from thirty to ninety days. Importers received assurance that any peace treaty would protect them by exempting goods imported during the war from future Mexican taxes or confiscation. A further modification in November extended the 30 per cent *ad valorem* rate to cloth, tea, coffee, tobacco, glass, china, iron, steel and sugar. The pre-war Mexican export taxes were also re-established.[22]

No modifications could compensate for the inability to get the goods to interior markets and the Mexicans' refusal to buy. From 1 May to August only $70,000 was collected at Tampico, the second most active port. As of 20 October only one small shipload of European-owned goods had been landed at Vera Cruz. American merchants accounted for most of the limited activity. As long as the Mexican government controlled the central valley and possessed sufficient force to deny the passage of goods, or make the journey hazardous, little could be expected from this source. Polk reported to Congress that about $500,000 in duties had been obtained through 31 October 1847. Both he and Walker assured the nation that occupation of Mexico City would increase the yield and contribute significantly to the cost of pacifying the country. Walker optimistically predicted that modest rates and honest collectors would produce import revenues equal to the pre-war level. This projection assumed that the army occupied the ports, Mexico City and the mining district. The more territory controlled, the greater the revenue. At this time Walker was in the camp of those advocating the annexation of all of Mexico. By 31 December 1847, revenues from the tariff had risen to $1,077,366 consisting of $1,050,129 in duties, $21,560 in tonnage and $5,676 in miscellaneous items and penalties. Collection expenses of $40,604 reduced net proceeds to $1,036,762. Of the revenue collected, 65 per cent came from Vera Cruz.[23]

The capture of Mexico City allowed Scott to implement the administration's policy of demanding contributions from Mexico's civil authorities. On 16 September 1847, two days after capturing the city, Scott issued General Order 287 demanding a $150,000 contribution be paid in four weekly instalments beginning on 20 September. The contribution was in return for a promise to maintain order and was used for treating the wounded, buying supplies and other military purposes. Included in the amount was a 5 per cent commission to which Scott felt personally entitled. Scott also required the city government to assume responsibility for feeding the nearly three thousand prisoners-of-war. The city government, the *Ayuntamiento*, secured the funds from the moneylenders. The *Agiotistas* demanded a 15 per cent commission and a pledge of future city revenues.[24]

The time now seemed favourable to increase receipts from the Mexican tariff. On 14 December Marcy forwarded Scott a copy of the president's recent annual message containing the administration's war policy and instructing him to hold Mexico City, maintain safe lines of communication and open the country to goods from ports held by American forces. Army units were to safeguard the wagon trains inbound to Mexico City and then assist in distributing the goods to outlying areas. Scott was encouraged to occupy as much territory as possible, both for the distribution of goods and the collection of internal taxes. The moves, it was hoped, would increase revenues and force Mexico to make peace on American terms.[25]

The cessation of organized resistance provided an opportunity to confiscate the revenues previously paid to the civil governments. In an attempt to implement the administration's policy, Scott issued a series of General Orders beginning with Number 358 on 25 November 1847. This directive and subsequent General Orders set out demands and procedures for the collection of Mexican internal taxes. Assessments were also proposed against the state governments and the export of gold and silver. Since the army lacked the resources to physically enforce the decrees little actual money was collected. A populace skilled at avoiding the taxes of its own government could be made to do so by a foreign power only by force.[26]

The agreement on peace terms reached by Nicholas Trist and the Mexican commissioners on 2 February 1848 dulled the military's already flagging enthusiasm for levying revenue. General William O. Butler, who replaced Scott on 18 February, sought mainly to keep the peace until the treaty was ratified and then withdraw his army. Peace required a government in Mexico strong enough to carry out the treaty's terms. Butler was prepared to assume successful ratification and work with the Mexican Congress and the newly organized government of Manuel de la Pena y Pena located at the temporary capital of Queretaro. On 29 February he entered into a truce that preserved the existing occupational zones, rescinded the internal revenue levies and recognized the Mexican government's authority to tax and administrate its remaining territory. Ratification by the United States Senate and the Mexican Congress allowed Butler to begin evacuating Mexico City on 12 July and by the end of July the army was out of Mexico. The Vera Cruz custom house was turned over to Mexican officials on 11 July. The Mexican government restored the revenue laws in effect in 1845.[27]

The United States Congress assembled in December 1848 determined to find out the amount extracted from the Mexicans and, more importantly, how it was spent. The House appointed a select investigating committee to discover if the president had exceeded his authority. The Whigs, now the majority party in the House, brought in a report critical of Polk's actions. The majority report expressed doubts as to Polk's authority to levy such assessments or spend the proceeds without congressional approval. Accounting for the expenditures was the greater issue.[28] The majority concluded that Polk's acts 'were not warranted by the constitution and the laws of the United States, but were in derogation of both'.[29] The Democrats, in the minority report, denied any illegal acts and pointed out that the Whigs had approved appropriations for the war and sat silently during the prior session when the assessment policy was explained.[30]

Both Polk and Congress wanted to end the controversy. Polk needed a way to settle the accounts of the military officers who had collected and disbursed the money. To end the impasse the select committee prepared and shepherded through Congress a measure entitled, 'A Bill to Provide for the Settlement of the Accounts of Public Officer'. The bill passed on 3 March 1849. It provided belated authority to make the expenditures and required a settlement of all accounts.[31]

Army officers acting as collectors at the Gulf ports of Vera Cruz, Tampico and Matamoros collected $3,359,098 in duties and tonnage. An additional $75,566 obtained in California brought the army's total to $3,434,664. Naval officers at the smaller ports of Frontera de Tabasco, Laguna, Tuspan, Alvarado, Tlocatalpan and the Guazacolcus River added another $131,836, bringing the total duties collected to $3,566,503. The army obtained an additional $553,055 in the interior of Mexico. Assessments on Mexico City and state governments provided $225,649, sale of captured public property, $163,573, and the diversion of internal taxes, municipal revenues and miscellaneous items another $163,833 (see Table 6.1).[32]

Table 6.1: Revenue from Mexican Assessments[33]

Tariff Duties	Amount ($)	Total ($)
Vera Cruz		
Scott's Order of 28 March 1847	287,187	
War Department Order of 3 April 1847	1,986,753	
Total		2,273,940
Tampico		728,976
Matamoras		356,186
California		75,566
Navy – Small Ports		131,835
Total Tariff		3,566,503
Other Revenue		
Internal taxes, municipal and Misc. Revenues		163,833
State and Municipal Assessments		225,649
Captured Property		163,573
Total Other Revenue		553,055
All Revenues from Assessments		4,119,558

After deducting collection expenses of about 3.5 per cent, the military spent the money mostly on commissary and quartermaster supplies and pay. Smaller sums supported occupied city governments, hospitals and medical services. Scott, for example, in Mexico City, spent $64,000 on blankets and shoes for his troops and gave $10 each to the wounded on their release from the hospital. The military officers acting as custom officials also paid themselves handsomely for their additional duties. Captain Francis Dimond, collector at Vera Cruz, claimed a commission of $18,862 on the collection of $287,187 made under Scott's decree and a salary of $7,617 for the subsequent period.[34]

The most controversial expenditure was a personal commission retained by General Winfield Scott. As commanding general, Scott felt the rules of war entitled him to 5 per cent of enemy property seized. He therefore appropriated $11,585 for his personal use. The amount represented 5 per cent of $231,691, derived from the Mexico City assessment, $150,000; the sale of captured tobacco, $49,569; proceeds of a captured Mexican pay chest, $11,791; and miscellaneous items, totalling $20,331. Scott argued that the funds were never the property of the United States and not subject to the Settlement Act of 3 March 1849. He equated it to naval prize money.[35]

Unlike the Zachary Taylor and Millard Fillmore administrations, the Democrats refused to ignore such a potent political issue. During the campaign of 1852 they belaboured candidate Scott (Whig presidential nominee) with accusations of plundering the public Treasury. In 1853 the new secretary of war, Jefferson Davis, demanded a final accounting from the defeated candidate. The real issue between Davis and Scott was not money but power and authority. As commander-in-chief of the army, Scott believed he had only one superior, the president. In no way did he feel himself subject to the orders of the secretary of war.[36]

Both Scott and Davis brought their case to a harassed president. In settling his accounts after returning from Mexico, Scott had submitted a list of expenses that, he believed, reduced the actual commissions outstanding to $6,149. The president allowed Scott to retain this amount. However, Davis subsequently found that Scott had been reimbursed $5,485 of the amount applied against the commission. Davis forced repayment of the later figure, but failed to prevent Scott's promotion to lieutenant general retroactive to 29 March 1847, with back pay to that date.[37]

Except for the tariff collected at the occupied Mexican ports, the effort to extract tribute from the Mexican people proved an exercise in futility. The American decrees demanding payment did not have credence because the army occupied insufficient territory and lacked administrators and tax collectors. The effort was also too short-lived to be effective. The key to exportable wealth in Mexico was the mines. A ruthless conqueror could have occupied the mining district, exploited it and supplemented the proceeds with levies against Mexican cities and states collected under the threat of plunder and destruction. However, neither Scott nor Taylor was one of Napoleon's marshals or Gustavus Adolphus's seventeenth-century Swedish generals living off the land and making war pay for itself. Given time and a commitment by the American people to occupy all of Mexico, they might have developed these skills. The success in the ports resulted from unchallenged control by the American military and the fact that most of the duties were paid by American merchants bringing goods into Mexico. Even this source was limited by the ability or willingness of the Mexican people to consume in the midst of war.

7 THE INDEPENDENT TREASURY AT WAR

Neither Polk nor Walker flinched from implementing the new financial system in the midst of war. They were confident it would survive, prosper and prove its worth under this stress. To the astonishment of its critics, the organization performed adequately in receiving, safeguarding, paying out and transferring the government's money. By a variety of means funds were made available where the military needed it. The government received gold and silver for its treasury notes and bonds without unduly disrupting the money market. Unlike the War of 1812 and the Civil War, both the government and banks remained on the gold standard. Prices rose and fell, mostly because of conditions in Europe, but the nation avoided runaway inflation. The private sector remained healthy and prosperous throughout the war.[1]

For an organization that raised so much passion and controversy, the Independent Treasury was physically small. At its inception, it consisted of fourteen full-time employees, the assistant treasurers in New York, Boston, Charleston and St Louis and ten clerks. The treasurers of the Philadelphia mint and of the branch mint in New Orleans were also designated assistant treasurers. The two mint treasurers received an additional $500 a year as compensation for their increased duties. The assistant treasurer in New York received a salary of $4,000 per annum and the other three $2,500 each. The Treasurer of the United States in Washington operated the seventh large depository and assumed executive responsibility, but without additional compensation. The ten clerks were apportioned one each to Boston, Philadelphia, Washington, Charleston, New Orleans and St Louis and four to the most important office, New York City.[2]

The enabling legislation made the system nationwide by assigning Independent Treasury duties to all collectors of customs, receivers of public money at the land offices, postmasters and other federal officers who were empowered to receive public dues. The Independent Treasury and its officials assumed responsibility for receiving (but not collecting), safeguarding, disbursing and transferring government funds. In the larger offices the duties were separated. In the smaller ones the collector or receiver likely performed all functions.[3]

To extend the reach of the Independent Treasury, provide greater safety and concentrate government funds, Walker designated twenty-one offices as depositories. In addition to the seven major offices, fourteen more were established at the custom house or land office at Buffalo, Wilmington (North Carolina), Savannah, Mobile, Nashville, Cincinnati, Little Rock, Jeffersonville (Indiana), Chicago, Detroit, Baltimore, Richmond, Norfolk and Pittsburgh. By 1854 the number had grown to twenty-four with the addition of Tallahassee (Florida), Dubuque (Iowa) and San Francisco. Seventeen of the depositories, the seven major offices and the first ten listed above, were also empowered to accept deposits from federal marshals, district attorneys and other federal officers. The remaining four were responsible only for the money collected in their own custom houses or land offices.[4]

To concentrate public money, Walker issued a series of letters dated 28 September 1846 ordering officials at the small custom houses and land offices to make periodic deposits with the nearest of the seventeen depositories. For example, the receivers and collectors in Mississippi and Alabama were to deposit their funds with the collector and depository in Mobile and those in Indiana and Southern Illinois with the receiver and depository in Jeffersonville, Indiana. Collectors and receivers located in the same city as an assistant treasurer were required to make weekly, not periodic, deposits. The exceptions to these rules were the collectors in Boston and New York. Because of the large receipts in these offices, they were required to deposit daily with the local assistant treasurer.[5]

The requirement of the small offices to make deposits from time to time was realistic since little in the way of actual funds was expected. Until 1 July 1849, the collectors and receivers first paid the expenses of their offices from the proceeds collected and then turned over anything remaining to the credit of the treasurer of the United States. The Treasury reported only the net amount in its quarterly and annual reports. Collection expenses exceeding $2 million a year were hidden in this manner. In many medium and small offices expenses absorbed the income and little or nothing remained for the national Treasury. This happened in offices as large as Norfolk, Virginia.[6]

Not only was the Independent Treasury limited in personnel, it was also woefully underfunded and dependent on the custom service and land offices for space and equipment. Since Congress only appropriated $5,000 to institute the new system, strict economy was necessary. Even the quarterly pay of the assistant treasurers and clerks was made on the assumption that Congress would pass a supplemental appropriation when it met in December 1846. The enabling legislation assumed, erroneously, that the quarters prepared under the 1840 act creating the first Independent Treasury were still available. Eventually, temporary quarters were found in the New York and Charleston custom houses and temporary offices rented in Boston and St Louis. An audit in May 1847 revealed that the assistant treasurer in St Louis possessed $611,811 in specie and stored it in a very insecure building. After this report a contract was let by the Treasury to construct a substantial building with a fireproof vault.[7]

Conditions in the smaller offices were worse. In the Ohio River Valley none of the buildings contained fireproof vaults. The depository in Jeffersonville, Indiana, across the Ohio River from Louisville, Kentucky, shared quarters with the town's chief tavern. The tavern was considered the strongest building in town. The bar and the depository were separated by a grated door, fastened with an iron chain. To protect the hundreds of thousands of dollars passing through the depository, the receiver often slept in his office with an assortment of pistols, knives and guns. Independent Treasury officers frequently purchased necessary equipment with personal funds. As late as 1854, an inspection by William Gouge found most depositories lacked the security deemed necessary by the banking community.[8]

The efforts by the depository officers to improve the security of public money ran afoul of Walker's need to economize. Unlike expenses incurred in collecting revenues from customs and land sales, expenses at the Independent Treasury were on the books in the sense they required congressional appropriations. Expenditures also needed the advance approval of the secretary. Walker's close control extended so far that the assistant treasurer in New York was required to obtain his written approval before spending $42 on coal stoves, paper and fixtures. In response to the collector at Norfolk's request to buy an iron safe, Walker demanded an estimate and then pointed out that since expenses exceeded revenues there was unlikely to be much money to protect. Walker refused approval to rent a bank vault at Little Rock and instead demanded the old iron safe be repaired. Walker's wish to separate the government from bank influence extended to the use of vaults in local banks to store the government's money. He advised the collector at Portland, Maine, that such action was not prohibited, assuming the collector retained the key, but that the iron safe at the custom house was preferable.[9]

Accounting for receipts and expenditures consumed much of the Independent Treasury officials' time. Record-keeping instructions were issued in a Treasury Circular dated 15 September 1846. In the seven major offices the assistant treasurers (or the treasurer in Washington) accepted deposits from collectors and other federal officers and credited the proceeds to the account of the treasurer of the United States. In the smaller offices officials wore two hats, that of collector of customs or receiver of public monies and that of a depository of the Independent Treasury. These officials collected the money for taxes, land sales and fees, paid the collection expenses, and credited the net amount to the account of the treasurer of the United States. Once the office, regardless of its size, credited the treasurer's account, the funds could be paid out or transferred only on the expressed orders of the treasurer.[10]

Bookkeeping entries for the Independent Treasury were made on what Walker referred to as a ledger account current. It consisted of a double-sheeted cash book with deposits recorded on one side and expenditures and transfers on the other. The pages were printed with columns and bound into a book. Entries were relatively easy for those officers responsible for their own collections. After recording tax receipts in a separate journal, the officer entered the date, an explanation and the net amount being credited to the treasurer on the deposit side of the ledger. Information on the expenditure side included the date, the number of the treasury or transfer draft being paid, the number of the warrant on which the treasury draft was issued, the type of warrant being paid and the amount and type of money being paid out. Additional information was required of the assistant treasurers and the ten designated depositories. These officials recorded information on the deposit including the depositor's name, to whom the money was to be credited, the purpose of the deposit and the kinds of funds (bank notes, specie, treasury notes, etc.) deposited. Ledgers were balanced weekly and at the end of the quarter. Each week a transcript of the account was extracted and two copies forwarded to Washington. In addition to the ledger cash current, Walker recommended a separate register of transfer drafts and, in the larger offices, a day book be maintained. In large centres such as New York record-keeping was extensive. Not only did the assistant treasurer receive large sums daily from the collector of customs and weekly deposits from marshals, district attorney and others, he also took in massive amounts of specie from the public in payment for treasury notes and bonds.[11]

The Independent Treasury became fully operational on 1 January 1847, when its most important provision, the Specie Clause, became effective. This clause was implemented in two stages. On 1 January 1847, the Independent Treasury began to accept only gold and silver coins or treasury notes. Disbursement officers paying expenses and debts of the federal government were allowed to pay out bank notes until 1 April, if the creditor was willing to accept them. In anticipation of the change Walker advised the local offices to dispose of their supply of bank notes by paying them out, if possible, before 31 December 1846. On that date any remaining bank notes over $5,000 were to be exchanged for specie. The officers were further instructed both to weigh and count any large deposit of coins.[12]

The mandate to receive only specie or treasury notes failed to attain instant compliance. There was much confusion in the hinterlands. The convenience of bank notes was too attractive, particularly when transporting money. Many collectors and receivers continued to accept bank notes well after 1 January 1847. An audit in April discovered $200,000 in bank notes in the Charleston assistant treasurer's vault. Walker pointed out the illegality of this action and angrily demanded an explanation. The receiver in Jeffersonville, Indiana, D. G. Bright, also received criticism when bank notes were found in his possession. The receiver explained that some of the notes had been accepted by district clerks before 1 January and deposited with him after that date. The aggravated receiver demanded to be relieved from his depository duties. Walker explained this was impossible regardless of how inconvenient and burdensome he found the new duties. To escape, the receiver would have to give up the lucrative land office position. Fortunately for Bright, the notes were issued by the highly respected Bank of Indiana.[13]

The problems in the Ohio Valley continued into 1848 with the discovery of both bank notes and cheques in the possession of the surveyor of customs in Cincinnati. The surveyor, Patrick Collins, assigned blame to the receivers at Upper Sandusky, Ohio, Chillicothe, Ohio, and Fort Wayne, Indiana. The Upper Sandusky and Fort Wayne receivers denied any breach of the regulations. John Hough, the receiver in Chillicothe, argued that he acted within the spirit of the law if not its letter. Because of the weather and conditions of the roads it was impractical to move specie by wagon. Hough vented his frustrations in a letter to Senator William Allen of Ohio. He complained that on one trip he was required to carry over one hundred pounds of specie a hundred yards across a ravine. His health was still affected.[14]

The first business day of the Independent Treasury, 2 January 1847, passed quietly. In Charleston the *Courier* reported that the 'monster's' effect was minimum with little traffic and a bored clerk waiting for customers in vain. The paper concluded that the Warehouse Act neutralized the Independent Treasury's inconvenience. In New York stocks were up and in Philadelphia the *Public Ledger* reported that operations commenced quietly and easily. Even the *Washington National Intelligencer* admitted the Independent Treasury was not intrusive and only those paying or receiving government funds were aware it was in full operation. The mercantile community began to accommodate itself to the new system though they disliked carting specie to the offices of the collectors and assistant treasurers. Some expressed their dissatisfaction by paying in dimes and half-dimes. The *New York Journal of Commerce* found the specie requirement ridiculous. The coins were in a continuous circle to everyone's inconvenience. Merchants obtained specie from the banks and paid it in at the Independent Treasury or custom house. The Treasury paid the specie out to the government's creditors, who in turn carted it back to the banks and re-deposited it. In spite of this, many observers believed the inconvenience a small price to pay if the experiment resulted in a sounder currency.[15]

Walker's next step, on 4 February, was to order the transfer of the government's remaining bank deposits to the Independent Treasury. The transfers were to be completed by 1 April. The government was moving a step closer to separating itself from the banks. Since deposits had already been reduced significantly by war expenses, little inconvenience to the banks or money market was expected. The drafts were drawn and the money trickled out of the banks. In the case of Corcoran & Riggs the last federal money was not transferred until August. Simon Cameron's Bank of Middleton, Pennsylvania, delayed until November. This bank provided the loan of $50,000 that allowed administration supporters to purchase the old *Washington Globe* in 1845 and convert it into the *Union*. Because of this service it was the last bank to lose its deposits.[16]

Despite its peaceful inauguration, the organization came into existence during a period of heightened financial activity. Its most important mission was to support the war effort. During the first twenty-two months the Independent Treasury received $91,484,823 and paid out $92,142,512. This was twice the normal volume and unlike prior years the transactions were made in specie or treasury notes. The Independent Treasury also assisted in the conversion of the treasury notes to bonds, the redemption of matured notes and the sale of treasury notes and bonds authorized by the Loan Acts of 1846, 1847 and 1848. Additionally, massive amounts of specie were transferred around the country and into Mexico.[17]

During its first two years the sale of bonds and treasury notes greatly increased the Independent Treasury's responsibilities. It accepted funds from purchasers and prepared certificates of deposit, which became the basis for the issuance of the loan certificates by the Register of the Treasury. The certificates of deposit consisted of a pre-printed form slightly larger than a modern bank cheque. The assistant treasurer numbered the certificate, and entered the date, the depositor's name and amount. The certificates were prepared in duplicate, one for each party.[18]

In addition to receiving funds from individuals or firms wishing to purchase government securities, the Independent Treasury also accepted treasury notes from holders wishing to exchange or convert them. Because of the differences in the loan laws and Treasury announcements procedures for exchange or conversion varied. The first chore, beginning in the fourth calendar quarter of 1846, was the exchange of the one mill notes for those bearing 5.4 per cent. The Treasury instructed the assistant treasurers to cancel the one mill notes by punching holes in them and forward the cancelled notes to the first auditor. The register issued new 5.4 per cent notes in replacement.[19]

The Loan Act of 28 January 1847, with its conversion privilege, caused a large influx of treasury notes from holders seeking to take advantage. On 15 February 1847, Walker set out the procedures for converting the notes into the new 6 per cent twenty-year bonds. In addition to cancelling the notes the assistant treasurers were to prepare a certificate of deposit and issue a copy to the person or firm submitting the notes. Submission of treasury notes was the equivalent of making a specie deposit. The certificate credited the customer with the principal amount of the notes only. The accounting officers in Washington computed the interest due. The holder received 6 per cent bonds for the face value of the notes and a treasury draft for any interest due. The interest was redeemed for cash, not bonds. Periodically, the Treasury issued a warrant to the assistant treasurers authorizing them to draw upon funds in their possession to redeem the interest drafts.[20]

Until 1 July 1848, the Independent Treasury paid the interest on the notes, but not the semi-annual payments on the bonds. Unlike the interest on the bonds, which was due on 1 January and 1 July, interest was due on the notes every six months from the date the purchase price was deposited. Every day a note holder or his agent was likely to show up for payment. The Independent Treasury officer paid the interest in specie, stamped on the note's face a statement indicating interest for a six-month period ended on a certain date had been paid and gave the note back to the holder. If a treasury note matured and the holder wanted cash instead of converting it, the note was forwarded to the treasurer in Washington who authorized payment.[21]

Prior to 1 July 1848, major banks such as the Bank of America in New York, Merchants Bank in Boston, Corcoran & Riggs in Washington and the Southwestern Railroad Bank in Charleston paid the interest on the bonds without charging the government a fee. The Register of the Treasury provided a transcript to each bank listing the bondholders in their area and the amount of interest to be paid. A separate transcript was provided for the bond issues of 1842, 1843, 1846, 1847 and 1848. As part of the process the treasurer issued a treasury draft to the paying banks so they could obtain the specie needed to pay the interest from the local assistant treasurer. The banks used the money until the holder or his agent called for it. By June 1848, bankers such as George Newbold concluded that the cost outweighed the benefits. In response to their complaints the Treasury shifted responsibility to the assistant treasurers late in June 1848.[22]

The last-minute decision led to confusion and long lines at the Independent Treasury on 1 July. Newbold reported the assistant treasurer in New York was getting along slowly with his new duties. The problems were procedural and a strict interpretation of the specie clause. The clerks were required to verify the owner or agent's credentials, count out the specie and obtain the holder's signature on the transcript.[23]

The coupon bonds issued as part of the loan of 1848 posed a special problem. On 1 July 1848, the assistant treasurer in New York refused to pay the interest. The Bank of America paid instead and charged Corcoran & Riggs's account. Because the coupon bonds were readily transferable, the Treasury in Washington was unable to maintain an ownership list and issue a transcript for interest payments. At first, the assistant treasurers were requested to forward the unpaid coupons to the treasurer in Washington. Eventually the Treasury came to depend on Corcoran & Riggs to accept the coupons and pay the interest. The Treasury Department deposited the necessary funds with the firm shortly before the interest date. Corcoran & Riggs, in turn, maintained deposits with banks in the major money centres. The holder or his agent presented the coupon to the local correspondent bank or forwarded it directly to Corcoran & Riggs for payment. Corcoran & Riggs presented the paid coupons to the Treasury and received credit against the deposit. There was no charge to the Treasury and Corcoran & Riggs or the holder's agent was responsible for any loss. Corcoran & Riggs's benefit came from the use of the money before paying it out. By 1850 the firm had $100,000 in unclaimed interest on hand.[24]

The heavy transfer of funds from one depository to another during the war provided the Independent Treasury's most severe test and produced the most criticism. Before 1 January 1847, most transfers were made by banks at no cost. To facilitate the transfer banks accepted government funds, then sold bills of exchange in their home market, but payable at the location desired, New Orleans for example. The government's bank account increased in New Orleans and decreased in the eastern money centres. The banks made a profit on the sale of the bill of exchange and on the use of the money for the several weeks needed to complete the transaction. In additions to transfers to New Orleans and Mexico, the Independent Treasury sent funds from the smaller depositories to the larger ones, and moved foreign coins to the mints and newly minted American coins back. The Treasury could have easily moved funds by selling its own bills of exchange or drafts. However, Walker believed the Independent Treasury Act prevented him from doing so.[25]

Because of the sensitive nature of specie transfers to both the North and the South, discretion and fairness was needed. A decrease in specie tightened the local money market. This led to northern complaints about any large shipments and demands from the merchants and newspapers in New Orleans for a larger flow. As early as 1 September 1846, the Senate demanded information on transfers from the Atlantic States to New Orleans. The influx of specie in response to the export of foodstuffs eventually dulled, but did not eliminate, the criticism. Administration opponents challenged both the wisdom of the transfers and the methods used. The *New York Journal of Commerce* considered the Treasury's physical transfer of gold and silver coins unwise. The paper believed that banks were much more efficient than the Independent Treasury.[26]

Walker used three methods to transfer specie from New York, Boston, Philadelphia and Charleston to New Orleans and Mexico. First, the gold and silver coins were transported by steamer under the care of an express company. Treasury agents accompanied the shipments. The government assumed all risks from shipwreck, fire or unavoidable accidents. Second, contracts were made with bankers and brokers to provide a specific amount of specie in New Orleans at a future date. The funds were provided by the Treasury to the contractor in New York or Philadelphia in advance. The contractor either sold bills of exchange payable in New Orleans, assumed the risk of shipping specie or a combination. The contractor received a fee plus the use of the money while it was 'purported' to be in transit. Third, government disbursement officers (not the Treasury directly) were allowed to sell the treasury drafts issued to them. Once a disbursement officer received a draft he could sell it in New Orleans or Mexico at par (but not less than par). This is the reason General Scott pressured the foreign merchants in Vera Cruz. The disbursement officers were able to do things as individuals that the Treasury could not. Walker preferred to use contractors because he believed it involved less risk.[27]

The 1 April 1847 deadline requiring disbursement officers to pay out specie caused considerable alarm in the army and navy. To reduce the risk to his subordinates, the secretary of war insisted that the Treasury assume responsibility for moving the money from New York and Philadelphia to New Orleans where it would be made available to his officers. In April 1847 Secretary Marcy estimated the army would need $1 million a month in specie delivered to New Orleans. Before 1 April both the War Department and the Treasury moved money south. For example, in November 1846 the quartermaster general obtained $503,000 in American gold coins from the assistant treasurer in New York and transported the funds to New Orleans at a cost of $3,950. A few weeks later, on 7 December 1846, the quartermaster general entered into a contract with Matthew Morgan to provide $1.3 million in New Orleans at a fee of $9,000. Before the cut-off date, the Treasury secured New Orleans funds in a variety of ways. Between 1 September 1846 and January 1847 it moved $1,689,315 of its deposits by means of bank transfers. Additionally, it obtained $2 million in New Orleans from the first contract on the 1847 treasury notes. In April 1847 the last of the Treasury's deposits, $212,104, in the northern banks were ordered south. From this point forward the Independent Treasury had to make its own arrangements.[28]

The most active of the Treasury's contractors was Corcoran & Riggs, who sublet the actual work. On 20 April 1847, the firm entered into an agreement with the Treasury to provide $1.5 million in specie to disbursement officers in New Orleans for a fee of 0.75 per cent ($11,250). The funds were to be delivered in ten weekly instalments. Corcoran & Riggs accepted delivery of $1 million in specie from the Treasury and another $500,000 in treasury notes on 21 April. The firm then entered into separate agreements with Corning & Company and Matthew Morgan & Company, both of New York. Corning & Company obligated itself to provide $1 million at the rate of $100,000 a week in New Orleans for a fee of 0.7 per cent. Morgan & Company agreed to provide the remaining

$500,000 for a fee of 0.5 per cent. Morgan's assistance was critical because of his alliance with the Canal and Banking Company of New Orleans. The bank and its allies, the Rothschilds, were the strongest factors in the New Orleans exchange market. The venturers expected to raise most of the money through the sale of exchange in New Orleans.[29]

On 5 May 1847, the *New Orleans Bulletin* reported the arrival of $150,000 in specie. It could not arrive fast enough for the local merchants or the mint treasurer. The treasurer's balance was below $100,000 on 24 May and by 21 June the heavy drafts issued on him resulted in a $2,853,831 overdraft. If all the treasury drafts were presented, he could not pay. The *Bulletin* questioned the advisability of raising most of the specie needed by the military in New Orleans instead of shipping it from the North. The paper accused Walker of creating a credit crunch in New Orleans to the detriment of its merchants. Shipments of specie to Mexico further reduced the local supply. Treasury drafts payable in New York were trading in New Orleans at a 1 per cent discount.[30]

The *Washington Union* defended Walker by pointing out that treasury drafts were drawn on the depositories in which money was available. The paper believed Walker had no power or control over a treasury draft once issued. The disbursement officer receiving it could cash, sell or negotiate it in the manner the officer believed best as long as he received par. The conditions in New Orleans would be alleviated by the large transfers on the way. The *Union* optimistically predicted any amount could be sent to New Orleans at a cost of 0.375 per cent. The paper believed the Treasury would move quickly when the need arose. Additionally, the *Union* argued that the Mexican tariff would reduce the drain on New Orleans.[31]

In addition to the New Orleans press, Corcoran & Riggs's associates were also pressing for actual shipments of specie. On 27 May Morgan advised Corcoran that his friends in New Orleans wanted coins. Morgan had just shipped $150,000 in two steamers. The money had been borrowed at 5 per cent and shipping cost another 1 per cent. Because of the additional expense he asked Corcoran to provide him with an additional $1 million. Half would be immediately shipped and the other half used for a while to offset the increased cost.[32]

In June 1847 Corcoran proposed to make another $2 million available to disbursement officers in New Orleans. Under this proposal no fee would be charged the government. The agreement required the Treasury to pay the money over in New York immediately and Corcoran & Riggs to make $400,000 available in New Orleans a month later on 15 July, $500,000 more on 5 August, a further $500,000 on 20 August, and the final $600,000 by 15 September. Corcoran & Riggs's profit came from loaning the money in the New York call market before paying it over. At the request of the Treasury Department, General T. S. Jesup, the quartermaster general, prepared a requisition for $2 million in specie to be delivered in New Orleans. Based on this document the Treasury Department paid the $2 million over to Corcoran on 17 June and credited the army's account.[33]

The contract caused Walker considerable difficulty with an irate president. In making inquiries about the army's unspent appropriations, Polk discovered it had $4 million in specie on hand. The total included the $2 million in the possession of Corcoran & Riggs. Polk demanded to know why it possessed so much. In defending the army's actions General Jesup informed Polk of the contract with Corcoran & Riggs and told him that as of 25 August only $400,000 had been delivered in New Orleans. Further, he informed the president that Corcoran & Riggs and Morgan were using the remaining funds for speculation in Wall Street. Polk reacted angrily and demanded Walker return from New York immediately and explain. Despite Walker's spirited defence of the use of contractors, Polk censured him for both the size of the contract and the length of time allowed the contractors to make the transfer. Two days after Walker's interview with Polk, the Treasury informed the president that the second instalment of $500,000 had been provided to the disbursement officers in New Orleans. Additionally, since neither the War nor Treasury Departments had received information otherwise it was assumed the third instalment was timely paid. The fourth instalment of $600,000 was not due until 15 September.[34]

At the time of the president's inquiry Walker had gone north for his health. The week before he was summoned home he entered into a $2 million contract with Matthew Morgan & Company and the Canal and Banking Company (New Orleans). The final arrangements of this contract delayed Walker's return to Washington until 24 August 1847. This contract also proved embarrassing. The bank assumed it had some latitude under the contract terms and was not prepared to meet the New Orleans mint treasurer's demand for the funds on 29 November. The bank delivered $1.2 million and prevailed on the treasurer to give them a receipt for the entire $2 million. The bank completed the contract within a few days but the entire affair proved embarrassing to the administration and contractors.[35]

In addition to using contractors, the critical condition of the Independent Treasury in New Orleans during the summer of 1847 caused the Treasury to ship specie south under the care of its own agents. On 3 June 1847, the Treasury instructed the assistant treasurers in New York and Philadelphia to prepare $500,000 each in coin for immediate shipment to New Orleans. Greene & Company of New York was selected to transport the funds. Treasury agent B. Mackall took possession of the funds on 8 June and accompanied the shipment to New Orleans. On 14 June the Treasury requested another $1 million from the assistant treasurer in New York. The funds, consisting of fourteen boxes of gold, were delivered to treasury agent Lewis Jones on 16 June. Jones hired Adams (Express) & Company to transfer the gold.[36]

On 19 June William Bouck, assistant treasurer in New York, received news that a further $1 million, half each from New York and Philadelphia, would be needed shortly. On 21 July a further $2 million was demanded from New York. In August the Treasury arranged a $300,000 transfer from Charleston to New Orleans. A further transfer of $100,000 was made from Charleston in late October and early November. In December the Treasury made arrangements with H. W. Connors, president of the Bank of Charleston, to move $300,000 from New York and Charleston to New Orleans. Early in 1848 the Treasury supplemented the transfers by requiring some of the proceeds from the loan of 1847 to be deposited in the delta city.[37]

The disbursement agents responsible for paying the troops or purchasing supplies in Mexico obtained specie by selling or exchanging treasury drafts in New Orleans with the suppliers, contractors or the mint treasurer. Additionally, treasury drafts were sold to foreign merchants in Mexico, particularly in Vera Cruz. The major factors in the Mexican exchange market were Britons Lionel Davidson, the Rothschilds' agent, and Manning & Mackintosh, agents for the Barings. Both groups viewed the American army's need for specie as a lucrative business opportunity. The army needed vast sums to purchase supplies in Mexico and pay its troops. On 2 July 1847, August Belmont, American agent for the Rothschilds, wrote to Walker advising him that Lionel Davidson possessed a large amount of funds which he and the Rothschilds would gladly make available to American authorities in Mexico. Interest at 6 per cent from the date of payment in Mexico until reimbursement by the government was made in New York would suffice. The Rothschilds' real objective was to move money safely from Mexico to London via New York by using bills of exchange. Silver obtained in Mexico from the sale of goods or collection of debts could be given to the American army in Vera Cruz, Mexico City or points in between, thereby avoiding the danger of transporting it out of Mexico. Reimbursements made in New York could easily be remitted to London. The advantage for the Americans was the avoidance of the expense and bother of transporting specie from New Orleans into the interior of Mexico.[38]

Agreement was reached in August. The contract required Davidson to make two equal payments of $200,000 each to General Scott's quartermaster in Mexico. Neither party knew the exact location of Scott's advancing army. If Scott had failed to occupy Mexico City, Davidson was to attempt to make delivery in Puebla. Walker insisted, successfully, that the interest commenced when notification of the payment reached Washington, not when the payment was actually made in Mexico. The agreement gave the Rothschilds the sole right to make future payments to the army. When the army occupied Mexico City, Davidson attempted to carry out the agreement, but the army initially refused to accept delivery of the specie. Finally, on 1 March 1848, Belmont was able to advise Walker that the contract had been completed.[39]

In the meantime, in January 1848, the parties entered into a second contract for an additional $400,000. Belmont furnished the Treasury with two bills of exchange of $200,000 each payable in Mexico City. The first was payable in thirty days, the second in sixty. The Treasury was responsible for transporting the bills to Mexico so army officers could present them to Davidson for payment. Reimbursement to Belmont was in the form of treasury notes, one half immediately and the remainder when notice of the payment of the first bill was received. Scott's paymaster and quartermaster again proved difficult, demanding to wait until the sixty-day bill matured and then take possession of the entire $400,000. Eventually, during May and June, Davidson got the two officers to accept payment in four equal instalments of $100,000 each. Davidson was forced to hold the money for five months and Belmont made Walker aware of his displeasure with the confusion and additional cost.[40]

Belmont and the Treasury entered into a third and much larger contract in March 1848. As part of the agreement Belmont delivered three bills of exchange, one payable twenty days after presentation (sight) in Mexico City, in the amount of $400,000, a second payable forty days after sight, $400,000, and the third, $450,000 payable sixty days after sight. The agreement was associated with the Rothschilds and Corcoran & Riggs's bid for the third contract on the 1847 treasury notes. Reimbursement was to be made in the 6 per cent notes at par. Problems were again encountered. On 9 May 1848, Davidson reported the receipt of the bills by General Scott's successor, General William O. Butler. However, Butler was not anxious to present the bills and assume responsibility for the gold and silver. Eventually Butler did present the first two. The $800,000 obtained plus $100,000 remaining from the previous payments made up part of the first $3 million paid to Mexico on the ratification of the treaty. The last bill of $450,000 was returned to Belmont.[41]

The Independent Treasury also moved considerable amounts of foreign coins from Boston and New York to the Philadelphia mint for coinage. During 1847 the mint coined $22,655,206 in new money, the greatest year up to that time in its history. The effort exceeded that of the prior year by three times and of the previous high, 1843, by almost twice. The express firm of Adams & Company transported the coins and bullion for 25¢ per each $1,000. After some confusion between the mint and the new assistant treasurers, regulations were adopted. Adams and Company would pick up the coins at the assistant treasurers office or on the return trip from the mint and provide the sender with a receipt. The receipt would be mailed to the receiver and serve as notification. The mint assumed responsibility for all expenses.[42]

The smaller depositories encountered transfer problems of a different nature. They physically transported sums of a few thousand dollars over bad roads and swollen streams. The receiver personally escorted the money or hired trustworthy agents. To cover expenses the receiver was paid a fee based on a percentage of the amount transferred. The fee covered risks, travel, transportation and all other expenses. The fee paid to the Chicago receiver was 0.33 per cent on the funds he sent to the assistant treasurer in St Louis.[43]

In his annual reports Walker made an elaborate defence of the new system. In his view it had proved its worth during a period of war with unprecedented demands caused by the large loans, expenditures and transfers. The Independent Treasury and specie clause prevented over-expansion of bank notes, inflation and the inevitable crash resulting from over-trading. Instead of bank notes, specie circulated among the people. Walker claimed responsibility for the high state of the government's credit and the nation's prosperity. He believed that under the old system the European financial crisis of 1847 would have brought the American economy down.[44]

The most important contemporary repudiation of Walker's claims was made by Professor George Tucker of the University of Virginia. Tucker, with good reason, assigned the nation's prosperity to the export of foodstuffs. The benefits of the high volume and good prices filtered down to all levels of society. The importation of specie from this fortunate occurrence provided the wherewithal to pay taxes in specie, avoid a credit contraction at the banks and allow the export of specie to Mexico. Tucker believed the state of things would have been the same whether the Independent Treasury existed or not. In his view, the benefits of the system were illusory. Tucker believed the demands of the Mexican War, not the financial system, saved the country from over-expansion.[45]

The major criticism of the Independent Treasury's war effort concerns the transfer of funds. Walker was charged with favouritism and inefficiency. There is no doubt the system was used for private gain. However, with the strict constructionism of the Polk administration preventing the Treasury from selling its own bills of exchange, there was little option. Walker was willing to accept some profiteering from the use of government funds as a reward for services rendered. The military's need for quick delivery restricted the gross abuses that surfaced during the Whig administrations that succeeded Polk's. Under Walker the money was out of the Treasury an average of thirty-eight days during transfers to New Orleans. Between October 1850 and 3 March 1853, during the Fillmore administration, between $15 and $16 million was transferred and remained out of the Treasury for an average of sixty days.[46]

The Independent Treasury continued to serve the nation until succeeded by the Federal Reserve System in 1913. It proved neither the monster feared by its critics nor the panacea envisioned by its supporters. It successfully protected government funds. William Gouge in 1854 identified only one loss by theft. The system could thank the diligence of its employees for this good fortune. On the other hand, the Independent Treasury proved ineffective in preventing credit over-expansion leading to the Panics of 1857, 1873 and 1893. Professor Tucker's argument that the government's ability to finance the war was due to favourable economic conditions is very persuasive. Much of the credit must be given to this, not the Independent Treasury. However, the new organization caused little harm and displayed reasonable competency in processing the loan, making payments and transferring funds. The insistence on specie did strengthen the currency and ensured that the government received full value for its bonds.[47] Unlike latter-day advocates of central banking, contemporaries viewed its performance favourably enough to ensure its continued existence. The American Civil War would reveal it weaknesses and bring change, but not extinction.[48]

8 THE LOAN OF 1848

Neither the expectation of peace nor its occurrence diminished the government's need to borrow. One last major loan remained to be approved and sold before financing of the Mexican–American War was complete. Unlike the Twentieth-Ninth Congress which met in 1846 and 1847, the Whigs were now in a position to exercise considerable influence over the loan legislation. As a result, the Loan Act of 31 March 1848 authorized a straightforward loan of $16 million to be obtained through the issuance of 6 per cent twenty-year bonds. The legislation increased the bonds' marketability by allowing the secretary to sell both coupon and registered bonds. The issue provided funds for demobilization, bonuses for soldiers and sailors, treaty payments and other expenses related to winding up the war. Because the loans of 1846 and 1847 saturated the American market, it became necessary to sell many of the bonds abroad. William Corcoran, with assistance from the Treasury, eventually accomplished this task. The successful marketing of the bonds in Europe and their subsequent rise in price was a major step in re-establishing American credit internationally.[1]

The likelihood of an immediate peace was not apparent in the late autumn of 1847 as the administration prepared to meet the newly elected Thirtieth Congress. Without a treaty three alternatives were open to Polk and his cabinet. The first, withdrawal to a defensive line encompassing the territory demanded as an indemnity (California and New Mexico), was rejected. Polk favoured a second option, occupation of sufficient Mexican territory to force a favourable treaty. Walker and Buchanan advocated occupying all of Mexico. Both were posturing for the 1848 Democratic presidential nomination.[2]

Polk's plan and that of his two leading subordinates required more troops and vast amounts of money. The secretary of war estimated his department needed an additional $18 million for the last seven months remaining in fiscal year 1848 and a total of $41 million for the fiscal year beginning 1 July 1848 (1849). The amount horrified both Polk and Walker. Such amounts, they feared, would alarm the public, shake the government's credit and make it difficult to negotiate new loans. Walker pointed out that the Treasury was beginning to receive many of the 1847 treasury notes back in payment for public dues. If this trend continued, it would be impossible to sell new notes and bonds at par. Walker advocated additional levies in Mexico, including an export duty on specie. Polk, more realistic, pressured the bureau chiefs to reduce their estimates.[3]

In his third annual message, 7 December 1847, Polk reiterated his determination to wage war until a suitable treaty was obtained. Additionally, his frustration with the Mexicans had reached the point where he was willing to consider the 'all of Mexico' option. Polk acknowledged the war's high cost and proposed to finance the anticipated deficits with an immediate loan of $18.5 million to cover the fiscal year 1848 deficit and a further loan of $20.5 million in fiscal year 1849. Consideration of the second loan, he believed, could be delayed until Congress met again in December 1848. A duty on tea and coffee and the graduated sale of land, which he again endorsed, would reduce the loans to $17 million each. To make the duty more palatable, Polk recommended it be limited to the duration of the war.[4]

Polk based his proposals on information furnished by Secretary Walker. The secretary estimated expenditures for the remainder of fiscal year 1848 would exceed available means (including $6.3 million in 1847 treasury notes still to be sold), by $15,729,114. The need for a reserve of $3 million brought the total amount to be borrowed to $18.5 million. Walker urged passage of legislation authorizing an issue of fundable treasury notes. In his annual report accompanying Polk's message, Walker predicted great benefits from the Mexican levies and added his voice to the call for taxing tea and coffee. Regardless of official optimism Walker realized Congress was unlikely to increase taxes and that the Mexican levies were uncertain. To be safe, he requested that Congress authorize the Treasury to borrow the entire $18.5 million.[5]

Many in the financial community lacked Walker's confidence in the success of a new loan. Thomas Ward, Baring Brothers' agent in the United States, advised his employer that Walker was likely to receive authority to issue $18 million in treasury notes, but that it would be necessary to sell the notes off in small lots as the Treasury needed money. Ward predicted a gradual tightening of credit and a decline in the price of all stocks and bonds. He believed the government's notes and bonds would encounter stiff competition for funds in the money market from state securities and borrowing by private enterprise. However, Ward considered it important to sustain the government's credit. Like Walker, he favoured an issue of fundable treasury notes. Albert Gallatin echoed Ward's theme on the competition for funds. The war, he believed, was absorbing too much of the country's resources. Gallatin doubted the Polk administration's ability to make peace and foresaw increased pressure on the money market. Since a loan was necessary, Gallatin recommended it be raised through a simple, direct issue of bonds. He preferred 7 per cent ten-year bonds to 6 per cent twenty-year ones because of the ability to liquidate the debt sooner.[6]

The makeup of the Congress that assembled in December 1847 to consider the administration's proposals was entirely different from that of the last two sessions. The Whigs made large gains in the mid-term elections and, with the help of independents, organized the House of Representatives and elected Robert Winthrop of Massachusetts as speaker. Samuel F. Vinton (Whig, Ohio) assumed the chairmanship of the important Ways and Means Committee. Though the Senate remained strongly Democratic, the House Whigs possessed the power to put their imprint on the new loan bill and other financial measures.[7]

The economic picture also darkened somewhat as 1847 came to a close. Credit was tightening, 1847 treasury notes were at par or below and large amounts of the notes were being returned to the Treasury. *Bankers' Magazine* believed the money market would remained disturbed for the first half of 1848 and blamed six factors – first, the fall in the price of cotton; second, the need of the government to borrow large sums; third, the Independent Treasury; fourth, speculation by capitalists; fifth, the financial crisis in Great Britain and Europe; and sixth, the unfavourable balance of trade. The *New York Journal of Commerce* reported a contraction of bank credit as the institutions sought to solidify their positions by increasing specie reserves. The *Journal* believed any effort to sell 6 per cent government bonds for more than 95 would be unsuccessful as long as the nation remained at war and the Independent Treasury existed. Part of the pressure on the market arose from a steady increase in the export of specie. The favourable trade balance the nation enjoyed in 1846 and most of 1847 was no more. On 15 January 1848, *Niles' National Register* estimated that since the preceding October $7 million had gone abroad. Conditions in Europe were mixed. The financial crisis in Great Britain was easing, but there were signs of the unrest on the continent that broke out into widespread revolution in 1848. European capitalists were nervous and beginning to look towards the United States as a safe haven.[8]

Before Congress could seriously consider the loan bill, it became necessary to decide exactly how much the government needed for the remainder of fiscal year 1848. It quickly became apparent that the Treasury report contained serious errors. In computing the funds available to the government, veteran clerk J. D. Barclay erred in the amount of the loans of 1846 and 1847 that remained unsold and therefore available to meet the government's needs. Barclay picked up the amount available from those sources as of 1 October 1847 ($6,285,294) instead of as of the first day of the fiscal year, 1 July. In the interim, the July–September quarter, the Treasury received $6,915,078 from the sale of treasury notes and bonds. This amount should have been included in available means thereby reducing the deficit and the need to borrow by almost $7 million.[9] The lesser amount did not remain under consideration long. Ten days after acknowledging the error, acting secretary of the Treasury McClintock Young advised Congress that the secretary of war needed to increase his estimates by another $3,880,000. Young requested Congress authorize a loan of $16 million, which he believed sufficient until Congress met again.[10]

Failure by the Whigs to give the bill quick consideration caused concern in the administration and Democratic press. On 24 January 1848, Polk met with Representatives James McKay and George Smith Houston, Democratic members of the Ways and Means Committee, and urged passage of a loan bill that included treasury notes. Polk also sought to ensure that blame fell on the Whigs if the bill failed. Walker appealed to the committee's chairman in what Vinton described as an anxious letter. The *Washington Union* used less tact and blunter language in accusing the opposition of attempting to sabotage the administration's efforts to obtain an honourable peace.[11]

The House began consideration of the loan bill on 8 February. Chairman Vinton proposed to give the administration its $16 million but took the occasion to belabour the administration for its financial incompetency. He rightly pointed out that in its last session Congress was assured that $23 million would suffice for all of fiscal year 1848. Now the administration wanted $16 million more. Vinton accused the Democrats of deliberately underestimating the needs in December 1846 in order to deceive the people of the party's true goals and the costs. Other Whig Congressmen continued in the same vein, alternately accusing the administration of fomenting the war and concealing its true objectives.[12]

In the end little option existed except to approve a loan bill. Most Whigs, like freshman congressman Abraham Lincoln, distinguished between censuring the administration for its conduct of the war and voting supply. 'This vote' (declaring the war unnecessary and unconstitutional), Lincoln informed his law partner William Herndon,

> has nothing to do, in determining my votes on the questions of supplies. I have always intended, and still intend, to vote supplies; perhaps not in the precise form recommended by the president, but in a better form for all purposes, except loco foco party purposes.[13]

Lincoln failed to convince his friend. Like most Midwesterners Herndon viewed the war as both necessary and constitutional.[14]

The House passed the loan bill on 17 February but not in the form the administration sought. In spite of claims that they were putting the success of the loan in jeopardy the Whigs rejected Walker's request for fundable treasury notes and, instead, authorized an issue of $16 million in 6 per cent twenty-year bonds. The full faith and credit of the government backed the bonds, but no specific assets or revenues were pledged. To increase competition the secretary was required to advertise for bids in at least two newspapers in each state. The legislation also allowed the Treasury to repurchase the bonds before their due date at the market price as long as the purchase price was not below par.[15]

Any urgency the Senate felt for the bill evaporated on 23 February when Polk submitted the Treaty of Guadalupe Hidalgo for its consideration. Although Polk's indemnity demands had grown harsher the longer the war lasted, the treaty was within the bounds of envoy Nicholas Trist's original instructions and he felt obliged to submit it to the Senate. As the debate in the Senate over the treaty continued, Polk became more anxious to end the war and began to fear the treaty's rejection by a coalition of Whigs and dissident Democrats. His fears about the Whigs were misplaced and the treaty received approval on 10 March 1848 by a vote of 38–14. Given a choice between the treaty and continuation of the war, the Senate elected the former. The opposition came from senators who demanded a greater territorial indemnity.[16]

Before the Senate took up the loan bill again, a further error was discovered in the Treasury's computation. The Treasury's coffers contained $1,401,900 in treasury notes accepted in payment of public dues. The Treasury expected to reissue the notes and counted the amount as revenue in the estimates for fiscal year 1848. However, no offsetting entry was made expensing the redemption of the notes which took place during the first quarter of fiscal year 1848. The *New York Tribune* speculated that another $1.5 million would now be needed. The accumulation of errors, the *Tribune* editorialized, cast so much doubt on the Treasury's competency that little faith should be placed in its reports. Congress decided to ignore the error.[17]

With peace in the offing the Democratic leadership in the Senate decided to accept the House bill. The treaty improved the prospects of a straight bond sale and $16 million now seemed sufficient. Both parties were also busily increasing appropriations for politically popular items such as soldiers' bonuses and the payment of the outstanding claims of American citizens against the Mexican government. With neither side prepared to support a tax increase the need for the loan was clearly recognized. The loan bill passed the Senate on 29 March and Polk signed it into law two days later.[18]

The third contract on the loan of 1847 provided some relief in the interim, but with the Treasury's reserve hovering around $2 million the secretary needed to advertise for a new loan soon. On 8 April the cabinet met and agreed to invite proposals. This time the effort was not to be limited to the domestic market.[19]

The outlook for foreign sales was improving in early 1848. The British financial crisis was easing and the Bank of England's interest rate fell to 4 per cent on 27 January and continued to decline throughout 1848. The end of the British railroad boom freed up capital and left investors seeking profitable and safe places for their funds. Revolution on the continent, particularly in France and Germany, made the victorious Americans appear a better risk. In addition to the Rothschilds' participation in the third contract, both Baring Brothers and George Peabody were beginning to accept certificates of the previous loans for resale in Europe. A successful war, reasonable prosperity, a better appreciation in Europe of the federal government's credit standing, the efforts of the default- ing states to resume interest payments, the great need for capital to develop the United States and a nervous European market all made the British bankers revise their opinion of investments in the United States.[20]

On 17 April the Treasury Department announced its intention to accept bids on the entire $16 million of 6 per cent twenty-year bonds. The bonds were not redeemable before 1 July 1868 and paid interest semi-annually on 1 January and 1 July. Bids were required to be unconditional and to specify the amount of bonds desired and the premium offered. Bids below par were unacceptable. Sealed bids were due by 17 June and a deposit equal to 1 per cent of the amount requested required. To increase participation, or the illusion of it, bids as low as $50 would be entertained.

Several changes were introduced in response to the criticism cast on prior announcements. To prevent the contractors from inconveniencing the Treasury and profiting from domestic exchange operations by making deposits outside the eastern money centres, the successful bidders were required to make payments into the depository nearest their residency. Foreign residents were to deposit with any of the assistant treasurers in Boston, New York, Philadelphia or New Orleans. The bids were scheduled to be opened in a public ceremony at 3 p.m. on 17 June. Successful bidders were required to make payments in July, August, September, October and November at the rate of 20 per cent a month. As an added inducement, the purchaser might take either coupon or registered bonds. For its own convenience, the Treasury limited the coupon bonds to denomina- tions of $1,000 and above. Finally, the premium had to be paid with the July instalment.[21]

Wall Street conceded leadership in bringing out the loan to Corcoran & Riggs, and those wishing to participate eagerly sought to be included on the firm's list. Corcoran believed much of the loan must be sold abroad and actively solicited the support of Baring Brothers and George Peabody. Such sales would keep the bonds off the American market and ease credit by bringing specie into the United States (or at least reducing its export). Peabody expressed interest as early as 14 April, but restricted his commitment to $40,000. Eventually, he agreed to a joint venture that included Elisha Riggs, Corcoran & Riggs and him- self. Each was to share equally in the sale of $750,000 of the new bonds (the 3/3 account). Peabody agreed to sell most of the bonds in Europe. Elisha Riggs was to obtain the funds for deposit by selling bills of exchange in New York payable by Peabody in London.[22]

Both Thomas Ward, Baring Brothers' American agent, and James G. King & Son, their New York correspondent, were anxious for the British firm's participation in the offering. James G. King (son of New York senator and statesman Rufus King) wanted a small portion for his own firm. King believed the bonds a good investment even if a premium of 3 per cent was necessary. The Barings expressed a willingness to participate to the extent of $1 million. They preferred to do so as part of a larger bidding group. This would allow them to ease back into the American market and limit their risk.[23]

Corcoran began his own campaign to obtain the assistance of the Barings by approaching King on 1 June. He proposed a joint bid in the range of 101.5 to 102.5. Thomas Ward, two weeks away from his employer by steamer and acting somewhat in the dark, was prepared to listen. Ward and King met with Corcoran on 13 June and agreed in principal to a united bid. Corcoran still believed a premium of 1.5 to 2.5 per cent sufficient to obtain most of the loan. However, he indicated his intentions of going higher if this became necessary. On 16 June Ward committed the Barings to take $1,250,000 million of the loan and King agreed to take a further $250,000 for his own firm. They set a ceiling of 104. The same day Corcoran advised them of the likelihood of a bid in excess of that previously mentioned.[24]

In addition to Peabody and the Barings, Corcoran busily lined up other foreign and domestic participants. Applicants included erstwhile competitors such as Winslow & Perkins, Matthew Morgan and the Bank of Commerce (New York). The usual allies, Cammann & Whitehouse, the Riggs family and George Newbold, also joined for varying amounts. By the deadline, Corcoran & Riggs's list approached $10 million. Many of the would-be buyers specified a maximum price they were willing to pay. The Bank of Commerce, for example, expressed its willingness to take $1 million at 101, but only $750,000 at 101.5 and $650,000 if the price rose to 102. John Ward wanted $250,000 at 101.25 or below. James Robb of New Orleans limited his bid to 101.[25]

William Corcoran sought to control the loan for his firm regardless of price. Legally it was a new firm. The large-scale operations of his partner caused George Riggs grave concern and with a sizeable fortune in hand he elected to withdraw. In place of George, Corcoran accepted Elisha Riggs, Jr, George's half-brother and Elisha's youngest son. They agreed to share profits 75–25 per cent with Corcoran getting the larger share. Corcoran was now free to concentrate on the bidding process. His anxious fellow venturers weighed in with their advice. James G. King recommended a progressive bid starting with $12 million at 101.25 or below and bidding for the remainder in $2 million increments at 102.05 and 102.5. With the prospects of peace, the 1847 treasury note and bond prices had advanced in the spring of 1848 but had recently fallen, partially because of heavy sales by Corcoran & Riggs in order to depress the price and discourage bidding.

The 1847 6 per cent bonds were selling at 103. George Newbold left the decision to Corcoran but limited his share to an insignificant $50,000. He advised Corcoran that $7 or $8 million would be offered from New York.[26]

After receiving information on premium deposits and the actions of likely bidders, Corcoran concluded that a bid of 102.5 would leave $6 or $7 million to others. Assuming the bids of allies Winslow & Perkins and George Riggs were made to make the process appear more competitive, he was correct. Opening of the bids revealed $5.7 million at 102.5 or above by competitors. At the last moment Corcoran submitted a proposal to take the entire loan at 103.02. The bid was above the maximum price set by most of the individuals and firms on his list.[27]

The secretary and chief clerk of the Treasury opened the bids in a two-hour ceremony held in the entrance hall of the Treasury building. The Treasury's bureau chiefs and leading bidders attended. All but $54,000 of the $30,393,890 in bids submitted were above par. William C. Bestor submitted the highest bid at 104 for $5,000 of the new bonds. A total of $17,934,450 was at 103.02 or above. The premium totalled $487,168. Corcoran & Riggs obtained $14,065,500 of the $16 million issue.[28]

The Democratic press hailed the sale at the large premium as a complete success. The results, the *Washington Union* crowed, were worthy of 'universal congratulations by men of all parties throughout the country'.[29] The *Union's* New York correspondent reported that the Barings' participation gave Wall Street a sense of confidence. The reporter attributed the favourable outcome to the stability of the American government. The *United States Magazine and Democratic Review* believed the loan's success repudiated those 'croakers' who claimed Democratic policies would injure the financial interest of the country and destroy its credit. The magazine pointed out that in spite of war in Mexico, revolution in Europe and financial crises abroad, the credit of the American government stood higher than ever.[30]

Instead of criticism the Whig press down played the loan's success and refused to acknowledge the transaction as a great Democratic victory. The *Washington National Intelligencer* attributed the favourable outcome to the desires of nervous Europeans to invest in the United States. The paper pointed out that the State of Massachusetts recently obtained more favourable terms on an issue of 5 per cent bonds. In the long term, the contractors, not the government, stood to gain most. The *Intelligencer* passed on an opportunity to lambaste Corcoran & Riggs. Instead, it acknowledged that the firm was admirably suited to attract foreign capital. The *New York Tribune* also believed that the firm was the most capable of serving the interest of both the Treasury and financial community. However, the *Tribune* did complain that regardless of the terms the nation had committed itself to pay $960,000 annually in interest for the next twenty years.

The paper also discounted the prospects of the Barings sending great amounts of specie to the United States. The *Tribune* believed, correctly, that most of the funds would come from the collection of debts owed to the Barings in the United States. Thomas Ward was in the process of doing this very thing.[31]

Corcoran notified Thomas Ward and James G. King of the group's success in controlling the loan on 17 June. None of the loan, he believed, fell into weak hands.[32] Corcoran considered the prospects excellent and advised Ward that 'after having seen all the bids we would not vary our bid a fraction'.[33] He also passed along Walker's assurance that no further loans would be required for fiscal years 1848 and 1849. Corcoran believed this news increased the value of the bonds. In informing the Barings, Ward acknowledged that the price was higher than expected, but assured them the loan was still desirable.[34]

In addition to Baring Brothers, Corcoran obtained $1.4 million in other foreign commitments. Over half of this amount was the 3/3 account with George Peabody. Corcoran & Riggs expected to send $500,000 of the $750,000 to Peabody for sale in Europe. More would be sent if the venture proved profitable. Merchant John Cryder advised Peabody that the high price surprised observers and stocks and bonds on the New York market had risen in reaction. Elisha predicted the bonds would reach 105 by July. He quickly revised this to 110 in light of the probability of peace and news that no further loans were required. The more pessimistic Cryder predicted that European sales would be less than expected and that prices would fall if specie continued to be exported.[35]

E. W. Clark & Company was the second most successful bidder and acquired $950,000 at prices from 103.03 to 103.45. Clark & Company submitted a series of bids starting at 102.04 and becoming progressively higher. The firm received 60 per cent of the amount covered by its various bids. To circumvent the Treasury's restriction on the place of deposit, Clark & Company submitted its bid in the name of E. W. Clark & Brothers, its St Louis affiliate. This allowed the two firms to sell bills of exchange in St Louis for a premium, use the proceeds to make deposits with the assistant treasurer in the river city, and redeem the bills and take title to the bonds in New York and Philadelphia.[36]

Once the bidding was complete the Barings sought to resell their share as rapidly as possible. Ward deposited $240,000 on the first possible day, 1 July 1848, and asked Corcoran & Riggs to obtain $162,000 in coupon bonds and the remainder in registered bonds in order to fill British and French orders. Priority went to those Barings clients who, before the closing date, had committed to the purchase of $550,000 at the bid price plus a 1 per cent commission. American debt collections and sale of London exchange in New York supplied the funds for deposit.[37]

The wish of the Barings to obtain and dispose of their bonds quickly suited Corcoran's plan. He readily agreed to restrict the deposits of his other clients in order to allow the Barings to obtain their entire share in July. On 3 July Ward reiterated his intention of meeting this goal but requested an extension to 10 August if needed. Throughout July Ward concentrated on collecting debts and selling bills of exchange. Generally, he obtained 110 for London exchange. By 14 July he was able to report deposits of $500,000 with the assistant treasurers and the forwarding of $222,000 in coupon bonds and $115,000 in registered bonds. Eleven days later deposits had risen to $745,000. The 31 July deadline found deposits at only $825,000 but by 9 August Ward was within $48,000 of his goal of $1.25 million. On 22 August he reported success and informed his employer that the last of the bonds had gone out by steamer.[38]

In Europe the Barings and George Peabody quickly came to an understanding and agreed to maintain the bond price at 105.5 (New York price) and not to sell below that point. They supported the market by, when necessary, buying up bonds of the older issues offered by the Rothschilds and small lots sent from the United States on consignment or as remittances. The Rothschilds had cooperated by holding their 1847 notes and bonds off the market during the bidding process but were now anxious to dispose of them. In spite of the competition, the Barings were able to make sales in lots of $10,000 to $20,000 in Britain and larger amounts on the continent. Sales were particularly brisk in disturbed France. By 9 September the firm had sold $1.1 million of its allocation. However, they consistently rejected pleas to accept more bonds. Commercial commissions were at the time more profitable than government finance.[39]

The agreement between Elisha Riggs, Corcoran & Riggs and George Peabody was both an effort to sell bonds and an exchange operation. During the 1840s the international bill of exchange business was conducted in pounds sterling since London was the centre of international finance. At this point the reader should be advised of the manner in which sterling bills were quoted. The price of bills of exchange depended on the demand for specie in a particular location. Such demand usually arose from international settlements arising from trade imbalances and the flow of investments. In 1847 the great export of American foodstuffs produced an exchange rate highly favourable to the United States. American merchants were able to buy bills on London at a reduced price, as low as 104.5 in April 1847 but rising to 110.25 in December as conditions returned to normal.[40]

The quotation also reflected the relative gold content and the value of the dollar and pound. Neither government was averse to tampering with the official value. In 1792 Congress set a standard of twenty-seven grains per dollar in American gold coins. In 1834, because Congress believed there was insufficient gold in the country to conduct the nation's business, the gold content in the coins was reduced to 25.8 grains per dollar. The legislation also changed the monetary ratio of silver to gold from 15 to 1 to 16 to 1. In 1792 Alexander Hamilton had established the 15 to 1 ratio, thereby undervaluing gold and driving gold coins from circulation. Congress also adjusted the official exchange rate between the dollar and pound. In 1834 it established a rate of $4.8665 per pound. The rate was reduced in 1842 to $4.84 and again in 1843 to $4.83. The second reduction was on the premise that British coins were slightly worn and a small portion of the gold lost. The rate was used to compute the import duties on invoices quoted in pounds and in the Treasury's international transactions.[41]

The mercantile and banking communities who engaged in buying and sell-ing bills of exchange on London ignored both the official rate and the gold content of the American and British currencies and assigned a value of $4.44 to the pound (4 *s.* 6 *d.* to the dollar). This arbitrary and fictitious sum repre-sented a standard set a century previously and never changed. The marketplace adjusted for the increased value of the pound by assigning a premium of about 9.5 per cent on London exchange sold in New York. Assuming balanced trade and no financial crisis in Britain or the United States, bills of exchange pay-able in London were usually quoted at 109 to 110. If the rate varied from 1.5 to 2 per cent in either direction, it became profitable to assume the cost and ship specie instead of buying exchange. In 1847, with a huge American trade surplus, the price of London exchange fell below 105 in New York and the United States was flooded with specie. At 105 the market value of the pound was reduced to $4.66. The same system was used to quote American stocks and bonds in the London market. As a result most American bonds were quoted below par. A quotation of 96 for an American bond in London equalled a New York price of 105 to 105.5.[42]

During the early part of the exchange operation, both Thomas Ward and Elisha Riggs were able to obtain 110 in New York and Boston. For example, on 8 July, Elisha sold £20,000 on London at 110 and received payment of $97,602.19. This placed a value of $4.88 on the pound and represented a slight devaluation of the dollar. It was not sufficient to encourage massive shipments of specie to Europe. However, some movement was taking place.[43]

Corcoran & Riggs informed Peabody of the successful bid on 19 June and promised to start shipping bonds to him by 1 July. One day later, 20 June, the firm advised Peabody of their intention to send $230,000 in coupon bonds con-sisting of 120 of the $1,000 denomination, eighteen of the $5,000s and two of the $10,000s in the next few weeks. Peabody believed the bonds could not be forced on the European market and suggested a slower, steadier selling campaign. He wanted to start with an initial $120,000 and then receive further shipments according to market conditions. He expected to sell $100,000 a month. If sales proved brisker, then shipments could be accelerated. Throughout July and August Elisha sold exchange and Corcoran & Riggs shipped bonds to Peabody. By 16

August Elisha was able to announce sales of $227,593 in exchange and shipment of $177,000 in bonds. He was awaiting $51,000 in bonds from the Treasury. The operation proceeded until 29 September when Peabody reported receipts of $470,000 and asked that further shipments cease after the final $30,000.[44]

In spite of assisting the Barings support the European market, Peabody was able to sell $220,000 of the new bonds by late August. However, like the Barings, he was anxious to limit his commitment to $500,000. In a request that later became controversial he asked that the remaining $250,000 of the 3/3 account be sold in New York. As this point Corcoran suggested Peabody hold the bonds in his possession for two or three months. Peabody ignored the advice and continued to sell whenever a profit could be obtained. Subsequently, with the sale of the first $500,000 nearing completion and the price rising in Europe, Peabody changed his mind about the remaining $250,000 of the 3/3 account and sold a considerable portion of it. This posed some difficulty since Elisha Riggs was selling the same bonds on the New York market. An angry Peabody forced Corcoran & Riggs and Elisha Riggs to make up $120,000 of the sales from their own holdings at a loss of personal profit.[45]

E. W. Clark & Company sought to tap the European capital market through other means. The firm's principal, E. W. Clark, went to Europe early in July to negotiate a loan using the 6 per cent bonds as collateral. Peabody predicted that he could not borrow money even at 8 per cent. It is unlikely Clark had any success. The English were unwilling to assume the risks inherent in a loan without the profit potential ownership bestowed in the event of a price rise.[46]

Left to their own resources, E. W. Clark & Company and its St Louis affiliate got down to the business of selling exchange in St Louis on New York, depositing the proceeds with the St Louis assistant treasurer and selling the bonds in the North. By the end of November 1848 they had completed the sale of their $950,000 commitment. Bond sales were made to the firm's brokerage customers or on the open market. In marketing the bonds Clark & Company effectively used its network of related firms spread around the nation. Unlike in the Civil War, no appeal was made to patriotism and only the Boston office publicly advertised the bonds for sale. The firm drew profits from three sources: the sale of the bonds above the contract price, the commission on the sale of exchange and the interest on the bonds between the time the deposit was made in St Louis and the redemption of the bill of exchange in Philadelphia or New York (two or three weeks). As important as the profits were, notoriety proved more beneficial in the growth of the firm. Building on this success the firm expanded into marketing municipal, state and railroad securities during the 1850s.[47]

With the commitments from foreign buyers flowing in, Corcoran & Riggs easily met the July deposit requirements. The Independent Treasury credited the firm with almost $3 million during the month and a further $2 million in

August. After this initial surge it became more difficult. Many of the individuals and firms on Corcoran & Riggs's list had specified prices below the 103.02 bid and refused to take the bonds. The firm lost half of the original $10 million in commitments and struggled to find other markets. After eliminating those foreign and domestic buyers who bought the bonds in spite of the high price, Corcoran & Riggs had $6 or $7 million to sell. Those that went ahead with the purchase included the Bank of Commerce, $500,000, Elisha Riggs and his associates, $645,000 and Winslow & Perkins, $400,000.[48]

Corcoran & Riggs entered the open market early in July by selling at 104. After pushing the price to 104.5 the firm withdrew for several weeks. The objective was to restrict American sales and stabilize the New York market in order to assist overseas sales. Unfortunately for Corcoran & Riggs, the money market tightened in the interim. By mid-July New York papers were reporting interest rates of 11 to 12 per cent for good credit risks and demanding the return to New York of specie arriving in New Orleans from Mexico as the army withdrew its forces. Economic activity slowed as merchants and bankers became cautious and began to husband their resources.[49]

Corcoran & Riggs re-entered the market as sellers with difficulty. Competition for funds from states and railroads severely strained the money market and put pressure on bond prices. On 2 August the *New York Tribune* reported sales of the new bonds at 103.625 (including 50¢ in accrued interest). The price did rally in mid-August to 104.5. During August Corcoran & Riggs's brokers were selling generally at 104.375 less commission. With accrued interest and expenses, this left little profit. The depressed market complicated Corcoran's efforts to honour his contract with the Treasury. The deposits being made by the firm's clients would only sustain it for another month or two.[50]

The solution to his firm's inventory problems and the tight American money market, Corcoran believed, was large additional bond sales in Europe. He resolved to visit Great Britain personally and negotiate either a sale or a loan. This proved to be the most crucial event in the successful marketing of the loan of 1848. Corcoran reached this conclusion in late July and began to search for an influential Whig to accompany him. The goal was to impress on the Europeans the non-partisan nature of the loan and to show that it had the support of the American people. William Appleton suggested Daniel Webster who could, as usual, use the generous fee, but Abbott Lawrence, former American minister to Great Britain, was Corcoran's first choice. Lawrence refused the offer but recommended ex-governor and current senator John Davis of Massachusetts. After interviewing Davis, Corcoran selected him and promised a fee of $5,000 plus expenses.[51]

The Treasury Department also acknowledged the need for increased foreign sales and prepared to cooperate fully. At the time of the loan's announcement

Walker sent copies to American consuls in the leading British and continental cities in an effort to publicize the issue. The Treasury also arranged to make a demand on Corcoran & Riggs for a $5 million payment. Since the Treasury's reserves stood at $1.8 million on 31 July and large sums were being appropriated by a generous Congress, sufficient substance existed to give the demand legitimacy. The real purpose was to provide Corcoran an excuse for the trip. Walker made a formal demand for the funds on 2 August. As expected, Corcoran informed him two days later of the impossibility of providing the funds without serious embarrassment to the American money market.[52] However, Corcoran added, 'if a portion of the loan could be placed in London and a part of the proceeds brought home in coin the effect on the market would be felt at once, confidence would be restored [and] the commercial interests relieved'.[53] Corcoran offered to participate in this grand endeavour. Walker reacted as expected and appointed Corcoran a special agent of the Treasury with the authority to negotiate the sale of up to $5 million of the loan in Europe. On 9 August he advised George Bancroft, now the American minister in London, of Corcoran's mission and requested that he render the banker all assistance possible. Bancroft was also to recommend the bonds to the British bankers and assure them of the Treasury's interest and cooperation.[54]

Both Thomas Ward and James G. King sought their employer's cooperation. Ward personally vouched for Corcoran's knowledge, business sense and soberness. He recommended the Barings establish a long-term relationship with the Washington firm. King advocated cooperation because success would make the American market stronger. King expressed his confidence by asking to participate to the extent of £50,000 if an agreement to purchase was concluded. Abbott Lawrence added his influence, recommending both Corcoran and the loan. Lawrence argued that peace, prosperity and a low national debt provided adequate security. He believed the certainty of payment should ensure sales of $10 million in Europe.[55]

The Barings were less than enthusiastic about the visit and not convinced of Corcoran's financial conservatism. Joshua Bates, expatriate American and Barings partner, ridiculed the trip. 'There never was anything so absurd', he wrote to Ward, 'as Mr. Corcoran and Governor Davis coming over to dispose of U. S. 6 per cent' bonds.[56] The Barings considered both Corcoran and Peabody 'boosters' who always overstated their successes and wealth. The main objection was Corcoran's quick rise by his wits and the lack of a century-old tradition. The Barings also doubted the European market for American bonds could absorb another large influx. Demand was likely to decrease as stability returned to Europe. Regardless of the prospects of a lukewarm reception, Corcoran decided to go ahead and informed Ward of his intention of taking the 16 August steamer.

The 6 per cent 1848 bonds were selling at 104.5 (including 75¢ accrued interest) as he boarded ship.[57]

To allow Corcoran sufficient time to negotiate, the Treasury took two steps during his absence. First, Walker agreed to an extension of time to make the monthly deposits. This was based on the rationale that the government had no current need for the funds; certainly a great turnaround from 2 August when Walker was demanding $5 million from Corcoran. The Treasury's balance did not reflect this and only rose from $1.8 million to $2 million during August. Deposits against Corcoran & Riggs's contract dropped to $645,000 in September and $825,000 in October, well below the $2.8 million due each month under the original terms. In fairness, the suspension was as much an effort to ease a tight money market as to aid Corcoran.[58]

The second action taken in late September and early October was more controversial. In a further effort to supply funds for the New York money market, the Treasury entered into an agreement to buy $800,000 in 1847 treasury notes at par from William R. Morgan, one of Corcoran's New York associates. Between 29 September and 11 October the assistant treasurer in New York paid Morgan $813,505 for the notes and accrued interest. By law the Treasury could redeem the notes only at par. Since they were selling above that price, the agreement allowed Morgan to repurchase the notes at par. Morgan made a surety deposit of 2 per cent ($16,000).[59]

Historian Richard Timberlake praises the action as one of the first open market operations conducted by the Treasury. To Timberlake, Walker's effort was a precursor of central bank activity in the money market and an indication of the role Walker envisioned for the Independent Treasury. The possibility existed, Timberlake believed, of turning the Independent Treasury into a thoroughgoing monetary authority and a stepping stone to central banking.[60]

The press divided on the legality of the transaction and its effect. The *New York Journal of Commerce* believed it equivalent to a friendly loan but was ready to praise anything that reduced the gold locked up in the Independent Treasury. In late September and early October tight money and high interest brought the New York money market to near panic. The *Journal of Commerce* speculated that the expected payment of the Mexican claims and other expenses by the government would place sufficient funds in the market so that Morgan's later repurchase of the notes could be managed without undue stress. The paper continued its ongoing campaign against the Independent Treasury but praised Walker for his efforts to provide some relief. The *Journal* defended the action's legality by pointing out that Section 8 of the Loan Act of 28 January 1847 authorized the secretary to repurchase the notes at par. Further, leading New York bankers and merchants had petitioned Walker for some action. Morgan's promise to loan part of the money to others at 7 per cent helped stifle some of the criticism.[61]

The *Washington Union* argued that the transaction benefited the government by saving interest on the notes for thirty to sixty days and the public by making the funds available for commercial activity. The Democratic paper strayed by alleging that Walker and Corcoran had no part in devising and implementing the measure. It was unlikely that acting secretary, McClintock Young would have taken the responsibility and acted independently. The *Union* was correct in asserting that the action met the letter of the law. Whether such transactions were the actual intent of Congress is more debatable.[62]

Whig papers developed the theme of illegality and used it as a basis to attack the Independent Treasury. For the good of commerce and business, specie needed to be in circulation or the banks, not locked up. *Niles' National Register* labelled the Treasury's action a disguised loan. The paper found it strange that an administration committed to the principles of separation of the government and banks could engage in money lending and stock brokering. *Bankers' Magazine* believed the action proved the Independent Treasury possessed excess specie to the detriment of commerce. In truth, Walker sought relief, both for the money market and his friends. Walker and the administration had a great stake in the loan's success. Both the Treasury's interest and that of the loan contractors were served.[63]

Upon his arrival in London Corcoran sought out his strongest supporter, George Peabody. Peabody was an expatriate American conducting a merchant banking business in London. Originally from South Danver, Massachusetts, he moved to Washington, DC, in 1814 where he had the good fortune to impress Elisha Riggs during a short stint in the militia during the War of 1812. In 1815 Peabody readily accepted the junior partnership Riggs offered him in a firm engaged in importing dry goods in Baltimore. In 1829, when Riggs left for New York, Peabody reorganized the firm as Peabody, Riggs & Company, with Elisha's nephew Samuel as his partner. After several buying trips to England he elected to reside there permanently beginning in 1837. In addition to serving as a purchasing agent he moved steadily into banking. The transition to finance was completed in 1845 with the establishment of George Peabody & Company. The firm engaged in the purchase and sale of commodities, securities and foreign exchange. He was particularly active in making a market for the state bonds remaining in Europe.[64]

Corcoran proposed to sell Peabody $3 million of the new bonds. The sale was to be consummated over a three-month period starting in October 1848. Peabody was not willing to purchase such a large amount. Instead, he helped Corcoran prepare a proposal to Baring Brothers. He also recommended Corcoran visit Paris and Holland. Corcoran went to Paris but left the Dutch to Peabody.[65]

Chances of success were highest in London so Corcoran and Peabody concentrated their efforts on Threadneedle and Lombard Streets. Whatever their reservations, several factors pushed the Barings towards agreeing to participate in the purchase of additional bonds. The United States government and financial community supported Corcoran's mission and its failure would weigh heavily on the market. The British money market was recovering from a crisis and the bankers were reluctant to have another break-out across the Atlantic. Additionally, the United States was a major trading partner whose prosperity benefited British manufacturers and merchants. America's long-term prospects were bright and held the prospect of profitable investments and commissions. The Barings simply could not allow Corcoran to fail and he knew it. These factors, as much as profit, drove the parties towards an agreement.[66]

After three weeks of on-and-off negotiations, agreement was reached between Corcoran, acting for Corcoran & Riggs, and an investment group led by Baring Brothers. Corcoran & Riggs sold $3 million in bonds to six different firms. The Barings took $750,000 (including $250,000 for James G. King & Son), George Peabody, Morrison & Dillon, Overend Gurney and Denison & Company, $500,000 each, and Samuel Jones Lloyd & Company the remaining $250,000. The $500,000 taken by Peabody was on joint account with Corcoran & Riggs. The price was 93.75 in London or about 103.25 in New York.

Corcoran also gave the bankers an option, valid until 1 January 1849, for an additional $1 million on the same terms. The option was divided proportionately based on the initial purchase. In giving the option Corcoran assured the Barings that his firm would still hold $2 million or more of the bonds after the sale. To be valid, notification of the intent to exercise the option must be forwarded on a Cunard steamer leaving Liverpool before 1 January 1849.

The Britons agreed to pay in three equal monthly instalments beginning in October. Instead of coins the bankers gave Corcoran sixty-day bills of exchange at the fixed rate of 4 s. 6 d. per dollar ($4.44 per pound sterling, 210.18.9 pounds per $1,000 bond). Any change in the exchange rates on the bills was at Corcoran's risk. Corcoran agreed to limit his firm's sales in the United States to $1 million a month. As compensation, Corcoran & Riggs received 5 per cent of the 6 per cent interest earned on the bonds during the sixty-day period (21 September to 21 November) before the bills of exchange were redeemed in London. In his capacity as special agent to the Treasury, Corcoran agreed that the interest on the bonds would commence on 21 September, not the date of deposit with an assistant treasurer.

The *New York Tribune* calculated that at the current rate of exchange (108.5) Corcoran would lose 1.5 per cent. However, the 5 per cent interest offset much of this loss. The sale of the $3 million plus $833,000 of the option resulted in a net loss of $16,000, slightly over 0.25 per cent. Official blessing of the agreement came on 27 September from the American Legation in London. Bancroft assured the Barings that the secretary of the Treasury would honour the arrangement.[67]

In the United States news of the agreement arrived on 7 October and created a sense of relief, not elation. John Cryder believed the $3 million sale unaccompanied by the additional $2 million in loans that the market expected would prove insufficient to relieve the money market. Elisha Riggs was disappointed that Corcoran failed to bring back $500,000 to $1 million in coins. Such an influx of specie would push up bond prices by 1 per cent and exchange by 0.5 to 1 per cent. Riggs predicted a fall in the price of bills of exchange to 108 in New York as Corcoran attempted to negotiate those he brought back from London.[68] Even the *Washington Union* conceded the transaction was 'not calculated to relax the present pressure for money, but to prevent such further stringency'.[69] Wall Street reacted more favourably. The *New York Herald* reported that the news had a good effect and that the following day stocks were buoyant.[70]

In Corcoran's absence Elisha Riggs acted on his pessimism and prevailed on his son Elisha Jr to do likewise. Elisha energetically liquidated his holdings and by 29 September reported to Peabody that he had deposited nearly 75 per cent of his commitment and sold almost all of the bonds received. He professed confidence in the bonds but vowed that he was too old to speculate. Age did not prevent him from selling some of the new bonds short and when he attempted to make his sales good from the 3/3 account he encountered the ire of Peabody. Worse than the lack of confidence displayed by Elisha in Corcoran's mission was the action of his son, Corcoran's partner. At Elisha's instigation, Elisha Jr sold a large part of the firm's remaining bonds at 104.625 to 105. Corcoran placed the sales at $1.8 million and estimated the action cost him $150,000 in lost profits as bond prices rose.[71]

Despite continued tight credit in the United States, the London market rallied and the bonds advanced quickly from the purchase price of 93.75 to 97, the equivalent of a rise from 103 to 106.5–107 in New York prices. The Barings and Peabody worked together, buying up bonds in the open market and forcing up the price. The price rise attracted more bonds from the United States which, in turn, increased the New York price. In New York Corcoran supported the market with judicious purchases. Early on, Matthew Morgan, acting for Corcoran & Riggs, entered the market intending to force the price back up to 104.625 by purchasing $300,000 of the bonds. The task was accomplished by purchasing only $250,000. By the end of October the bonds were selling in New York at 105 to 105.5.[72]

Once the London price was advanced to 97, the Barings and Peabody began to slowly liquidate their holdings. Both found the English market dull and concentrated their efforts on the continent. The Barings worked France and Holland

and Peabody, Germany. The other four firms involved in the $3 million purchase held the bonds for investment. A substantial price rise did later bring many of these bonds on the market. By mid-November Bancroft was advising that United States government bonds were in great shape with demand increasing. Peabody attributed the success to his and the Barings' ability to excite the market.[73]

With the price now satisfactory the Barings on 6 October requested that the first $250,000 under the new agreement be sent to London. A week later they requested a further $250,000. Most of the bonds were $1,000 denomination coupon certificates for resale to small investors. By 18 December Corcoran & Riggs had forwarded all but $40,000 of the allotment. For the first few weeks of the new selling campaign the Barings acted cautiously, refused other bonds on consignment and steadily reduced their inventory. As profits piled up, however, their attitude changed, they exercised their option, and expressed a willingness to engage in other deals with Corcoran & Riggs. The Barings' selling effort was completed in January 1849. At that time the bonds were selling in London at 103.5 to 104.5 (113 to 114 in New York).[74]

Peabody also began selling in earnest as the market rose. The $500,000 of the joint account and the $167,000 option proved insufficient to meet the demand, so he purchased the $83,000 Jones Lloyd option and then demanded the final $250,000 of the original 3/3 contract. By November his most vexing problem was not sales but getting the bonds from America. Originally he requested that Corcoran & Riggs send him $50,000 by each weekly steamer. By 17 November, $350,000 had been forwarded and Peabody was requesting $150,000 be sent on the 13 December steamer. The bonds for London were packed in the diplomatic bag and forwarded to Minister Bancroft – another service for friends.[75]

The key to Peabody's success lay in the network of brokers he built up in Germany and to a lesser extent in Amsterdam and Paris. Peabody set a minimum price and the amount of bonds the broker could sell. He paid a commission of 0.25 per cent. Typically, Peabody authorized the sale of bonds at a price that would net him a specific amount. Between 13 and 27 October, Hope & Company of Amsterdam sold $25,000 at a net price to Peabody of 96. On 31 October, Peabody increased the price to 97.5. Peabody assured Hope & Company of his ability to supply the firm regularly with bonds at the lowest market price.[76]

In Germany, Peabody used brokers in Hamburg (J. Berenben, Gassler & Company), Altoona (Hesse, Newman & Company), Bremen (Lurman & Company) and Frankfurt (L. Speyer, Ellison & Company). The market proved profitable as Germans hedged against revolution in their own country. Immigrants, preparing for their trip to America, added to the volume by converting their assets into movable property. Peabody gradually raised the price his agents charged. As the brokers completed the sale of one agreed-upon lot, Peabody authorized further sales. Peabody forwarded the bonds from London by registered mail and received payment in twenty-day bills of exchange. The brokers paid the postage and insurance.[77]

European sales remained brisk and by January 1849 Peabody had completed the sale of the bonds under the second agreement and was beginning to sell the final third of the first 3/3 account despite Elisha's and Corcoran's protest. Final liquidation was completed in the early spring of 1849. The sale of the last of the original issue of the bonds did not finish Peabody's activity. He continued to buy in New York and resell in Europe. In May 1849 he requested that Corcoran & Riggs purchase $200,000 in coupon bonds in New York at 113 if exchange could be sold at 107. He was willing to increase the price to 114 if bills of exchange brought 108. His total dealings in United States bonds approached $2 million by April 1849.[78]

Peabody reaped a profit in money and prestige from his dealings in United States bonds. Profits totalled £8,817 on the 3/3 account, £4,013 on the $500,000 joint account and the option and £1,703 on the Jones Lloyd option. The sale of $1.25 million in bonds in Europe yielded a total profit of £14,533 ($70,194 at an exchange rate of $4.83). Peabody's share was £5,797. More important than the money was the enhanced reputation of being associated in the transactions with the leading British banking houses.[79]

Unlike with the loan of 1847, Corcoran & Riggs did not engage in an extensive domestic selling campaign. After Corcoran's sales in Europe and Elisha Jr's unwise action in his absence, the firm only had $1 to $2 million left and Corcoran intended to get the best possible price. The firm concentrated on selling the bills of exchange given in payment for the London sales and acting as liaison between its clients and the Treasury Department. Sale of the exchange became a problem because the volume involved brought them into unwelcome competition with Brown Brothers, the dominant American dealer. The controversy was ended by giving the Browns the right to negotiate the bills for Corcoran & Riggs.[80]

Corcoran & Riggs, like Peabody, later engaged in large-scale open market operations involving the bonds and maintained an inventory of over $1 million. The inventory was carried by arranging loans with Barings ($600,000), the Baltimore & Ohio Railroad ($350,000) and others. Since the firm borrowed at a lesser rate than the 6 per cent the bonds paid the arrangement proved profitable. The holdings of the firm and partners were sold in late 1849 and early 1850 at prices from 116 to 120. During the period 1 July 1848 through 30 June 1850, Corcoran earned personal profits of $400,000 from the firm and in private dealings in government bonds.[81]

In late 1848 the Treasury Department took several additional steps to alleviate the money market and facilitate the sale of the bonds. Walker publicly announced on 9 November that the Treasury's means were ample and that any bidder who wished could postpone the November and December deposits to

1 January 1849. Walker stressed the interest savings to the government. *Niles' National Register* reported that the act accommodated those bidders short of funds and in the Wall Street phrase allowed the government to carry the bonds for them. Naturally the bidders assured the secretary they would accede to his wishes and not call for more bonds than necessary to meet existing sales commitments.[82]

In November the Treasury again went into the market. Cornelius Lawrence, the collector of customs in New York, arranged for the brokerage firm of Cammann & Whitehouse to purchase $500,000 in government bonds secretly. The transaction was only partially to relieve the money market. As early as 21 October Polk expressed a great desire to begin repayment of the debt before the end of his term.[83] He told the cabinet that 'the payment of the public debt should be regarded as a vital principle of the future policy of the government'.[84] After learning that $500,000 to $1 million was available, Polk quickly authorized the repurchase of $500,000.[85]

The government's action did not remain secret long. George Newbold demanded Corcoran advise him of when and how much the secretary would purchase. Two days later, on 29 November, Newbold had ferreted out the $500,000 deposit with Cammann & Whitehouse and wanted to know if these were the funds meant for the repurchase. Newbold sought to sell the secretary $350,000 of his holdings of the 5 per cent bonds issued in 1843. He was to be disappointed. By 5 December the purchases were complete. The Treasury obtained $80,700 of the 1842 6 per cent bonds, $136,000 of the 5 per cent bonds of 1843 and $260,000 of the 6 per cent bonds of 1848. The difference of $23,300 represents the premium paid by the government. The 1848 bonds, for example, were selling at 106.25 (ex-dividend). The government was in the uncomfortable position of buying bonds at 106 while still selling the last of the 1848 bonds at 103.[86]

With his term ending Walker turned conservative. Instead of relieving the markets, he engineered a credit crunch by increasing specie reserves at the Independent Treasury. Reserves reached $5.5 million on 27 February. The actions forced the new secretary of the Treasury, William Meredith, to continue Walker's policies. Meredith continued the services of Corcoran & Riggs, again suspended instalment payments on the loan of 1848 and purchased $382,000 of the 1847 bonds in the market. Walker was able to go into retirement with little criticism of his performance.[87]

The Treasury Department accepted the last deposit and issued the last bond in September 1849, almost a year after the original deadline of 30 November 1848. Altogether it issued $7,740,000 in coupon and $8,260,000 in registered bonds (Table 8.1), 80 per cent of which was in the $1,000 denomination. The repurchase in December 1848 left $15,740,000 outstanding. The sale of many of the bonds abroad or their use as remittance by the original purchasers eased the money market as 1849 progressed. The price rise in particular helped restore confidence in American securities and raised the nation's prestige. A huge mass of government notes and bonds were in the market being traded by brokers on both sides of the Atlantic. Appetites in the United States and Europe were whetted and ready for the large numbers of railroad and state improvement bonds to be issued in the early and mid-1850s. Participants in the sale of the $49 million in federal bonds moved aggressively into the new field.[88]

Table 8.1: Loan of 1848, Monthly Deposits[89]

Date	Coupon ($)	Registered Certificates ($)
1848		
July	898,000	1,928,500
August	552,000	2,117,950
September	279,000	753,200
October	402,000	1,112,400
November	1,354,000	961,800
December	480,000	652,300
1849		
January	976,000	493,300
February	392,000	65,050
March	136,000	15,000
April	14,000	7,050
May	331,000	50,000
June	1,575,000	77,400
July	213,000	13,700
August	135,000	12,350
September	3,000	0
	7,740,000	8,260,000

9 MEXICAN INDEMNITY AND BOUNTY LAND

In addition to the three major loan acts Congress authorized the issuance of two smaller types of debt obligations to compensate American citizens and soldiers. The first Act, passed in August 1846, provided for the payment of two instalments due to Americans holding valid claims against Mexico under the Convention of 1843. Instead of cash the claimants received five-year bonds paying 5 per cent interest. At the close of the war provisions were made for paying the remaining fifteen instalments. In 1847 as an inducement for enlistment and reward for serving, non-commissioned officers and privates were granted land. Recipients had the option of taking land warrants or bounty land script (bonds) paying interest at 6 per cent.[1]

The civil strife that periodically racked Mexico led to losses by foreign merchants doing business in that country. Commercial activities held the prospect of high profits but were also very risky. The Mexican government believed that foreign merchants should assume the same risk as its own businessmen and treat the losses as part of the cost of doing business. The foreigners felt differently and appealed to their own governments. They benefited from an emerging international trend by powerful commercial nations of demanding protection for their citizens. The British, French and American governments brought pressure on Mexico for compensation. The French resorted to force in 1837, sent out a squadron of ships and blockaded the major Gulf ports. Eventually, after capturing Vera Cruz's citadel and making Santa Anna a national hero by shooting off his leg, the French, with British assistance, received their money.[2]

The United States government, relying on negotiation and threats, secured Mexico's agreement to submit the claims of American citizens to arbitration. The Convention of 1839 provided for a commission consisting of two members appointed by each government and a fifth appointed by the King of Prussia. The commission considered $11,850,589 in claims and reached agreement on $6,650,000 before its mandate expired. The balance of $5.2 million remained unresolved. Much of the $6,650,000 in claims considered by the commission was greatly inflated and only $2,026,139 was allowed. A second agreement, the Convention of January 1843, specified that Mexico was to pay accrued interest on the $2 million on 30 April 1843, and pay the principle plus accruing interest in twenty equal quarterly instalments commencing 30 July 1843. By means of forced loans the Santa Anna government secured the funds to pay the interest and the first three instalments. Payments were made in Mexico City to an American agent appointed for that purpose. Mexico was also responsible for paying an additional 2.5 per cent in lieu of expenses involved in collecting and transporting the funds to the United States.[3]

When Polk entered office on 3 March 1845, the status of the fourth and fifth instalments was in doubt. Based on the expectation that the funds would be collected in Mexico City, Congress on 3 March 1845 appropriated $275,000 to pay American claimants the overdue instalments of 30 April and 30 July 1844. However, before payment could be made the new administration was required to determine whether the funds were actually received in Mexico City. The American agent had given the Mexican government a receipt under mysterious circumstances but there were indications that no money changed hands.

John Slidell's mission to Mexico provided an opportunity to ascertain the facts concerning the payment of the fourth and fifth instalments. Slidell's real objective as minister plenipotentiary to Mexico was to negotiate the purchase of California, at least, and hopefully New Mexico also. In investigating the status of the instalments he found that the agent, Emilio Voss, had obtained the services of the British firm, Tayleur, Jameson & Company. The Britons were in the process of collecting other claims against the Mexican government. Tayleur, Jameson obtained vouchers payable against specific duties and taxes due to the Mexican Treasury. Based on these promises to pay Voss gave the Mexicans a receipt. Revolution in December 1844 made it impossible to collect on the vouchers. Further, Slidell reported, because of financial difficulties and the Mexican public's reaction to the annexation of Texas there was little prospects of collection in the future. The Mexican populace was enraged over Texas and the methods used by Santa Anna to secure the funds used to pay the first three instalments.[4]

To Polk, non-payment of the claims represented both an affront to the United States and an opportunity to pressure Mexico on territorial cessions. In his first annual message, 2 December 1845, Polk advised Congress that a serious misunderstanding existed between the United States and Mexico 'growing out of unredressed injuries inflicted by the Mexican authorities and people on the persons and property of citizens of the United States through a long series of years'.[5] In conducting the negotiations Slidell was instructed by Polk and Buchanan to assume a threatening attitude on the claims issue and inform the Mexican government that the Americans were running out of patience. Polk sought to obtain payment on the past due instalments and to resume negotiations on the $5.2 million in unresolved claims. He wanted an answer before Congress adjourned in August 1846. Slidell was authorized to waive the claims if Mexico agreed to a border that incorporated that part of New Mexico east of the upper Rio Grande into the United States. Forgiveness of the claims might also be included in any purchase of New Mexico and California.[6]

The war resolution effectively suspended efforts to collect the instalments and Congress decided to take action on the fourth and fifth. It authorized the issuance of $320,000 in five-year 5 per cent bonds as payment. The claimants were required to assign their rights to the two instalments to the United States government and accept the bonds. In keeping with the quarterly nature of the instalments, Congress specified quarterly interest payments. The Treasury actually issued $303,573.92 in bonds. One third of the total represented past due interest. No provision was made for the $1,519,605 due on the remaining fifteen instalments. The bonds were redeemed after the war out of ordinary revenue during the January–March and July–September quarters of 1851.[7]

By the terms of the Treaty of Guadalupe Hidalgo ending the war, the American government assumed responsibility for all claims by its citizens against Mexico. The treaty recognized two types. Under Article 13 the United States agreed to reimburse its citizens for the unpaid balance of $1,519,605 still due under the Convention of 1843. Article 14 exempted Mexico from responsibility on any further claims up to 2 February 1848. The American government assumed responsibility for any remaining claims by its citizenry but limited its liability to $3.25 million. Any claims beyond this amount would be lost. Article 15 provided for an American Board of Commissioners to set the second group of awards.[8]

Polk considered the territory ceded a sufficient reward for the cost of the war and claims assumed. Immediately upon completion of the ratification process, he recommended payment of the remaining fifteen instalments. Since Congress was assured that sufficient funds were in the Treasury they quickly responded with the Act of 29 July 1848. The Treasury Department also displayed considerable energy. Secretary Walker issued notice to the claimants on 16 August requesting that the certificates documenting their claims be submitted. Cash payments started in October and served to further alleviate the tight money market and to ease Corcoran & Riggs's efforts to market the loan of 1848. By 31 October, $542,000 had been paid out. The process was completed by the end of the fiscal year, 30 June 1849. The Treasury disbursed $2,090,253 in principle ($1,519,605) and interest in cash from general revenues and the proceeds of the loan of 1848.[9]

As in most such transactions, speculators reaped much of the reward. The *New York Tribune* reported that two or three years previously the claims had been selling for 15 to 20 per cent of their value. Including interest they were now worth 128 per cent. According to the *Tribune*, one speculator realized a $100,000 profit. Elisha Riggs and Corcoran & Riggs were actively involved, particularly in respect to the bonds issued in payment of the fourth and fifth instalments. Elisha obtained $25,000 in bonds for claims that he had purchased. Corcoran & Riggs provided services to the claim holders. Acting as agent the firm presented documentation to the Treasury and obtained the bonds. It also sold the claimants' bonds on commission. The speculators did not receive everything they sought. Congress refused to include loans made to the revolutionary Mexican government during its war of independence.[10]

On 3 March 1849, Congress established the Board of Commissioners to consider the unresolved (under the Convention of 1843) and all subsequent claims against Mexico. The Board submitted its report in February 1852. It considered 292 claims and approved 198. A total of $3,208,314.96 was awarded. The successful claimants were paid in full from general revenues. This brought the final liability on Mexican claims assumed by the American government to $5,031,494.[11]

Congress's effort to stimulate enlistment and reward the soldiers (and voters) by a distribution of the public lands was incorporated in the much debated Ten Regiment bill. Though most of the debate centred on the appointment of officers in the new regiments, the land bounty section came in for considerable attention. The question centred on the effect of the land distribution on the national Treasury and, if passed, how much those serving should receive. Proponents argued that a bounty of 160 acres for twelve-month men was justified in light of the sacrifices expected. Opponents pointed out that 12–16 million acres was a sizeable reduction of the public domain. Additionally, so much land coming on the market, they believed, would surely reduce the government's own revenue from land sales. The opponents preferred a one-time cash bonus.[12]

Two separate sets of concerns were aired in the Senate debate. Proponents sought to extend the benefits to the officers of the volunteer regiments and to restrict the sale or conveyance of the land warrants. Senator Thomas Hart Benton, in particular, viewed the grant as a means of providing homes to veterans. Senator Daniel Webster disagreed. He believed the ranks could better be filled by giving the enlisted men the option of selling the warrants if they had no desire to relocate to the western frontier.[13]

The House addressed the measure's cost, its effect on government revenues and who should receive the largesse. Representative Linn Boyd (Democrat, Kentucky) argued that the grant was due to all that served in recognition of their patriotism and service. Other representatives attempted to expand the benefits to veterans of the Indians Wars and to the heirs of soldiers killed in the War of 1812. The eastern representatives raised the question of cost. They estimated the cost at $10 million (low) and over 10 million acres. Representative Thomas Perry (Democrat, Maryland), pointed out that the land warrants would be sold and compete with government land sales. He foresaw a sharp drop in government revenues from this source resulting in the impairment of the government's credit and increased taxation. One further point bothered Perry. Congress was considering a massive land grant after it had only recently pledged the public domain as security for the loan of 1847.[14]

In the end Congress agreed to allow a land bounty to each non-commissioned officer, musician and private, regular or volunteer, who served. Those who served at least twelve months or the heirs of those who died in service received a warrant entitling them to 160 acres. Soldiers serving less than a year received 40 acres. To be eligible, the soldier or marine must have entered the war zone in Mexico or along the border. Since a major purpose of the bill was to fill the army's ranks, sailors were not included. The warrants could not be assigned to another individual before they were issued. Once issued by the War Department they were negotiable. Instead of land warrants the soldiers could elect to receive Treasury script in the amount of $100 or $25 (40 acres). The script paid 6 per cent interest, semi-annually. The Bounty Land Act of 28 September 1850 extended the privilege to army officers. This subsequent bill also made provision for the officers and men of all prior wars not already included. Naval personnel were again denied land on the premise that they received better pay and shared in prize money. Marines did receive land.[15]

The soldiers began to return home in mass during 1848 and in the main elected to take land warrants instead of script. The *American Review* predicted little of the script would be taken since it was selling at $98 while the warrants were being priced much higher. The Treasury only issued $233,075 of the script and redeemed the entire amount for cash in 1849.[16]

The land warrants became a means of speculation and fuelled another land mania in the late 1840s and early 1850s. Speculators organized companies to buy up the warrants and locate large blocks of land. Corcoran & Riggs entered the market in earnest in the autumn of 1848. The firm advertised its willingness to pay the highest price and in September 1848 was purchasing warrants through broker Charles Manley at $109. E. W. Clark & Company and its related firms also advertised and promised the highest prices. The firm and its St Louis affiliate, E. W. Clark & Brothers, acquired extensive acreage in Illinois. Jay Cooke acquired large amounts of land in Iowa.[17]

The Pension Office in the War Department issued the first warrant in March 1847. From that point until 30 November 1848, a total of 39,825 warrants for quarter sections (6,372,000 acres) were issued. A further 3,349 warrants representing 133,900 acres went to those eligible for 40 acres. At that time the Land Commissioner estimated that half of the eligible 90,000 soldiers had applied. The Commissioner also anticipated a falling off of land revenues to $2.8 million for the fiscal year ending 30 June 1849 and further to $2.4 million in fiscal year 1850. During fiscal year 1848 the government received $3.3 million. The Commissioner proved too optimistic. Receipts actually fell to $1,688,959 for fiscal year 1849 and to $1,859,894 for fiscal year 1850.[18]

By 30 September 1859 the distribution was almost complete. At that time 88,012 land warrants had been issued embracing 13,174,000 acres, of which 90 per cent had been located and land patents issued. A few bounty land claims based on the Mexican War warrants continued to be filed well into the twentieth century. The Commissioner of the General Land Office's report in 1907 indicated a total of 88,274 warrants issued on 13,213,640 acres. Of this amount 12,956,520 acres had been located. At a price of $1.25 an acre the 13.2 million acres represented $16.5 million in lost revenue. However, the amount paled into insignificance when compared to the land obtained by the Treaty of Guadalupe Hidalgo.[19]

The actual debt obligations issued for $303,574 and $233,075 are insignificant when compared to the $49 million borrowed under the Loan Acts of 1846, 1847 and 1848. What is important is the commitment to pay the Mexican claimants $5 million and the distribution of $16.5 million in government land. Both raised the cost of the war significantly.

CONCLUSION

The exchange of the ratified treaty in May 1848 and withdrawal of the American army of occupation ended the conflict and allowed reconstruction to begin. The Americans counted the war's cost and addressed the task of absorbing the new lands and repaying the debt. The Mexicans strove to rebuild their institutions and find civil and financial stability. Neither nation's efforts proved entirely satisfactory. In the United States the struggle over the expansion of slavery into the new territories inflamed sectional feelings. A promising start towards redeeming the debt was halted by the Panic of 1857 and then the Civil War. The treaty payments allowed the new government in Mexico City to keep the peace for a few years. By 1853 this resource was exhausted or squandered and Mexico entered into another round of revolutions.[1]

The American territorial gains came at a high price in human misery. Of the 104,184 American soldiers and marines enrolled, 13 per cent died. Emory Upton, the accepted authority, estimates battlefield deaths at 1,551, including 944 regulars and 607 volunteers. An additional 3,300 were wounded. Disease and accident were the greatest killers. Seven times more troops died of these causes than were killed in action. The final total of 13,780 fatalities included 12,229 non-combat deaths.[2]

The financial cost of the war to the United States is less precise. The Whigs came to power in March 1849 anxious to blame the increased cost of government on the Democrats' war. To some extent the Whigs were correct. The increased size of the nation required more government services and a larger military and civil bureaucracy. The nation assumed responsibility for additional interest, treaty payments, rewards to its fighting men and pensions. Most of the costs associated with the war were incurred after the fighting ceased.[3]

In December 1849 the secretary of the Treasury, William Meredith, estimated the actual cost of waging the war at $63,605,621. Meredith computed the army's expenditures for the period 1 April 1846 to 1 April 1849, and the navy's from 1 April 1846 to 1 October 1848, and then deducted what should have been their normal peacetime expenditures. The excess expenditures, $58,853,993 for the army and $4,751,627 for the navy, made up the war's military cost. Meredith recognized that subsequent appropriations would raise the total cost substantially but made no effort to arrive at a final figure.[4]

The following year, Thomas Corwin, Meredith's successor, made a more sweeping attempt to count the financial cost. Corwin sought to justify budget expenditures almost twice pre-war levels. He blamed the increase on fulfilling treaty obligations and administering the new territories. Corwin assumed fiscal year 1845 was normal and then computed total expenditures for the next seven years. The total expenditures for the period 1 July 1845 through 30 June 1852 over the base period (fiscal year 1845) he placed at $124 million. Additionally, expenses such as interest, bounty land, Mexican claims and Texas boundary bonds remained to be paid. The final bill, Corwin believed, exceeded $217 million.[5]

Historian Justin Smith accepts Meredith's computation of $63,605,621 as the cost of military operations. He then adds treaty payments, Mexican claims, bounty land and several smaller liabilities. Military pensions receive little weight. From the total he deducts the value of supplies, equipment and ships purchased during the war but still in inventory at its conclusion. His final figure of $100 million is at best a rough estimate.[6]

A more recent estimate of the cost is provided by Professor James L. Clayton of the University of Utah. In 1969, testifying before the Joint Congressional Economic Committee on military budgets, Professor Clayton calculated the cost of all of America's wars. The total cost of the Mexican War he computed to be $147 million. He estimated the cost of fighting the war at $73 million then added $64 million in veteran's benefits and $10 million in interest. Clayton assumed the cost of waging the war ran from 1 July 1845 to 30 June 1849. His computations are accurate for the cost of the actual fighting and for veteran's pensions, but he grossly underestimates the interest on the war debt.[7]

The actual cost in money greatly exceeded Smith's estimate and approached that of Corwin. In addition to land bounties Congress in 1848 authorized pensions for the widows and orphans of those killed. In 1861 benefits were extended to those veterans disabled in service. The largest increment to the pension rolls for Mexican War veterans came with the Act of 29 January 1887. This Act provided a pension of $8 a month to surviving officers and men or their widows and dependent children. The applicant or his widow must have attained the age of sixty-two or be disabled. Periodic raises were authorized to $12, $20, $30, $50, and finally, $65 a month. The last veteran died during fiscal year 1930 and the last widow during fiscal year 1964. The final total for Mexican War pensions was $64,284,000.[8] Assuming that the treaty payments to Mexico were part of the cost, the total exceeded $200 million (see Table C.1).

Table C.1: Schedule of Expenditures Chargeable to the American–Mexican War

Expenditure	Costs ($)	Total Costs ($)
Cost of fighting		73,000,000
Mexican Claims		
4th & 5th instalments	303,574	
Remaining unpaid instalments	1,519,605	
Final claims settlement	3,208,315	
		5,031,494
Treaty Payments plus interest		15,400,746
Interest		
Treasury notes of 1846	96,525	
Bonds of 1846	2,414,257	
Mexican indemnity bonds	75,413	
Treasury notes of 1847	1,576,883	
Bonds of 1847	17,435,857	
Bounty land script	13,783	
Bonds of 1848	13,125,719	
		34,738,437
Net Premiums paid on repurchases	4,720,812	
Less: Premium on sales	563,084	
		4,157,728
Land		
Land Warrants:	16,500,000	
Bounty land script	233,075	
		16,733,075
Pensions		64,284,000
Total cost		213,345,480

Interest, cost of repurchasing the bonds in the open market, land and veterans benefits, cost incurred well after the end of the war, made up 57 per cent of the total.[9]

The sale of the last bond in September 1849 allowed the nation to take stock of its new obligations. The national debt stood at $64,704,693. Mexican War loans represented $48,661,073 of this total (Table C.2). Obligations associated with the war such as treaty payments to Mexico absorbed much of the government's resources in the early 1850s and restricted loan repayment. Some progress, however, was made during the last part of the Polk administration and that of Zachary Taylor and Millard Fillmore. The loan of 1847 was reduced by $3.6 million and those of 1846 and 1848 by $68,200 and $453,300 respectively. The bounty land script and Mexican indemnity bonds were paid in full.[10]

Table C.2: Public Debt Attributable to the Mexican War, 30 November 1849[11]

Loan	Amount ($)	Total ($)
Loan of 1846		4,999,149
Loan of 1847 – Treasury Notes and Bonds	28,000,850	
Less: Repurchased – January 1849	382,500	
		27,618,350
Loan of 1848	16,000,000	
Less: Repurchased – December 1848	260,000	
		15,740,000
Mexican Indemnity Stock		303,574
Bounty Land Script	233,075	
Less: Repurchased Fiscal Year 1849	233,075	
		0
Total		48,661,073

The new administration of Franklin Pierce that took office in March 1853 was favoured with a growing budget surplus and a large cash balance. Pierce endeavoured to make real progress in reducing the debt. The secretary of the Treasury, James Guthrie, announced on 3 July 1853 his intention of purchasing $5 million of the bonds of 1847 and 1848 at a price of 121 plus interest due. Guthrie followed this with a second announcement offering to buy $2 million of the bonds of 1842 and 1846. He offered a lower price for the 1846 bonds, 108.5, because of their shorter maturity date. From 1 July 1853 through 30 June 1858 the Democrats succeeded in purchasing or redeeming $26.8 million of the outstanding Mexican War bonds.[12]

Efforts to liquidate the debt ceased with the Panic of 1857 and the coming of the Civil War. On 1 July 1858, $7,600 of the loan of 1846, $9,412,700 of the loan of 1847, and $8,908.341 of the loan of 1848 remained. The small balance due on the 1846 loan was paid as the holders submitted the certificates, but the other two loans remained unpaid until after the Civil War. In the years immediately following that war the Treasury was able to go into the market and purchase $5.2 million of the outstanding bonds at a discount.

Those bonds still outstanding reached their twenty-year maturity date in fiscal years 1868 and 1869. In fiscal year 1868 the Treasury redeemed $6.4 million of the 1847 bonds at par and a further $727,000 the next year. Small amounts continued to be submitted until 1874. Redemption of the matured 1848 bonds started in fiscal year 1869. In that year the Treasury purchased $7.7 million and in the next five years the remaining $91,150. An optimist can argue that the final part of the debt was paid from government surpluses. A pessimist has room to claim that they became involved in the massive Civil War funding operations and are still with us.[13]

The politicians engaged in Mexican War financing continued to influence events during the years preceding the Civil War. Polk had the least influence. He became ill on his trip home from Washington to Nashville and died in the latter city on 15 June 1849. He was spared the struggle over his expansionist legacy. James Buchanan, with the aid of Corcoran, achieved his lifelong ambition of becoming president in 1857. He reaped the whirlwind of the angry passions over the expansion of slavery and left office broken in spirit and reputation. William Marcy returned to public life as Franklin Pierce's secretary of state in 1853. Pierce's cabinet included Jefferson Davis as secretary of war. In his position as secretary of state, Marcy was able to exploit Mexico's financial instability one last time and acquire southern New Mexico and Arizona in the Gadsden Purchase.[14]

Robert Walker resumed the practice of law and attempted to attain wealth by exploiting contacts made during his years of public service. A return to the Senate was not practical since the slaveholders of Mississippi were not impressed with his nationalistic performance at the Treasury. Walker sought riches through railroad, land and mining speculations with varying degrees of success. He was often associated with Corcoran in these endeavours. Though some profits were derived from the New Almadan mine, he was still in financial difficulties at the end of the Civil War. In 1857 Walker responded favourably to Buchanan's request to become governor of the embattled Territory of Kansas. His opposition to the pro-slavery LeCompton Constitution and belief that most Kansans wanted to enter the Union as a free state led to a break with the pro-southern Buchanan administration. By 1863 Walker had come full circle and was now a war Democrat and supporter of Lincoln. In that year he went to Britain as a Union agent in an effort to prevent the Confederacy from borrowing money and obtaining supplies in Europe. In Britain he attacked slavery as vigorously as he had defended it in Mississippi thirty years previously.[15]

Though not as profound, the influence of the financiers was longer lasting than that of the politicians. E. W. Clark & Company failed in the late 1850s and though revived remained a regional private banking firm. Jay Cooke, however, organized his own firm and became the dominant personality in Civil War financing. The firm, Jay Cooke & Company, failed in 1873 after an unsuccessful attempt to finance the Northern Pacific Railroad. It did not remain a corpse long. Cooke's son-in-law, Charles Barney resurrected it and, as Smith Barney & Company, it became one of the most influential investment bankers of the twentieth century. Eventually the firm was acquired by the Travelers Group, a large insurance firm. As part of this firm it was merged in 1998 into Citigroup, the largest financial service firm in the world with assets exceeding $1 trillion.[16]

The House of Barings' status as the greatest financial house in London continued until 1890 when speculative investments and overexpansion in Argentina brought the firm close to collapse. Though rescued by the Rothschilds and Bank of England, the house never regained its dominant position. Its reputation did revive sufficiently by 1952 for it to be named one of the managers' of the royal family's fortune. Disaster revisited the firm in 1995. Reckless speculation by a futures trader in the Singapore office led to losses exceeding $1 billion and brought the firm down. ING, a Dutch firm, picked up the pieces.[17]

George Newbold's institution, the Bank of America, turned conservative after his retirement and lost its position as one of New York's premier banks. Harold Cleveland describes its performance as solid yet stuffy in the years between 1860 and 1920. In the 1920s it sustained considerable losses in Latin America. Weakened, it was acquired by the Transamerica Company, a holding company dominated by California's leading banker, A. P. Giannini. In 1931 Giannini arranged to merge the institution into the National City Bank, the predecessor of Citigroup. Giannini liked the named and eventually consolidated his California banking interests into a new firm, Bank of America, NA.[18]

William Corcoran continued as senior partner in Corcoran & Riggs until 1854. The firm expanded into state, municipal and railroad financing. With an income approaching $100,000 a year Corcoran retired to manage his investments and engage in philanthropic activities. An outspoken southern sympathizer he was forced into European exile during the Civil War. His reputation among the permanent residents of Washington did not suffer and upon his return he resumed his position as a leading citizen. His primary interest and beneficiary in his later years was the Corcoran Gallery of Art which opened in 1871. To some extent Corcoran can be credited with starting the trend by wealthy individuals of endowing art and cultural institutions.[19]

After Corcoran's retirement George Washington Riggs, Corcoran's first partner, returned and reorganized Corcoran & Riggs as Riggs & Company. The private banking firm continued to be banker to the presidents and the provider of discreet services to politicians. One of the services it provided the government was to loan the $7.2 million needed to purchase the Territory of Alaska from Russia. By the beginning of the twentieth century the firm had been incorporated as a national bank and was the largest bank in Washington. In 2000 its assets totalled $5.5 billion. In 2005 the Riggs National Corporation was acquired by PNC Financial, a Pennsylvania banking concern headquartered in Pittsburgh.[20]

Of all the major participants, George Peabody influenced the history of finance the most. This influence was chiefly indirect and involved establishing the Morgan family in investment banking. In 1854 Peabody invited a middle-aged Boston dry goods merchant, Junius Spencer Morgan, to London as a junior partner. During college vacations Junius's teenage son, John Pierpont (J. P.), apprenticed at the firm. Upon Peabody's retirement in 1864, Junius reorganized the private banking firm as J. S. Morgan & Company in London. Junius also assisted, with capital and influence, J. P.'s successful effort to go into business in New York in 1862. The London house prospered and became a major factor in government finance. Upon Junius's death in 1890, J. P. made the firm part of the worldwide activities of J. P. Morgan & Company. As Morgan Grenfell, the firm continued as a major player in European finance until 1989 when it was acquired by the Deutsche Bank. It continued in existence as a wholly owned subsidiary.[21]

The house of Morgan exceeded all its predecessors and attained the dominant position in American finance. J. P. began his American apprenticeship with Duncan, Sherman & Company, a firm heavily involved in railroad financing and a participant in distributing Mexican War bonds. He also cultivated relationships with other firms engaged in financing the war such as Winslow, Lanier (formerly Winslow and Perkins). From J. P. Morgan & Company evolved two of America's most powerful companies, the investment banking firm of Morgan Stanley and the commercial bank J. P. Morgan & Company. Both participated in the consolidation of financial service firms that occurred in the United States during the 1990s and early 2000s. Morgan Stanley merged with Dean Witter to form Morgan Stanley Dean Witter, a giant investment banking and brokerage firm. J. P. Morgan merged with the Chase Manhattan Bank to form J. P. Morgan Chase and Company, the third largest banking group in the United States.[22]

Peabody also profoundly influenced American philanthropy. His gifts exceeded $8.6 million, a great sum in the mid-1800s. His major beneficiaries included the Peabody Institutes, particularly the one in Baltimore, which supported cultural and educational efforts. The Peabody Fund for Southern Education did much to revive learning in the South after the Civil War. In an effort at social engineering Peabody donated $2.5 million to the Peabody Donation Fund in London to provide homes for the poor. The activity still continues. Like Corcoran, Peabody's greatest impact on philanthropy was the example he set.[23]

The successful conclusion of the war raised American prestige in foreign capitals. Europeans were surprised that a democracy such as the United States was able to raise the men and money to prosecute a foreign war. Both the nation's economic strength and its will proved up to the task. Dissent certainly existed as to the war's cause, conduct and aims. However, at no time was there any serious effort to deprive the military of the means to wage war. Polk's parsimony had a greater effect on limiting resources than Whig opposition. This trend by the American people of supporting their military once committed, regardless of the righteousness of the cause, would become more pronounced in the twentieth century and beyond.

Great economic and financial changes were sweeping the United States as the war began. The story of the war's financing provides one window into which the historian can view these changes and the economic activities of the robust young nation. Ongoing trends were accelerated by the conflict's demands. War orders gave a further impetus to manufacturing and agriculture. The move towards financial specialization became more pronounced. The state chartered banks concentrated on serving their commercial and manufacturing clients and began to forego the marketing of securities. Federal bonds were now viewed by the banks as a long-term investment and collateral for bank notes, not as a commodity to be sold. Private bankers moved into the void of marketing securities and raising capital from the public. As the underwriting of securities grew in importance, speciality firms rose to dominate this important branch of finance. National growth provided the opportunity and the investment bankers seized it. Many of the most successful of these financiers rose to prominence during the Mexican War. Directly or indirectly, war financing provided an opportunity for men such as Jay Cooke and the Morgans. The nation emerged from the war with the means and talent to face an uncertain but promising future.

The Mexican War was the most successfully financed of all of the United States' wars down to the dawn of the twentieth century. It behoves the historian to consider why. Foremost is the increase in the economic strength and wealth of the United States in the thirty-two years since the War of 1812. The transportation revolution, particularly the steamship, had given the military the ability to move men and supplies and extend its reach. The rising industrial sector was quite capable of providing the material. A wealthier country meant that money was available if the means could be found to coax it into the national treasury. The administration was able to do so through three major loans. To accomplish this task Jacksonian economic purity often gave way to financial reality. The Treasury was not omnipotent and consideration had to be given to powerful and influential interest. The new financial system proved adaptable.

Secretary Walker learned this lesson early. The failure of the treasury notes in the autumn of 1846 clearly revealed that the Treasury must seek the financial community's cooperation and assistance. Success was more important to Walker than Democratic orthodoxy. As the war progressed he became more and more inclined to work with the bankers and accept their advice. William Corcoran served as the conduit. The price for this cooperation was profit. The key was to keep the financial gains within reasonable bounds. After a shaky start Secretary Walker and the Treasury managed the loans competently and, under the watchful eye of Polk, honestly.

Each of the three loans had its peculiarities and faced a unique challenge in the marketplace. The $5 million bond issue of 1846 was the first such effort by the federal government since 1843. Despite initial fumbling the 6 per cent ten-year bonds proved suitable. Even with this issue Walker realized the need for the Treasury to assist the contractors. He agreed to accept certified cheques in lieu of specie and slowed his withdrawal of government deposits at critical times in order to maintain liquidity. Marketing the issue provided valuable experience to the Treasury and loan contractors.

The loan of 1847 was the most crucial to the successful prosecution of the war. It came at the height of the fighting and ensured the resources for the military conquest of Mexico. The loan's size, $23 million, dwarfed previous efforts. Importantly, the loan was sold above par and for specie. It was absorbed almost entirely within the United States. The conversion feature again reflected Walker's willingness to accept advice and adapt. The ability to convert the treasury notes into 6 per cent twenty-year bonds increased marketability and spared the Treasury the need to float a new note issue every year to pay off the old notes.

Sale of much of the loan of 1848 abroad helped restore European confidence in American securities and created a thirst for more stocks and bonds. A 20 per cent rise in the price of the bonds of 1848 greatly encouraged foreign investors. American railroads, state governments and investment bankers were happy to supply this demand. Foreign capital provided a significant portion of the money that fuelled the expansion of the 1850s.

The Tariff of 1846, the Independent Treasury and the Warehouse Act were also legacies of the era. To the surprise of its opponents the financial system functioned creditably until the Civil War. The tariff produced sufficient revenue for ordinary governmental expenses, treaty payments, and the repurchase of 63 per cent of the war debt. Much of the tariff's success was due to good fortune. Neither party anticipated the import boom of the 1850s generated by widespread prosperity or the California gold rush.

The Independent Treasury enjoyed a longer life than the tariff. Except for the Federal Reserve System, it is the longest lived of the government's banking systems. The new system did not break under the stress of financing the Mexican War and this, along with the prosperity enjoyed by the country, ensured its survival. Much of its longevity can be attributed to inertia and the lack of a viable alternative. In receiving, safeguarding, disbursing and transferring government funds it was a clumsy and inefficient system. However, this inefficiency was a price the Jacksonians were willing to pay.

In spite of drawbacks, enough flexibility was found in the Independent Treasury to aid the banks and financial markets. Often the aid was delivered in a manner not anticipated by Polk and Jacksonian purists. The most notable example was the intervention in the money market during the latter part of 1848 and the Treasury's willingness to adjust loan instalment payments during periods of crises. Intervention left Walker open to charges of favouritism but it also assisted the hard-pressed New York money market. Both the market and his friends were aided. Cooperation, not antagonism, became the policy between the Independent Treasury and financial community.

Having acknowledged the nation's success in financing the Mexican–American War, it must be stated that Walker possessed considerable advantages not available to his predecessors, Albert Gallatin and Alexander Dallas, in the War of 1812, or his successors, Salmon Chase and William Fessenden, during the Civil War. Most important was the quality of the opposition. Financial needs to defeat Mexico were modest when compared to the demands of fighting the British or subduing the South. In 1846 the American economy was up to the challenge. The nation's financial institutions, particularly investment banking, were sufficiently mature to sell the debt obligations to the investing public. The nation had emerged from a depression and conditions were favourable with rising wealth and a large trade surplus. In the War of 1812 the demands of the conflict against a great power overwhelmed an immature system. During the Civil War the money was raised but at a fearsome cost. In the other two wars rampant inflation was a by-product of the financial strain.

The United States emerged from the war much enlarged geographically and stronger financially and economically. Though fractured politically, it was able to take the expansive steps in transportation, manufacturing and agriculture that made it a world-class economic power. Despite interruptions occasioned by war and depression, the advance still continues. Polk's efforts in the long term undermined the agrarian society he advocated. Instead of holding back modernization, his efforts led to its acceleration. Economic expansion and money-making gained over the Jeffersonian ideal of the yeoman farmer and civic virtue. Territorial expansion hastened the sectional conflict and civil war that destroyed the political influence of the agricultural South. The political upheaval led to policies Polk opposed – a protective tariff, a national banking system, paper currency and a strong federal government.

NOTES

Introduction

1. J. D. Richardson (ed.), *A Compilation of the Messages and Papers of the Presidents, 1789–1902*, 10 vols (Washington, DC: Bureau of National Literature and Arts, 1904), vol. 4, p. 438.
2. *The Diary of James K. Polk during his Presidency, 1845–1849*, ed. M. M. Quaife, 4 vols (Chicago, IL: A. C. McClurg & Company, 1910), vol. 1, pp. 227–9, 248–9, 353–4, 384–5, 386–93, 342–8, 451–6, 461; C. G. Sellers, *James K. Polk, Continentalist, 1843–1846* (Princeton, NJ: Princeton University Press, 1966), pp. 405–11, 398–400; P. Bergeron, *The Presidency of James K. Polk* (Lawrence, KS: University Press of Kansas, 1987), pp. 128–35; J. M. McPherson, *Ordeal by Fire: The Civil War and Reconstruction*, 2nd edn (New York: McGraw-Hill, 1992), pp. 60–1.
3. Richardson (ed.), *Messages of the Presidents*, vol. 4, p. 443.
4. *The Diary of Polk*, vol. 1, pp. 390–4; Sellers, *Polk, Continentalist*, pp. 416–23.
5. Varying interpretations on the cause(s) of the war are provided by D. M. Pletcher, *The Diplomacy of Annexation: Texas, Oregon and the Mexican War* (Columbus, MO: University of Missouri Press, 1973); J. H. Smith, *The War with Mexico*, 2 vols (New York: McMillan, 1919); N. Graebner, *An Empire on the Pacific: A Study in American Continental Expansion* (New York: Ronald Press, 1955); A. K. Weinberg, *Manifest Destiny: A Study of Nationalist Expansion in American History* (Baltimore, MD: Johns Hopkins University Press, 1935); F. Merk, *Manifest Destiny and Mission in American History* (New York: Alfred A. Knopf, 1963); G. M. Brack, *Mexico Views Manifest Destiny, 1821–1846: An Essay on the Origins of the Mexican War* (Albuquerque, NM: University of New Mexico Press, 1975); R. Horsman, *Race and Manifest Destiny* (Cambridge, MA: Harvard University Press, 1981); T. R. Hietala, *Manifest Design: Anxious Aggrandizement in Late Jacksonian America* (Ithaca, NY: Cornell University Press, 1985).
6. Bergeron, *The Presidency of Polk*, pp. 4–6, 261; P. Studenski and H. E. Krooss, *Financial History of the United States*, 2nd edn (New York: McGraw-Hill, 1963), pp. 119–20; H. Bodenhorn, *A History of Banking in Antebellum America: Financial Markets and Economic Development in an Era of Nation-Building* (Cambridge: Cambridge University Press, 2000), pp. 2–4; McPherson, *Ordeal by Fire*, pp. 1, 63–5; F. Redlich, *The Molding of American Banking: Men and Ideas*, 2nd edn, 2 vols (New York: Johnson Reprint Corporation, 1968), vol. 2, pp. 69–73, 343–4.
7. In American history the Jacksonian era is the period 1829–49. The breakdown of the political parties or factions between the 1790s and the American Civil War in 1861 is as

follows: Party politics emerged in the early 1790s as a result of disagreements between the nationalist supporters of Alexander Hamilton (Federalists – administrations of George Washington, 1789–97; and John Adams, 1797–1801) and the more agrarian states' rights followers of Thomas Jefferson (Democratic-Republicans/Jeffersonians – administrations of Jefferson, 1801–9; James Madison, 1809–17; and James Monroe, 1817–25). The Federalist Party disappeared shortly after the War of 1812. The dominant Democratic-Republicans split between the supporters of John Quincy Adams (National Republican – administration of John Quincy Adam, 1825–9) and Andrew Jackson (Democrats/Jacksonians – administrations of Andrew Jackson, 1829–37; Martin Van Buren, 1837–41; and James K. Polk, 1845–9) during the 1820s. The anti-Jackson forces cohered into the Whig Party (administrations of William Harrison/John Tyler, 1841–5; and Zachary Taylor/Millard Fillmore, 1849–53) in the 1830s. This party disintegrated in the 1850s as a result of disagreements within its ranks over the expansion of slavery. The present-day Republican Party was formed in 1854 from old-line Whigs such as Abraham Lincoln, the anti-immigrant American party and disaffected northern Democrats. See J. F. Biddy and B. F. Schaffner, *Politics, Parties and Elections in America*, 6th edn (Boston, MA: Thomson & Wadsworth, 2008), pp. 21–7; D. McSweeny and J. Zvesper, *American Political Parties: The Formation, Decline and Reform of the American Party System* (London: Routledge, 1991), pp. 13–26.

8. S. W. Haynes, *James K. Polk and the Expansionist Impulse* (New York: Longman, 1997), pp. ix, 80–3, 92; Sellers, *Polk, Continentalist,* pp. v, 310, 343–6, 468; F. Tick, 'The Political and Economic Policies of Robert J. Walker' (PhD dissertation, University of California at Los Angeles, 1947), pp. 328–9; D. R, Stabile, *The Origins of American Public Finance* (Westport, CT: Greenwood Press, 1998), pp. 159–62.

9. J. M. McPherson, *Battle Cry of Freedom: The Civil War Era* (1988; New York: Oxford University Press, 2003), p. 23.

10. McPherson, *Battle Cry of Freedom,* pp. 23–6; H. L. Watson, *Liberty and Power: The Politics of Jacksonian America* (New York: Hill & Wang, 1990), pp. 43–53, 237–40.

11. H. Bodenhorn, *State Banking in Early America: A New Economic History* (New York: Oxford University Press, 2003), pp. 222–3; S. Bruchey, *The Roots of American Economic Growth, 1607–1861: An Essay in Social Causation* (New York: Harper & Row, 1965), pp. 200–7; R. E. Wright and D. J. Cowens, *Financial Founding Fathers: The Men Who Made America Rich* (Chicago, IL: University of Chicago Press, 2006), p. 184; R. V. Remini, *Andrew Jackson and the Bank War: A Study in Presidential Power* (New York: Norton, 1967), pp. 22–3; E. J. Perkins, *American Public Finance and Financial Services, 1700–1815* (Columbus, OH: Ohio State University Press, 1994), pp. 3, 9; E. C. Ettin, 'The Development of American Financial Intermediaries', in J. V. Fenstermaker (comp.), *Readings in Financial Markets and Institutions* (New York: Appleton-Century-Crofts, 1969), pp. 241–61, on p. 243.

12. E. J. Perkins, *The Economy of Colonial America* (New York: Columbia University Press, 1980), pp. 99–100; R. D. Hormats, *The Price of Liberty: Paying for America's Wars* (New York: Times Books, 2007), p. 24; R. Sylla, 'Shaping the United States Financial System, 1690–1913: The Dominance of Public Finance', in R. Sylla, R. Tilly and G. Tortello (eds), *The State, the Financial System and Economic Modernization* (Cambridge: Cambridge University Press, 1999), pp. 249–70, on pp. 249–51.

13. Sylla, 'Shaping the United States Financial System', p. 251.

14. R. W. Michener and R. E. Wright, 'State "Currencies" and the Transition to the U. S. Dollar: Clarifying some Confusion', *American Economic Review*, 95 (June 2005), pp.

682–703, on p. 683; R. Sylla, R. Tilly and G. Tortella, 'Introduction: Comparative Historical Perspectives', in Sylla et al. (eds), *The State, the Financial System and Economic Modernization*, pp. 1–19, p. 3; R. Levine and S. Zervos, 'Stock Markets, Banks and Economic Growth', *American Economic Review*, 88 (June 1998), pp. 537–58, on p. 554; Bodenhorn, *A History of Banking in Antebellum America*, pp. xvii–xviii; McPherson, *Battle Cry of Freedom*, p. 9; R. E. Wright, *Wealth of Nations Rediscovered: Integration and Expansion in American Financial Markets, 1780–1850* (Cambridge: Cambridge University Press, 2002), p. 193.

15. Robert E. Wright has been good enough to provide a list. See Wright, *Wealth of Nations Rediscovered*, p. 2, n. 4; Bodenhorn, *State Banking in Early America*, p. 4; Bodenhorn, *A History of Banking in Antebellum America*, pp. 15, 27, 80–3; Levine and Zervos, 'Stock Markets', p. 554.

16. Redlich, *The Molding of American Banking*, vol. 2, pp. 70, 343–4; M. G. Myers, *A Financial History of the United States* (New York: Columbia University Press, 1970), p. 118.

17. Redlich, *The Molding of American Banking*, vol. 2, p. 323.

18. Bruchey, *The Roots of American Growth*, p. 150; Bodenhorn, *State Banking in Early America*, pp. 6, 191; Ettin, 'The Development of American Financial Intermediaries', p. 243; Redlich, *The Molding of American Banking*, vol. 2, p. 70.

19. R. C. McGrane, *Foreign Bondholders and American State Debt* (New York: Macmillan Company, 1935), pp. 254–81; Myers, *A Financial History of the United States*, pp. 133–6; Redlich, *The Molding of American Banking*, vol. 2, p. 353–5; L. E. Davis and R. J. Cull, *International Capital Markets and American Economic Growth, 1820–1914* (Cambridge: Cambridge University Press, 1994), p. 125.

20. Bruchey, *The Roots of American Economic Growth*, pp. 150–3; Redlich, *The Molding of American Banking*, vol. 2, pp. 69–71, 343–9; S. Ratner, J. H. Soltow and R. Sylla, *The Evolution of the American Economy: Growth, Welfare and Decision Making* (New York: Basic Books, 1979), p. 220.

21. M. G. Myers, *The New York Money Market*, 4 vols (New York: Columbia University Press, 1931), vol. 1, pp. 184–5; D. Kinley, *The Independent Treasury of the United States and its Relationship to the Banks of the Country* (Washington, DC: Government Printing Office, 1910), pp. 8–9, 60–5; B. Hammond, *Sovereignty and an Empty Purse: Banks and Politics in the Civil War* (Princeton, NJ: Princeton University Press, 1970), pp. 20–3.

22. D. C. North, *The Economic Growth of the United States, 1790–1860* (1961; New York: W. W. Norton, 1966), pp. v–vii, 204; Bodenhorn, *A History of Banking in Antebellum America*, pp. 2–4; McPherson, *Ordeal by Fire*, pp. 5–6; Studenski and Krooss, *Financial History of the United States*, p. 123; B. Hammond, *Banks and Politics in America from the Revolution to the Civil War* (Princeton, NJ: Princeton University Press, 1957), p. 672.

23. R. P. Porter (comp.), 'Report on Valuation, Taxation and Public Indebtedness in the United States', vol. 7 of US Bureau of the Census, *Tenth Census of the United States, 1880*, 22 vols (1883–8; New York: Norman Ross Publishing, 1991), pp. 364–7; J. P. Shenton, *Robert John Walker: A Politician from Jackson to Lincoln* (New York: Columbia University Press, 1961), pp. 91–3; H. Cohen, *Business and Politics in America from the Age of Jackson to the Civil War: The Business Career of W. W. Corcoran* (Westwood, CT: Greenwood Press, 1971), pp. 40–1.

24. Porter (comp.), 'Report on Valuation', pp. 366, 351–3; Cohen, *Business and Politics*, p. 45–9; Shenton, *Walker*, pp. 95–8; W. F. DeKnight, *History of the Currency and of the Loans of the United States from the Earliest Period to June 30, 1896* (Washington, DC: Government Printing Office, 1897), pp. 64–8.

25. Porter (comp.), 'Report on Valuation', p. 367; M. E. Hidy, *George Peabody, Merchant and Financier, 1829–1854* (New York: Arno Press, 1978), 298–9.
26. Smith, *The War with Mexico*, vol. 2, pp. 253–5; M. Wasserman, *Everyday Life and Politics in Nineteenth Century Mexico: Men, Women and War* (Albuquerque, NM: University of New Mexico Press, 2000), pp. 74–9; J. F. Ramirez, *Mexico during the War with the United States*, trans. E. Scherr (Columbia, MO: University of Missouri Press, 1950), pp. 17–22, 29; B. A. Tenenbaum, *The Politics of Penury: Debt and Taxes in Mexico, 1821–1856* (Albuquerque, NM: University of New Mexico Press, 1986), pp. xi–xii, 56, 76, 87; T. M. Davies, 'Assessments during the Mexican War, an Exercise in Futility', *New Mexico Historical Review*, 41 (July 1966), pp. 197–216, on pp. 211–12.
27. Smith, *The War with Mexico*, vol. 2, pp. 253–67.
28. Shenton, *Walker*, pp. 91–8, 114–16; Tick, 'The Political and Economic Policies of Walker', pp. 189–224; Cohen, *Business and Politics*, pp. 40–62; H. Cohen, 'Business and Politics from the Age of Jackson to the Civil War: A Study from the Life of W. W. Corcoran' (PhD dissertation, Cornell University, 1965), pp. 80–139.

1 Financial and Economic Background

1. Michener and Wright, 'State "Currencies"', p. 683; Perkins, *The Economy of Colonial America*, pp. 107–8; Myers, *A Financial History of the United States*, p. 8.
2. T. Hutchinson, *The History of the Colony and Province of Massachusetts Bay*, ed. L. S. Mayo, 3 vols (1936; New York: Kraus Reprint Co., 1970), vol. 1, pp. 337–41; Myers, *A Financial History of the United States*, pp. 8–12; Perkins, *The Economy of Colonial America*, pp. 105–7; Sylla, 'Shaping the United States Financial System', pp. 252–4.
3. Hutchinson, *The History of Massachusetts Bay*, vol. 2, pp. 248, 298–304; Myers, *A Financial History of the United States*, pp. 8–9; M. G. Kammen, *Colonial New York: A History* (New York: Charles Scribner's Sons, 1975), pp. 188–9; R. Sylla, 'Monetary Innovations in America', *Journal of Economic History*, 42 (March 1982), pp. 21–30, on pp. 22–5.
4. A. Hamilton, 'Report on the Public Credit', in US Congress, *New American State Papers, Public Finance*, 32 vols (Wilmington, DE: Scholarly Resources, 1972–3), vol. 1, pp. 29–57, on p. 40 (hereafter *NASP*).
5. Hutchinson, *The History of Massachusetts Bay*, vol. 2, pp. 333–7; Myers, *A Financial History of the United States*, pp. 8–9; Perkins, *The Economy of Colonial America*, pp. 112–13; R. E. Wright, *The First Wall Street: Chestnut Street, Philadelphia, and the Birth of American Finance* (Chicago, IL: University of Chicago Press, 2005), pp. 25–6.
6. Perkins, *The Economy of Colonial America*, pp. 112–14; Myers, *A Financial History of the United States*, pp. 11–12; J. A. Ernst, *Money and Politics in America, 1755–1775* (Chapel Hill, NC: University of North Carolina Press, 1973), pp. 49–53.
7. J. W. Markham, *A Financial History of the United States*, 3 vols (Armonk, NY: M. E. Sharpe, 2002), p. 58; Kammen, *Colonial New York*, p. 350; R. E. Wright, *Hamilton Unbound: Finance and the Creation of the American Republic* (New York: Praeger, 2002), pp. 14–18; Wright, *The First Wall Street*, pp. 29–32.
8. E. J. Ferguson, *The Power of the Purse: A History of American Public Finance, 1776–1790* (Chapel Hill, NC: University of North Carolina Press, 1961), p. 27.
9. Studenski and Krooss, *Financial History of the United States*, pp. 27–8; Myers, *A Financial History of the United States*, pp. 24–5; Continental Congress, *Journal of the Continental Congress, 1774–1789*, ed. W. C. Ford et al., 34 vols (Washington, DC: Government

Printing Office, 1904–37), vol. 2 (1775), pp. 103, 105–6, vol. 3 (1775), p. 390; Ferguson, *The Power of the Purse*, p. 30.

10. Myers, *A Financial History of the United States*, pp. 32–3; *Journal of the Continental Congress*, vol. 5 (1776), pp. 845–6; ibid., vol. 7 (1777), p. 36; ibid., vol. 10 (1778), pp. 59, 322; Ferguson, *The Power of the Purse*, pp. 35–40; W. G. Anderson, *The Price of Liberty: The Public Debt of the American Revolution* (Charlottesville, VA: University Press of Virginia, 1983), pp. 6–10.

11. Anderson, *The Price of Liberty*, pp. 11–12; *Journal of the Continental Congress*, vol. 16 (1780), pp. 262–6; Porter (comp.), 'Report on Valuation', pp. 299–316; Ferguson, *The Power of the Purse*, pp. 40–2, 235.

12. Myers, *A Financial History of the United States*, pp. 41–3; Studenski and Krooss, *Financial History of the United States*, pp. 20, 42; Wright and Cowens, *Financial Founding Fathers*, pp. 129–32.

13. Myers, *A Financial History of the United States*, pp. 50–2; Anderson, *The Price of Liberty*, pp. 16–17; H. E. Krooss, (ed.), *Documentary History of Banking and Currency in the United States*, 4 vols (New York: Chelsea House Publishers, 1969), vol. 1, pp. 159–61.

14. Benjamin Franklin to Thomas Ruston, 9 October 1780, quoted in Myers, *A Financial History of the United States*, p. 51.

15. Sylla, 'Monetary Innovations in America', p. 26; Wright, *The First Wall Street*, pp. 37–8.

16. Sylla, 'Shaping the United States Financial System', pp. 249–50.

17. Wright, *The First Wall Street*, p. 32.

18. R. Chernow, *Alexander Hamilton* (New York: Penquin Press, 2004), pp. 344–5.

19. Alexander Hamilton to Robert Morris, 30 April 1781, in *The Papers of Alexander Hamilton*, ed. H. C. Syrett et al., 27 vols (New York: Columbia University Press, 1961–87), vol. 2, p. 635.

20. Sylla, 'Shaping the United States Financial System', pp. 257–9; Chernow, *Hamilton*, p. 299; Wright and Cowens, *Financial Founding Fathers*, p. 22.

21. Hamilton, 'Report on the Public Credit', pp. 34, 44–5; Porter (comp.), 'Report on Valuation', pp. 324–8, 403–5.

22. R. Buel, Jr, *America on the Brink: How the Political Struggle over the War of 1812 almost Destroyed the Young Republic* (New York: Palgrave Macmillan, 2005), p. 2; Sylla, 'Shaping the United States Financial System', pp. 259–60; Bruchey, *The Roots of American Economic Growth*, pp. 110–11; Hamilton, 'Report on the Public Credit', pp. 31–2; Chernow, *Hamilton*, pp. 297–8.

23. Chernow, *Hamilton*, pp. 347–50; Sylla, 'Shaping the United States Financial System', p. 262.

24. Wright, *The First Wall Street*, p. 67.

25. Perkins, *American Public Finance*, pp. 327–9; Wright and Cowens, *Financial Founding Fathers*, p. 157.

26. Perkins, *American Public Finance*, pp. 328–9.

27. Ibid., pp. 329, 368–9.

28. D. R. Adams, Jr, 'The Beginning of Investment Banking in the United States', *Pennsylvania History*, 45 (April 1978), pp. 99–116, on p. 102; Porter (comp.), 'Report on Valuation', p. 343; Perkins, *American Public Finance*, pp. 329–31.

29. *US Statutes at Large*, 2 (1812), p. 767. All issues of treasury notes carried this provision until 1862 when the need for specie to pay interest on the public debt led Congress to exclude custom duties; *US Statutes at Large*, 12 (1862), p. 345; Porter (comp.), 'Report on Valuation', pp. 374–5.

30. Adams, 'The Beginning of Investment Banking', p. 102.
31. Ibid., pp. 103–12; D. R. Adams, Jr, *Finance and Enterprise in Early America: A Study of Stephen Girard's Bank, 1812–1831* (Philadelphia, PA: University of Pennsylvania Press, 1978), pp. 26–37; Perkins, *American Public Finance*, pp. 331–3; Wright and Cowens, *Financial Founding Fathers*, pp. 158–9; Redlich, *The Molding of American Banking*, vol. 2, p. 316.
32. Report of the Secretary of the Treasury, 1816, in *NASP*, vol. 2, pp. 251–2; *US Statutes at Large*, 3 (1816), pp. 266–77; Porter (comp.), 'Report on Valuation', pp. 354–5.
33. H. N. Scheiber, *Ohio Canal Era: A Case Study of Government and the Economy, 1820–1861* (Athens, OH: Ohio University Press, 1969), pp. 38–49, 140–58; Redlich, *The Molding of American Banking*, vol. 2, pp. 324–44.
34. Remini, *Jackson and the Bank War*, pp. 18–20; M. F. Holt, *The Rise and Fall of the American Whig Party: Jacksonian Politics and the Onset of the Civil War* (New York: Oxford University Press, 1999), pp. 16–17; Watson, *Liberty and Power*, pp. 138–40; Wright and Cowens, *Financial Founding Fathers*, p. 180; S. Wilentz, *The Rise of American Democracy: Jefferson to Lincoln* (New York: W. W. Norton, 2005), pp. 361–7; S. Huffmann, *Politics and Banking: Public Policy and the Creation of Financial Institutions* (Baltimore, MD: Johns Hopkins University Press, 2001), pp. 59–61.
35. Remini, *Jackson and the Bank War*, pp. 18–20; Watson, *Liberty and Power*, pp. 140–3; Holt, *The Rise and Fall of the American Whig Party*, pp. 15–16; Wilentz, *The Rise of American Democracy*, pp. 61–8.
36. Richardson (ed.), *Messages of the Presidents*, vol. 2, p. 590.
37. Remini, *Jackson and the Bank War*, pp. 10, 81–7, 177–8; Watson, *Liberty and Power*, pp. 144–8; Wilentz, *The Rise of American Democracy*, pp. 368–71.
38. Remini, *Jackson and the Bank War*, p. 176.
39. Ibid.
40. Ibid., pp. 109–29, 170–3; Watson, *Liberty and Power*, pp. 155–61; Holt, *The Rise and Fall of the American Whig Party*, pp. 23–7; Wright and Cowens, *Financial Founding Fathers*, p. 181.
41. Bodenhorn, *A History of Banking in Antebellum America*, pp. 2–3; North, *The Economic Growth of the United States*, pp. v–vii, 204; McPherson, *Ordeal by Fire*, pp. 1, 5–6.
42. P. Temin, *The Jacksonian Economy* (New York: W. W. Norton & Company, 1969), pp. 22–3, 174–7; S. P. Lee and P. Passell, *A New Economic View of American History* (New York: W. W. Norton, 1979), pp. 117–22, 126–7. Scholarly agreement on the cause of the Panic is by no means universal. Peter Rosseau attributes the Panic to a series of inter-bank transfers of funds in late 1836 and early 1837 and an increased demand in the West for specie after issuance of the Specie Circular. The specie transfers weakened the reserves of eastern banks leading to a credit contraction. He acknowledged that part of the pressure on the eastern banks came from the hard-pressed British money market. P. L. Rosseau, 'Jacksonian Monetary Policy, Specie Flow, and the Panic of 1837', *Journal of Economic History*, 62 (June 2002), pp. 457–88, p. 458; Richard Holcombe Kilbourne, Jr, argues that the Panic resulted from the pricking of a credit bubble originally created by the Bank of the United States in the early 1830s. Subsequent efforts by the bank to wind up its affairs, particularly in the Mississippi River Valley, led to a domestic credit contraction. State banks were unable to fill the void and credit dried up. R. H. Kilbourne, Jr, *Slave Agriculture and Financial Markets in Antebellum America: The Bank of the United States in Mississippi, 1831–1852* (London: Pickering & Chatto, 2006), pp. 149–53; Henry Clay to Alexander W. Stowe, 26 April 1837, in *The Papers of Henry Clay*, ed. J. F.

Hopkins, R. Seager II, and M. P. Hayes, 10 vols (Lexington, KY: The University of Kentucky Press, 1959–91), vol. 9, p. 43; Clay's Speech in the Senate, 25 September 1837, in *The Papers of Henry Clay*, vol. 9, pp. 75–9; I. H. Bartlett, *John C. Calhoun, A Biography* (New York: W. W. Norton & Company, 1953), pp. 237–8.

43. James K. Polk to Martin Van Buren, 29 May 1837, in *Correspondence of James K. Polk*, ed. H. Weaver and W. Cutler, 10 vols (vols 1–7: Nashville, TN: Vanderbilt University; vols 8–10: Knoxville, TN: University of Tennessee Press, 1969–2004), vol. 4, p. 131.

44. Polk to Van Buren, 29 May 1836, in ibid., vol. 4, pp. 130–3; Polk to William M. Warner, 19 June 1837, in ibid., pp. 152–5; T. H. Benton, *Thirty Year View*, 2 vols (1856; New York: D. Appleton & Company, 1893), vol. 2, pp. 9–11.

45. North, *The Economic Growth of the United States*, pp. 200–3; Ratner et al., *The Evolution of the American Economy*, p. 171.

46. J. C. Curtis, *The Fox at Bay: Martin Van Buren and the Presidency, 1837–1841* (Lexington, KY: University of Kentucky Press, 1970), pp. 64–151. Curtis provides the most comprehensive story of the first struggle for the Independent Treasury. Throughout the period the organization is referred to by several names: Independent Treasury, Sub-Treasury and Constitutional Treasury. Polk preferred the latter; US Congress, *Annals of the Congress of the United States, 1789–1824*, 42 vols (Washington, DC, 1834–56), 14th Congress, 1st Session, pp. 1919–20; Myers, *The New York Money Market*, vol. 1, pp. 174–81.

47. Myers, *The New York Money Market*, vol. 1, p. 181; Richardson (ed.), *Messages of the Presidents*, vol. 4, pp. 45–7, 63–8, 68–73, 346; R. Seager II, *And Tyler Too, A Biography of John and Julia Gardiner Tyler* (New York: McGraw-Hill, 1963), pp. 153–68; E. P. Crapol, *John Tyler, the Accidental President* (Chapel Hill, NC: University of North Carolina Press, 2006), pp. 12, 18–21, 106–7.

48. US Congress, Report of the Secretary of the Treasury on the State of the Finances, 11 December 1843, 28th Congress, 1st Session, Senate Document 3, Serial 432, p. 3; ibid., 16 December 1844, 28th Congress, 2nd Session, Senate Document 6, Serial 449, p. 28; ibid., 3 December 1845, 29th Congress, 1st Session, Senate Document 2, Serial 471, p. 1. A fiscal year is an accounting period of twelve months used by business firms or governmental bodies to report revenues and expenses. It ends on a date other than 31 December. In 1842 Congress established a fiscal year beginning 1 July and ending the following 30 June for the federal government. Richardson (ed.), *Messages of the Presidents*, vol. 4, p. 264.

49. Tick, 'The Political and Economic Policies of Walker', pp. 101, 106–8; Holt, *The Rise and Fall of the American Whig Party*, pp. 166–7; Benton, *Thirty Year View*, vol. 2, p. 307; Seller, *Polk, Continentalist*, pp. 42–5; Richardson, *Messages of the Presidents*, vol. 4, pp. 200–1, 346–7.

50. Report of the Secretary of the Treasury, 1845, pp. 1, 3–4; ibid., 9 December 1846, 29th Congress, 2nd Session, Senate Document 2, Serial 493, pp. 1, 6.

51. Ibid., 1845, pp. 24–5; ibid., 1846, pp. 21–2; *United States Magazine and Democratic Review* (New York), 19 (September 1846), p. 234.

52. Treasurer's Weekly Statement, 24 March 1845, in *Washington National Intelligencer* (Washington, DC), 2 April 1845.

53. Report of the Secretary of the Treasury, 1845, p. 25; ibid., 1846, p. 22; Treasurer's Weekly Statement, 29 December 1845, 27 April 1846, in *Washington National Intelligencer*, 6 January, 2 May 1846; Richardson (ed.), *Messages of the Presidents*, vol. 4, pp. 402–3.

54. *US Statutes at Large*, 5 (1836), pp. 52–6; Shenton, *Walker*, pp. 87–8; Cohen, *Business and Politics*, pp. 24–5, 28–9; 34–6; Sellers, *Polk, Continentalist*, pp. 344–5; Report of the Secretary of the Treasury, 1844, p. 25; Ratner et al., *The Evolution of the American Economy*, pp. 163–5. Specie paying meant the bank was prepared and able to redeem its bank notes with gold or silver coins. Banks suspended whenever they were unable to do so. Suspended banks continued to operate, accepting deposits and making loans using their own depreciated notes.

55. Source: Treasurer's Weekly Statements printed in the *Washington National Intelligencer*, 1845–9.

56. Redlich, *The Molding of American Banking*, vol. 2, pp. 69–70; H. M. Larson, 'E. W. Clark & Company, 1837–1857: The Beginning of an American Private Bank', *Journal of Commerce and Business History*, 4 (July 1932), pp. 429–60, on pp. 429, 435; Myers, *A Financial History of the United States*, pp. 72–3; Ratner et al., *The Evolution of the American Economy*, pp. 163–5.

57. Redlich, *The Molding of American Banking*, vol. 2, pp. 66–71, 363; Cohen, 'Business and Politics', pp. 8–13; R. Sylla, 'Forgotten Men of Money: Private Bankers in Early U. S. History', *Journal of Economic History*, 36 (March 1976), pp. 173–88, on pp. 180–1; Larson, 'E. W. Clark and Company', pp. 429–30, 435–6; Hidy, *Peabody*, p. 139; P. Ziegler, *The Sixth Greatest Power: A History of one of the Greatest of all Banking Families, the House of Barings, 1792–1929* (New York: Alfred A. Knopf, 1988), pp. 5–11; H. Bodenhorn, 'Capital Mobility and Financial Integration in Antebellum America', *Journal of Economic History*, 52 (September 1992), pp. 585–602, on p. 587; Bruchey, *The Roots of American Economic Growth*, pp. 150–2; Bodenhorn, *A History of Banking in Antebellum America*, pp. 148–9.

58. E. J. Perkins, *Financing Anglo-American Trade: The House of Brown, 1800–1880* (Cambridge, MA: Harvard University Press, 1975), pp. 5–12; Hidy, *Peabody*, pp. 200–9.

59. V. P. Carosso, *Investment Banking in America, a History* (Cambridge, MA: Harvard University Press, 1970), pp. ix, 1–13; J. P. Williamson (ed.), *The Investment Banking Handbook* (New York: John Wiley & Son, 1988), pp. 12–15; Ziegler, *The Sixth Greatest Power*, pp. 5–6, 8–11; R. L. Kuhn, *Investment Banking: The Art and Science of High-Stake Dealmaking* (New York: Harper & Roe, 1990), pp. 5–6.

60. Redlich, *The Molding of American Banking*, vol. 2, pp. 1–12; Ratner et al., *The Evolution of the American Economy*, pp. 162–5; Bodenhorn, *State Banking in Early America*, pp. 291–3.

61. Report of the Secretary of the Treasury, 3 December 1816, in *NASP*, vol. 3, pp. 251–2; Report of the Secretary of the Treasury, 9 December 1828, 20th Congress, 2nd Session Senate Document 7, Serial 181, pp. 3–5.

62. Report of the Secretary of the Treasury, 15 December 1829, 21st Congress, 1st Session, Senate Document 3, Serial 192, pp. 3–4; ibid., 8 December 1835, 24th Congress, 1st Session, Senate Document 2, Serial 279, p. 3; Porter (comp.), 'Report on Valuation', p. 361.

63. Porter (comp.), 'Report on Valuation', pp. 361–4; DeKnight, *History of the Currency*, pp. 62–8.

64. DeKnight, *History of the Currency*, pp. 64, 66, 68; Porter (comp.), 'Report on Valuation', pp. 362–4; Cohen, *Business and Politics*, pp. 19–23, 243–6, nn. 1, 11, 12; *New York Tribune*, 2 April 1842, 5, 25 May 1842, 1, 2 January 1843.

65. Source: Porter (comp.), 'Report on Valuation', pp. 362–4.

66. J. C. Spencer, Secretary of the Treasury, 'Notice of Redemption of Treasury Notes', 26 April 1843, Entry 585 (E-585), Miscellaneous Correspondence and Reports, folder titled Letters Related to Bonds and Certificates, Records of the Bureau of the Public Debt, Record Group 53 (hereafter RG 53), National Archives and Record Administration II, College Park, MD (hereafter NARA II); J. C. Spencer, Secretary of the Treasury, 28 June 1843, E-585, RG 53, NARA II.

67. Report of the Secretary of the Treasury, 1846, p. 27.

68. Source: ibid., p. 27.

69. James Rothschild to his nephew, 2 January 1842, cited in N. Ferguson, *The House of Rothschild, Money's Prophets, 1798–1848* (New York: Viking, 1998), p. 374.

70. McGrane, *Foreign Bondholders*, pp. 1–2; Hidy, *Peabody*, pp. 174–9; *The Times* (London), 28 April, 13 May, 24 September 1842; Davis and Cull, *International Capital Markets*, p. 6; 'Report of the Commissioners Sent to Europe to Negotiate a Loan', US Congress, in Sundry Reports, 27th Congress, 3rd Session, House Document 197, Serial 422, pp. 1–6.

71. *Baltimore American*, quoted in *New Orleans Picayune*, 6 February 1847; Myers, *A Financial History of the United States*, pp. 143–5; *United States Magazine*, 18 (March 1846), pp. 232–3; J. G. M. Ramsey to James K. Polk, 26 October 1839, in *Correspondence of Polk*, vol. 5, pp. 274–6; editors' notes, in ibid., vol. 5, p. 350, vol. 6, p. 21.

72. *The Times*, 28 April 1842.

73. *The Times*, 24 September, 31 October, 20 November, 26 August, 26 September 1846, 2 January 1847; 'Report of the Commissioners Sent to Europe to Negotiate a Loan', pp. 1–6.

74. McGrane, *Foreign Bondholders*, pp. 34–40; Myers, *A Financial History of the United States*, pp. 143–6; Sundry Reports, 27th Congress, 3rd Session, House Report 120, Serial 426, pp. 3–7, 14–17; William Appleton to Baring Brothers, 2 April 1842, Letters Received (Series A), reel C-1373, Baring Brother and Company Papers (microform), National Archives of Canada, Ottawa (hereafter BPOC).

75. G. L. Rives, *The United States and Mexico, 1821–1848*, 2 vols (New York: Charles Scribner's Sons, 1913), vol. 2, pp. 101–3; E. Turlington, *Mexico and Her Foreign Creditors* (New York: Columbia University Press, 1930), pp. 16–20; Tenenbaum, *The Politics of Penury*, pp. xi–xiii.

76. Turlington, *Mexico and Her Foreign Creditors*, pp. 16–21, 24–5; Tenenbaum, *The Politics of Penury*, pp. 14–20.

77. Tenenbaum, *The Politics of Penury*, pp. xi–xv, 20–5; Turlington, *Mexico and Her Foreign Creditors*, pp. 24–6; Smith, *The War with Mexico*, vol. 2, pp. 6–7; Rives, *The United States and Mexico*, vol. 1, pp. 90–1; P. Santoni, *Mexicans at Arms: Puro Federalists and the Politics of War, 1845–1848* (Fort Worth, TX: Texas Christian University Press, 1996), p. 1.

78. Turlington, *Mexico and Her Foreign Creditors*, pp. 35–45; Rives, *The United States and Mexico*, vol. 1, pp. 91–3; Tenenbaum, *The Politics of Penury*, pp. 20–2.

79. Tenenbaum, *The Politics of Penury*, pp. 22–5; Turlington, *Mexico and Her Foreign Creditors*, pp. 49–51, 92–4.

80. B. A. Tenenbaum, 'Merchants, Money and Mischief: The British in Mexico, 1821–1862', *Americas*, 35 (January 1979), pp. 317–39, on pp. 319–21; Tenenbaum, *The Politics of Penury*, pp. 32–5, 49, 56–9, 79; Turlington, *Mexico and Her Foreign Creditors*, pp. 81–3, 88.

81. Smith, *The War with Mexico*, vol. 1, pp. 6–8, vol. 2, pp. 8–9; G. M. McBride, *The Land System of Mexico* (New York: National Geographical Society, 1923), pp. 59–60, 68; W.

H. Callcott, *Church and State in Mexico, 1822–1857* (Durham, NC: Duke University Press, 1926), pp. 160–5; Tenenbaum, *The Politics of Penury*, p. 78.

82. Turlington, *Mexico and Her Foreign Creditors*, pp. 88–9; *Washington Union* (Washington, DC), 3 February 1846.

83. *The Times*, 6 October 1845.

84. Smith, *The War with Mexico*, vol. 2, p. 253.

2 Ideology, Revenue and Financial System

1. Sellers, *Polk, Continentalist*, pp. 213, 421–6, 445–6; C. A. McCoy, *Polk and the Presidency* (Austin, TX: University of Texas Press, 1960), p. 50; Richardson (ed.), *Messages of the Presidents*, vol. 4, pp. 403–9; *The Diary of Polk*, vol. 1, pp. 376–7, 397–8, 403–4, 438–40, 447–8, 451–4, 467; C. G. Sellers, *Market Revolution: Jacksonian America, 1815–1846* (New York: Oxford University Press, 1991), pp. 417–18; Bergeron, *The Presidency of Polk*, pp. 132–5.

2. *The Diary of Polk*, vol. 1, pp. 368–9.

3. Sellers, *Polk, Continentalist*, p. 310. Sellers's main interest is the first half of the nineteenth century. In making this statement he obviously does not give adequate attention to the legislation passed by the Civil War Congresses – the National Bank Act, protective tariffs, Greenbacks, Homestead Act, Pacific Railroad Act, National Bank notes, and massive loans. However, the legislation passed by the Twenty-Ninth Congress should still be considered very important; J. H. Silbey, *Shrine of Party: Congressional Voting Behavior, 1841–1852* (Pittsburgh, PA: University of Pittsburgh Press, 1967), pp. 67, 245, n. 2.

4. *The Diary of Polk*, vol. 2, pp. 95–6; Sellers, *Polk, Continentalist*, pp. 486–7.

5. Sellers, *Polk, Continentalist*, p. v. In his later writings Sellers credits Polk with accomplishing his objectives but believes his tactics agitated friends and foes alike and the strategy of using expansion to dampen sectional conflict had the opposite effect. Likewise the effort to defend patriarchal independence, equality and therefore honour against an activist capitalist state proved impossible. In the end, Sellers believes, Jacksonian Democracy strengthened the forces of capitalism by making the banking system more efficient and capital more mobile; Sellers, *Market Revolution*, pp. 417–18, 422–3, 425–7, 331, 359.

6. C. G. Sellers, *James K. Polk, Jacksonian, 1795–1843* (Princeton, NJ: Princeton University Press, 1957), pp. 17–33, 36–62; Haynes, *Polk and the Expansionist Impulse*, pp. ix, 2–19.

7. Haynes, *Polk and the Expansionist Impulse*, pp. ix, 14, 21–2; Sellers, *Polk, Jacksonian*, pp. 91–2, 96–9; editors' notes, in *Correspondence of Polk*, vol. 6, p. xi–xii; W. Dusinberre, *Slavemaster President: The Double Career of James Polk* (Oxford: Oxford University Press, 2003), pp. 5–6, 13, 58–62; Abbot Lawrence to James K. Polk, 21 September 1842, in *Correspondence of Polk*, vol. 6, pp. 115–16.

8. 'Address of James K. Polk to the people of Tennessee', 3 April 1839, reel 59, item 534, p. 17, James K. Polk Papers (microform), Library of Congress, Washington, DC (hereafter Polk Papers).

9. Ibid., pp. 14, 17–20; James K. Polk to Wyatt Christian et al., 15 May 1843, in *Correspondence of Polk*, vol. 6, pp. 288–97; J. George Harris to James K. Polk, 20 December 1842, in ibid., vol. 6, pp. 156–8; Richardson (ed.), *Messages of the Presidents*, vol. 4, pp. 374–9.

10. Richardson (ed.), *Messages of the Presidents*, vol. 4, p. 374.

11. Ibid., vol. 4, pp. 374–7; James K. Polk to James Buchanan, 17 February, 11 April 1845, in *Correspondence of Polk*, vol. 9, pp. 110–11, 275–7; McCoy, *Polk and the Presidency*, pp. 4–6, 148; Bergeron, *The Presidency of Polk*, pp. xii–xiv; Shenton, *Walker*, pp. 70–1.

12. McCoy, *Polk and the Presidency*, pp. 5–6, 74–82; Bergeron, *The Presidency of Polk*, pp. xii–xiv; *The Diary of Polk*, vol. 1, pp. 48, 314–15; Tick, 'The Political and Economic Policies of Walker', p. 143.

13. McCoy, *Polk and the Presidency*, pp. 5–6, 29, 139–40; *The Diary of Polk*, vol. 1, pp. 267, 367–9, 373–4, 400–1, 403–4, 407–10, 419–20, 424–5, 438–40, vol. 2, p. 10; *Washington Union*, 3, 18, 19 February, 18 June 1846, 21, 25 January 1847; Sellers, *Polk, Continentalist*, pp. 445–8; Sellers, *Market Revolution*, p. 425.

14. US Congress, *Congressional Globe*, 46 vols (Washington, DC, 1834–73), 23rd Congress, 1st session, pp. 68–9; Studenski and Krooss, *Financial History of the United States*, pp. 46–7; McCoy, *Polk and the Presidency*, p. 5.

15. Andrew Jackson to Polk, 2 May 1845, in *Correspondence of Polk*, vol. 9, pp. 333–4. In a like vein, see Jackson to Polk, 6 June 1845, in ibid., vol. 9, pp. 432–3.

16. Shenton, *Walker*, pp. 6–11, 22–31, 71; Tick, 'The Political and Economic Policies of Walker', pp. 71–7, 100–8, 143; *United States Magazine*, 16 (February 1845), pp. 157–64; *Congressional Globe*, 25th Congress, 1st Session, Appendix, pp. 77–85; *Congressional Globe*, 26th Congress, 1st Session, Appendix, pp. 137–43; *Congressional Globe*, 27th Congress, 1st Session, Appendix, pp. 260–1.

17. Robert J. Walker to James K. Polk, 30 May 1844, in *Correspondence of Polk*, vol. 7, p. 168.

18. James K. Polk to John K. Kane, 19 June 1844, in ibid., vol. 7, pp. 267–8.

19. Ibid., p. 267.

20. Historians disagree on whether Polk's reply was devious or an honest expression of deeply-held beliefs. Paul Bergeron in his favourable biography of Polk argues that it was actually a fairly forthright statement. Charles Sellers agrees. Michael F. Holt in his study of the American Whig Party accuses Polk of duplicity. The letter strongly resembles previous public statements; Bergeron, *The Presidency of Polk*, pp. 18–19; Sellers, *Polk, Continentalist*, pp. 120–1; Holt, *The Rise and Fall of the American Whig Party*, pp. 184, 1010, n. 73; US Congress, *Register of Debates in Congress, 1824–1837*, 14 vols (Washington, DC), 22nd Congress, 2nd Session, pp. 1163–4; James K. Polk to Wyatt Christian et al., 15 May 1843, in *Correspondence of Polk*, vol. 6, pp. 288–97.

21. Tick, 'The Political and Economic Policies of Walker', pp. 117–22; Sellers, *Polk, Continentalist*, pp. 116–23; Holt, *The Rise and Fall of the American Whig Party*, p. 184.

22. Richardson (ed.), *Messages of the Presidents*, vol. 4, pp. 378–9, 403–6.

23. Ibid., vol. 4, pp. 406–9.

24. Report of the Secretary of the Treasury, 1845, p. 4.

25. Ibid., pp. 4–15; 'Report of the Secretary of the Treasury in Reply to a Resolution of the Senate', 22 July 1846, in *Charleston Mercury* (SC), 28 July 1846.

26. Report of the Secretary of the Treasury, 1845, pp. 16–19.

27. *Congressional Globe*, 29th Congress, 1st Session, pp. 989–95, 1001–10, 1011–12, 1018–23, 1032–7.

28. Ibid., pp. 1043–5, 1046–53; Sellers, *Polk, Continentalist*, pp. 455–7.

29. *Congressional Globe*, 29th Congress, 1st Session, pp. 1081–4, 1103; *New York Herald*, 30 July 1846; *Charleston Mercury*, 21 July 1846.

30. *Congressional Globe*, 29th Congress, 1st Session, pp. 1090–2, 1102–3, 1156, 1158; *New Orleans Picayune*, 25 July 1846.

31. Report of the Secretary of the Treasury, 1846, p. 1; ibid., 9 December 1847, 30th Congress, 1st Session, House Executive Document 6, Serial 514, p. 1; ibid., 11 December 1848, 30th Congress 2nd Session, House Executive Document 7, Serial 538, p. 1; ibid., 1849, 31st Congress, 1st Session, Senate Executive Document 2, Serial 552, p. 1; ibid., 16 December 1850, 31st Congress 2nd Session, Senate Executive Document 4, Serial 588, p. 1; ibid., 6 January 1852 (1851), 32nd Congress, 1st Session, Senate Executive Document 11, Serial 614, p. 1; ibid., 15 January 1853 (1852) 32nd Congress, 2nd Session, Senate Executive Document 22, Serial 662, p. 1.

32. *Congressional Globe*, 29th Congress, 1st Session, pp. 574–6, 584–6, 595, Appendix, pp. 592–8; Shenton, *Walker*, pp. 87–9; Tick, 'The Political and Economic Policies of Walker', pp. 167–9.

33. *Congressional Globe*, 29th Congress, 1st Session, p. 591.

34. Ibid., pp. 1164, 1167, 1172, 1174–6; *New York Herald*, 1 July 1846; *American Review, A Whig Journal* (New York), 3 (May 1846), pp. 465–7.

35. *US Statutes at Large*, 1 (1789), pp. 65–7; Report of the Secretary of the Treasury, 1849, pp. 227–320; Report of the Commissioner of the General Land Office, 10 December 1846, 29th Congress, 2nd Session, House Document 9, Serial 498, pp. 11–27.

36. *US Statutes at Large*, 1 (1789), pp. 65–7; ibid., 4 (1830), pp. 414–16; E-103, 'Miscellaneous Letters Received' ('K' series, 1836–69), vol. 27, item 344, Record of the Department of Treasury, Record Group 56 (hereafter RG 56), NARA II; Sundry Reports, 30th Congress, 2nd Session, House Executive Document 46, Serial 541, pp. 2–31; Report of the Secretary of the Treasury, 1849, pp. 227–33.

37. *US Statutes at Large*, 9 (1846), pp. 59–66; Kinley, *The Independent Treasury*, pp. 53–7; Myers, *The New York Money Market*, vol. 1, pp. 182–5. The receiver of public money was one of the two officials at district land offices. The receiver kept and maintained the funds collected from the sale of public lands. The other official, the register, recorded land sales. In 1845 there were sixty-two land offices. Report of the Commissioner of the General Land Office, 1846, pp. 11–15.

38. Report of the Secretary of the Treasury, 1846, pp. 30–1; Kinley, *The Independent Treasury*, pp. 59–60; Myers, *The New York Money Market*, vol. 1, pp. 184–7.

39. *US Statutes at Large*, 9 (1846), pp. 53–5; *DeBow's Commercial Review of the South and West* (New Orleans, LA), 1 (January 1846), pp. 61–4; Sundry Reports, 29th Congress, 1st Session, House Report 411, Serial 489, pp. 1–7; Shenton, *Walker*, pp. 89–90; Report of the Secretary of the Treasury, 1845, pp. 14–15; Sellers, *Polk, Continentalist*, pp. 470–1; Charles August Davis to John C. Calhoun, 6 April 1846, in *The Papers of John C. Calhoun*, ed. W. E. Hemphill, C. N. Wilson and S. B. Cook, 26 vols (Columbia, SC: University of South Carolina Press, 1963–2001), vol. 23, p. 17; Solomon Townsend to Calhoun, 6 April 1846, in ibid., vol. 23, pp. 27–8; Eustis Prescott to Calhoun, 27 April 1846, in ibid., vol. 23, p. 64; Fitzwilliam Brydsell to Calhoun, 3 July 1846, in ibid., vol. 23, p. 269; M. Dix (comp.), *Memoirs of John Adams Dix*, 2 vols (New York: Harper & Brothers, 1883), vol. 1, pp. 200–1.

40. Richardson (ed.), *Messages of the Presidents*, vol. 4, pp. 408–9, 497, 555; Report of the Secretary of the Treasury, 1845, pp. 15–16; ibid., 1846, pp. 13–15.

41. Sellers, *Polk, Continentalist*, pp. 471–2; *Congressional Globe*, 29th Congress, 1st Session, pp. 1057, 1058–63, 1069, 1071–2, 1093–4, 1179–80, 1195–6.

42. Sellers, *Polk, Continentalist*, pp. 472–4, 477–8, 487; Richardson (ed.), *Messages of the Presidents*, vol. 4, pp. 460–6; Sellers, *Market Revolution*, pp. 425–7; Silbey, *Shrine of Party*, pp. 81–4.

3 The Loan of 1846

1. Report of the Secretary of the Treasury, 1845, pp. 24–5, 3; *Congressional Globe*, 29th Congress, 1st Session, pp. 510, 533–5, 549–52, 788–9; *The Diary of Polk*, vol. 1, pp. 257–8, 270, 294–5, 315.
2. Smith, *The War with Mexico*, vol. 1, pp, 139–40; A. H. Bill, *Rehearsal for Conflict: The War with Mexico, 1846–1848* (New York: Cooper Square Publishers, 1969), pp. 58–60; Report of the Secretary of War, 28 November 1845, in *Congressional Globe*, 29th Congress, 1st Session, Appendix, pp. 13–14.
3. Smith, *The War with Mexico*, vol. 1, pp. 142–6.
4. Tick, 'The Political and Economic Policies of Walker', pp. 191–3; *New Orleans Picayune*, 5 June 1846; George Newbold to William W. Corcoran, 29 May 1846, 2 June 1846, Box 135, Riggs Family Papers, Library of Congress, Washington, DC; Robert J. Walker to H. Wilkerson, President, Canal and Banking Company, 10 June 1846, E-59, 'Letters sent to Bankers' ('ZO' series), Box 5, item 174, RG 56, NARA II; Hidy, *Peabody*, p. 203.
5. George Newbold to William W. Corcoran, 2 June 1846, James J. Palmer to William W. Corcoran, 28 May 1846, Box 135, Riggs Family Papers; *New Orleans Weekly Picayune*, 18 May 1846; *New York Courier and Enquirer*, 28 May 1846, quoted in *New Orleans Picayune*, 6 June 1846.
6. Both Frank Tick and Robert Shenton assert that Walker moved funds from Whig-controlled banks, in order to prevent the bankers from embarrassing the government by restricting credit, while Congress debated the Independent Treasury bill. Both rely on Walker's letter of 30 June 1845 to J. L. O'Sullivan in which he indicates his intention of realizing government funds before the bankers create difficulties in December. An analysis of the deposits does not bear this out (see Table 3.1). Shenton, *Walker*, pp. 87, 237, n. 1; Tick, 'The Political and Economic Policies of Walker', pp. 185–7.
7. Treasurer's Weekly Statement, 24 March, 1 December 1845, 30 March 1846, in *Washington National Intelligencer*, 2 April, 8 December 1845, 3 April 1846; Sundry Reports, 29th Congress, 1st Session, House Executive Document 174, Serial 485, pp. 1–7.
8. Source: Treasurer's Weekly Statements, 24 March 1845, 1 December 1845, 30 March 1846, in *Washington National Intelligencer*, 2 April 1845, 8 December 1845, 3 April 1846.
9. *Congressional Globe*, 29th Congress, 1st Session, p. 804.
10. Ibid.
11. *New York Morning News*, 14 May 1846, quoted in *Washington National Intelligencer*, 16 May 1846.
12. Ibid.
13. Sundry Reports, 29th Congress, 1st Session, Senate Document 392, Serial 477, p. 1.
14. Ibid., pp. 1, 10–18.
15. Ibid., pp. 2–4.
16. Source: ibid., pp. 2–4.
17. Ibid., pp. 1–4; *New Orleans Picayune*, 25 June 1846; D. R. Hickey, *The War of 1812, A forgotten Conflict* (Urbana, IL: University of Illinois Press, 1990), pp. 35, 122; A. Balinky, *Albert Gallatin, Fiscal Theories and Policies* (New Brunswick, NJ: Rutgers University Press, 1958), pp. 185–7, 204; Stabile, *The Origins of American Public Finance*, pp. 160–1.
18. *Congressional Globe*, 29th Congress, 1st Session, p. 1094.
19. Ibid., pp. 1094–5.

20. Ibid., pp. 1098–100.
21. Ibid., pp. 1095, 1098–100, Appendix, pp. 826–9.
22. *Congressional Globe*, 29th Congress, 1st Session, pp. 1103, 1109–10, 1114–15, Appendix, pp. 1127–8.
23. W. N. Chambers, *'Old Bullion' Benton: Senator from the West, 1782*–1858 (Boston, MA: Little Brown, 1956), pp. 50–3; *Congressional Globe*, 29th Congress, 1st Session, pp. 1109–10.
24. Ibid., p. 1110.
25. Ibid., pp. 1114–15; DeKnight, *History of the Currency*, pp. 69–70; Porter (comp.), 'Report on Valuation', pp. 364–5.
26. Adams, 'The Beginning of Investment Banking', pp. 108–12; F. O. Gatell, 'Spoils of the Bank War: Political Bias in the Selection of Pet Banks', *American Historical Review*, 70 (October 1964), pp. 35–58, on pp. 43–5; Cohen, *Business and Politics*, pp. 10–13, 21–3.
27. George Newbold to William W. Corcoran, 29 May 1846, Box 135, Riggs Family Papers; Newbold to Corcoran, 6 June 1846, ibid.
28. Corcoran & Riggs to Elisha Riggs, 13, 22 June 1846, Box 23, Riggs Family Papers.
29. *Washington National Intelligencer*, 17 June 1846; *New York Tribune*, 11 June 1846.
30. Report of the Secretary of the Treasury, 1845, p. 26; ibid., 1846, pp. 18–22, 23; Treasurer's Weekly Statement, 27 April, 27 July, 24 August 1846, in *Washington National Intelligencer*, 2 May, 3 August, 4 September 1846.
31. 'Notice to Collecting, Receiving, and Disbursing Officers of the United States', 25 August 1846, Report of the Secretary of the Treasury, 1846, pp. 32–4; Treasurer's Weekly Statement, 23 November 1846, 30 April 1847, in *Washington National Intelligencer*, 3 December 1846, 3 May 1847.
32. Treasurer's Weekly Statement, 27 July, 26 October, 23 November 1846, in *Washington National Intelligencer*, 3 August, 4 November, 3 December 1846.
33. *Merchants' Magazine and Commercial Review* (New York), 14 (August 1846), pp. 192–3; E-369, 'Numerical Register for Treasury Notes of 1846', RG 53, NARA II; E-369, 5 vols, vol. 1, $50 1 mill notes, pp. 1–190, vol. 3, $100 1 mill notes, pp. 1–146, vol. 5, sundry, $500 1 mill notes, pp. 1–42, RG 53, NARA II; *Washington Union*, 28 August 1846.
34. E-369, vols 1–5, RG 53, NARA II.
35. Ibid., vol. 1, pp. 1–190, vol. 3, pp. 1–146, vol. 5, pp. 1–42, 70–1.
36. Tick, 'The Political and Economic Policies of Walker', pp. 191–2; *New Orleans Picayune*, 22, 23 September 1846; Newbold to Corcoran, 10 September 1846, Box 135, Riggs Family Papers.
37. Newbold to Corcoran, 10 September 1846, Box 135, Riggs Family Papers.
38. Walker to Cashier, Bank of Commerce, New York, et al., 1 September 1846, 'Letters Sent to Banks', ('ZO' series), E-59, Box 5, item 191, RG 56, NARA II.
39. Robert J. Walker to Cashier, Bank of Commerce, New York, 15 September 1846, E-59, Box 5, item 192, RG 56, NARA II; Treasurer's Weekly Statement, 24 August, 21 September, 26 October, 31 December 1846, in *Washington National Intelligencer*, 4 September, 5 October, 4 November 1846, 9 January 1847.
40. *The Diary of Polk*, vol. 2 pp. 163–4, 166–7.
41. *Philadelphia Public Ledger*, 29 September 1846; *New York Tribune*, 2 October 1846, quoted in *Philadelphia Public Ledger*, 3 October 1846; *New York Herald*, 3 March, 2 June, 8 October 1846.

42. *Niles' National Register* (Baltimore, MD), 26 September 1846; *Washington National Intelligencer*, quoted in *New Orleans Weekly Picayune*, 5 October 1846; *The Diary of Polk*, vol. 2, p. 166; *New Orleans Weekly Picayune*, 19 October 1846; Cohen, *Business and Politics*, p. 41; *New York Tribune*, 6 October 1846.

43. *New York Tribune*, 7 October 1846; *Washington National Intelligencer*, 7 October 1846; *New York Journal of Commerce*, 9 October 1846; *New York Express*, 8 October 1846 quoted in *Niles' National Register*, 17 October 1846; *Niles' National Register*, 10, 17 October 1846; *Philadelphia Public Ledger*, 12 October 1846; *The Diary of Polk*, vol. 2, p. 191.

44. *New York Journal of Commerce*, 12 October 1846; *New York Courier and Express*, 8 October 1846, quoted in *Washington National Intelligencer*, 13 October 1846; *New York Herald*, 12 October 1846; *New York Tribune*, 6 October 1846; *Philadelphia Public Ledger*, 24 October 1846; *Washington Union*, 22 October 1846; Tick, 'The Political and Economic Policies of Walker', pp. 192–3.

45. *Philadelphia Public Ledger*, 10 October 1846.

46. Ibid., 8, 10, 12 October 1846.

47. *New York Herald*, 8 October 1846.

48. Ibid.

49. Shenton, *Walker*, pp. 91–2; *New York Journal of Commerce*, 19 October 1846; *The Diary of Polk*, vol. 2, pp. 192, 194–5, 200–1, 205.

50. *Washington Union*, 22 October 1846.

51. Ibid.

52. *New York Herald*, 26, 27, 29 October 1846; *Washington National Intelligencer*, 26 October 1846; Treasurer's Weekly Statement, 26 October 1846, in *Washington National Intelligencer*, 4 November 1846.

53. *The Diary of Polk*, vol. 2, p. 213; 'Official Announcement, the Treasury Department', in *Washington Union*, 30 October 1846.

54. *Washington Union*, 30 October 1846, 2 November 1846; E-369, vol. 5, pp. 317–19, 341–2, RG 53, NARA II; Corcoran & Riggs to Elisha Riggs, 30 October 1846, Box 23, Riggs Family Papers; E-369, vols 2, 4, 5, RG 53, NARA II.

55. Report of the Secretary of the Treasury, 1846, pp. 27–8; $5,506,800 + $1,931,000 + $250,000 = $7,687,800, in ibid., 1847, pp. 36, 40, 47. It appears the Treasury Department issued the last $250,000 to W. W. Woodworth on 31 May 1847, but did not report the receipts until the following July; E-369, vol. 5, pp. 317–37, 341–53, 356, RG 53, NARA II.

56. *New York Tribune*, 2, 5, 7, 12 November 1846; *Washington National Intelligencer*, 4, 9 November 1846; James J. Palmer to Corcoran & Riggs, 10 November 1846, Box 179, Riggs Family Papers; *New York Journal of Commerce*, 5 November 1846; *New York Journal of Commerce*, 7 November 1846, quoted in *Charleston Mercury*, 11 November 1846; *Niles' National Register*, 7 November 1846.

57. *New York Journal of Commerce*, 7 November 1846, quoted in *Charleston Mercury*, 11 November 1846.

58. George Newbold to Corcoran & Riggs, 2, 9, 17 November 1846, Box 170, Riggs Family Papers; James J. Palmer to Corcoran & Riggs, 10, 11 November 1846, ibid.

59. *New York Journal of Commerce*, 17 November 1846; *Washington National Intelligencer*, 16, 18 November 1846; *New York Tribune*, 16 November 1846; *Niles' National Register*, 21 November 1846; *Washington Union*, 16, 19 November 1846; *The Diary of Polk*, vol. 2, p. 237.

60. The Treasury Department notified the successful bidders in a series of individual letters dated 17 through 19 November. The letters specified the amount of the bid accepted and terms. 'Letters Sent, November 1846 to March 1849', E-449, pp. 1–29, RG 53, NARA II.

61. Source: ibid.

62. Robert J. Walker to John Ward & Co., 17 November 1846, ibid., pp. 13–14; Walker to Henry Roland, 18 November, 21 November, 30 November 1846, ibid., pp. 26, 30, 32.

63. Walker to Thomas J. Abbott, 17 November 1846, ibid., p. 1; Walker to John V. Wilcox, 19 November 1846, ibid., pp, 27.

64. Walker to Manajeh H. Smith, 18 November 1846, ibid., p. 24; G. Morgensen and C. R. Harvey, *New York Times Dictionary of Money and Investing* (New York: Times Books, 2002), pp. 62, 270.

65. E-370, 'Records relating to the Loan of 1846', vol. 1, 'Register of Certificates of Loan of 1846', pp. 2–271, RG 53, NARA II. The original loan records are still available for inspection at NARA II.

66. Ibid., vol. 2, 'Journal of Loan of 1846', pp. 1–274.

67. Ibid., vol. 3, 'Ledger of the Loan of 1846', pp. 5–335; ibid., vol. 23, 'Dividends of Interest on the Loan of 1846'; J. Punnett, Cashier, Bank of America to R. H. Gillet, 26 December 1846, E-411, 'Letters on Loan of 1846', vol. 1, RG 53, NARA II; George Newbold to Corcoran & Riggs, 20 December 1846, Box 171, Riggs Family Papers.

68. E-370, vol. 1, pp. 2–5, 8–11, 21, RG 53, NARA II.

69. Ibid., vol. 1, pp. 2, 6, 14, 20, 23, 27.

70. Report of the Secretary of the Treasury, 1846, p. 28; Quarterly Treasury Statement, 31 December 1846, 31 March 1847, in *Washington National Intelligencer*, 4 February, 5 May 1847; Report of the Secretary of the Treasury, 1847, pp. 40, 45.

71. Quarterly Treasury Statement, 31 December 1846, 31 March 1847, in *Washington National Intelligencer*, 4 February, 5 May 1847; Report of the Secretary of the Treasury, 1847, pp. 36, 40. The Quarterly Treasury Statement of 30 June 1847 does not separate the avails from the bond issue, however subtraction of prior receipts from the yearly total gives the necessary figure. Quarterly Treasury Statement, 30 June 1847, in *Washington National Intelligencer*, 4 August 1847; E-370, vol. 1, pp. 2–171, RG 53, NARA II.

72. Quarterly Treasury Statement, 30 September, 31 December 1846, 31 March, 30 June 1847, in *Washington National Intelligencer*, 4 November 1846, 4 February, 5 May, 4 August 1847; Report of the Secretary of the Treasury, 1847, p. 36; ibid., 1846, p. 23.

73. Source: Quarterly Treasury Statement, 31 December 1846, 31 March 1847, 30 June 1847, in *Washington National Intelligencer*, 4 February 1847, 5 May 1847, 4 August 1847; Secretary of the Treasury Report, 1847 pp. 18, 40; E-370, vol. 1, pp. 2–171, RG 53, NARA II.

74. *New York Journal of Commerce*, 14 November 1846.

75. Ibid., 10 December 1846; *Washington National Intelligencer*, 16 November 1846; *New York Herald*, 15, 19 November, 13 December 1846.

76. Source: *New York Tribune* and *New York Herald*, 1 January 1847 through 30 June 1849.

77. Corcoran & Riggs to Elisha Riggs, 23, 24 November 1846, Box 23, Riggs Family Papers.

78. Corcoran & Riggs to Elisha Riggs, 23 November 1846, ibid.

79. Corcoran & Riggs to Elisha Riggs, 24, 17 November 1846, ibid.

80. Charnley & Whelen to R. H. Gillet, 23 December 1846, 22 January 1847, E-411, vol. 1, RG 53, NARA II; C. Macalester to R. H. Gillet, 23 December 1846, ibid.; Charnley

& Whelen to Corcoran & Riggs, 24 February 1847, Box 173, Riggs Family Papers; Accounts Current – Corcoran and Riggs with Charnley & Whelen, August through December, 1846, Box 171, Riggs Family Papers.

81. Cohen, *Business and Politics*, p. 42; John Ward & Company to Corcoran & Riggs, 14 December 1846, Box 171, Riggs Family Papers; Charnley & Whelen to Corcoran & Riggs, 27, 28 November 1846, Box 170, Riggs Family Papers; Accounts Current – Corcoran & Riggs with Charnley & Whelen, August through December, 1846, Box 171, Riggs Family Papers; Sam Harris & Sons to Corcoran & Riggs, 21, 28 November 1846, Box 170, Riggs Family Papers.

82. George Riggs to Corcoran & Riggs, 23, 25, 28 November 1846, Box 170, Riggs Family Papers; Elisha Riggs to Corcoran & Riggs, 27 November 1846, ibid.; Corcoran & Riggs to Elisha Riggs, 28 November 1846, Box 23, Riggs Family Papers; Charnley & Whelen to Corcoran & Riggs, 24 February 1847, Box 172, Riggs Family Papers; Cohen, *Business and Politics*, p. 42; Cohen, 'Business and Politics', pp. 83–5.

4 The Loan of 1847

1. Smith, *The War with Mexico*, vol. 1, pp. 156–80, 225–61, 282–3, 295–7, 331–46, 354–5; *The Diary of Polk*, vol. 2, pp. 211, 198–200, 219–22, 234–6, 240–1, 294.

2. Smith, *The War with Mexico*, vol. 1, pp. 216–23, 374–6; Santoni, *Mexicans at Arms*, pp. 99, 126–7; Rives, *The United States and Mexico*, vol. 2, pp. 308–10; Haynes, *Polk and the Expansionist Impulse*, pp. 154–7.

3. Holt, *The Rise and Fall of the American Whig Party*, pp. 231–4, 245–50; Silbey, *Shrine of Party*, pp. 22, 245, n. 1; R. H. Gillet to Polk, 16 November 1846, reel 47, Polk Papers; *Washington Union*, 29 December 1846, 21 January 1847; *The Diary of Polk*, vol. 2, pp. 217–18.

4. Treasurer's Weekly Statement, 26 October, 23 November, 31 December 1846, 25 January 1847, in *Washington National Intelligencer*, 4 November, 3 December 1846, 9 January, 3 February 1847; Quarterly Treasury Statement, 31 December 1846, in *Washington National Intelligencer*, 4 February 1847.

5. *Congressional Globe*, 29th Congress, 1st Session, p. xlvii; Report of the Secretary of the Treasury, 1846, pp. 1–3; *Congressional Globe*, 29th Congress, 2nd Session, pp. 2, 3.

6. Polk's Second Annual Message, 8 December 1846, in Richardson (ed.), *Messages of the Presidents*, vol. 4, pp. 497–8, 502; *Congressional Globe*, 29th Congress, 2nd Session, Appendix, pp. 7–8.

7. Report of the Secretary of the Treasury, 1846, pp. 4–5, 13–15.

8. Ibid., pp. 4–5.

9. *The Diary of Polk*, vol. 2, p. 303.

10. *Merchants' Magazine*, 16 (January 1847), pp. 72–3; *United States Magazine*, 20 (January 1847), p. 81; *Washington Union*, quoted in *Niles' National Register*, 3 April 1847.

11. *Washington Union*, quoted in *Niles' National Register*, 3 April 1847.

12. Ibid.; Report of the Secretary of the Treasury, 1847, p. 70; Hidy, *Peabody*, pp. 246–7; *Economist* (London), 5 (24 April 1847), pp. 466–7.

13. Daniel Ullman to Henry Clay, 12 July 1847, in *The Papers of Henry Clay*, vol. 10, p. 339; Clay to Ullman, 4 August 1847, in ibid., pp. 342–3.

14. Hidy, *Peabody*, p. 246.

15. Holt, *The Rise and Fall of the American Whig Party*, pp. 231–4, 245–50.

16. *New York Herald*, 16 December 1846, 1, 4 January 1847.

17. Ibid., 16 December 1846.
18. *New York Evening Express*, quoted in *The Times*, 1 January 1847.
19. *Niles' National Register*, 2 January 1847; *Washington Union*, 21, 25 January 1847; *Washington National Intelligencer*, 2 January 1847.
20. *Congressional Globe*, 29th Congress, 2nd Session, p. 102; *Niles' National Register*, 2 January 1847.
21. Quoted in *New Orleans Picayune*, 15 January 1847.
22. *New Orleans Picayune*, 15 January 1847; *The Times*, 1 January 1847; *New York Tribune*, 29 January 1847; *The Diary of Polk*, vol. 2, pp. 346–8; Silbey, *Shrine of Party*, pp. 83–4.
23. *Congressional Globe*, 29th Congress, 2nd Session, pp. 225, 230–1.
24. Ibid., pp. 228–31; *US Statutes at Large*, 9 (1847), pp. 118–22.
25. *Congressional Globe*, 29th Congress, 2nd Session, Appendix, pp. 255–8.
26. *Washington Union*, 31 December 1846, 14, 21, 25, 29 January 1847. The *Union*'s attacks became so resented after a temporary defeat of the Ten Regiment Bill in the Senate that the Whigs joined with the senators from South Carolina and Florida to expel Thomas Ritchie, the editor, from the Senate floor. The move followed the printing of an article on 9 February 1847 entitled 'Another Mexican Victory'; *The Diary of Polk*, vol. 2, pp. 375–9; *Congressional Globe*, 29th Congress, 2nd Session, p. 392.
27. *Congressional Globe*, 29th Congress, 2nd Session, pp. 228–30.
28. Ibid., p. 247.
29. Ibid., pp. 256–62, 267, 274.
30. Ibid., p. 259.
31. *US Statutes at Large*, 9 (1847), p. 121; Shenton, *Walker*, pp. 42–3; George Newbold to Corcoran & Riggs, 7 January 1847, Box 172, Riggs Family Papers; Newbold to Corcoran & Riggs, 27 January 1847, Box 135, Riggs Family Papers; Corcoran & Riggs to Elisha Riggs, 15 February 1847, Box 23, Riggs Family Papers; Elisha Riggs to George Peabody, 30 January 1847, Box 40, Folder 3, Riggs Family Papers.
32. *Niles' National Register*, 6 February 1847; *New York Journal of Commerce*, 3 February 1847; *Congressional Globe*, 29th Congress, 2nd Session, pp. 536–9, Appendix, pp. 180–3.
33. Ibid., pp. 572–4.
34. 'Advertisement for Proposal for a Loan – Official', 9 February 1847, in *Niles' National Register*, 13 February 1847; Report of the Secretary of the Treasury, 1847, p. 116.
35. *New York Journal of Commerce* and *New York Express*, quoted in *Niles' National Register*, 13 February 1847; *Niles' National Register*, 20 February 1847; Cohen, 'Business and Politics', pp. 88–9; Cohen, *Business and Politics*, pp. 44–5; Tick, 'The Political and Economic Policies of Walker', p. 209; *Merchants' Magazine*, 16 (March 1847), p. 291.
36. Report of the Secretary of the Treasury, 1847, pp. 46–7, 63; Quarterly Treasury Statement, 31 March 1847, in *Washington National Intelligencer*, 5 May 1847; E-369, 1846 Treasury Notes, vol. 2, pp. 4–5, RG 53, NARA II; Cohen in his study of Corcoran's business career speculates that the arrangement with Woodworth resulted in Woodworth changing his voting position on the Wilmot Proviso. At the time of the purchase the notes were selling at 105. The addition of $50,000 in new 1847 notes that he obtained at par on 31 May brought Woodworth's profits up to $15,000. The Treasury claimed the original proposal from Woodworth was received in February, but misplaced. At that time the notes were selling at par. Cohen, *Business and Politics*, pp. 43–4; Cohen, 'Business and Politics', pp. 87–8; Washington Hunt to Walker, 11, 15 February 1847, E-18, vol. 4, pp. 266, 272, RG 56, NARA II; Walker to E. Edwards, Cashier, Merchants

Bank of New York, 16 February 1847, E-59, Box 5, item 223, RG 56, NARA II; 'Letters advising congressmen of their allocation', E-18, vol. 4, pp. 278–304, RG 56, NARA II; Cohen, *Business and Politics*, p. 255, n. 6.

37. Cohen, *Business and Politics*, pp. 44–5; Cohen, 'Business and Politics', pp. 88–90; Report of the Secretary of the Treasury, 1847, pp. 48–63; Quarterly Treasury Statement, 31 March 1847, in *Washington National Intelligencer*, 5 May 1847. The Treasury reported $3,671,350 of the notes outstanding. This amount included $421,000 of the 1847 5.4 per cent notes.

38. Corcoran & Riggs to Elisha Riggs, 10, 12, 13, 22 February 1847, Box 23, Riggs Family Papers; Cohen, *Business and Politics*, pp. 44–5; John J. Palmer to Corcoran & Riggs, 18 March 1847, Box 174, Riggs Family Papers.

39. Charnley & Whelen to Elisha Riggs, 19, 20, 22, 23, 31 March 1847, Box 23, Riggs Family Papers; Corcoran & Riggs to Elisha Riggs, 10, 31 March 1847, ibid.

40. Charnley & Whelen to Corcoran & Riggs, 22 March 1847, Box 174, Riggs Family Papers; Account Current with Charnley & Whelen, 23 April 1847, Box 175, Riggs Family Papers; Account Current with Samuel Harris & Son, 15 April 1847, ibid.; Account Current with John Ward & Company – 6 per cent stock, Box 174, Riggs Family Papers; 'Statement of Treasury Note Account', January–May 1847 folder, Box 36, Riggs Family Papers; Corcoran & Riggs to Elisha Riggs, 13, 15, 18, 19, 25 March 1847, Box 23, Riggs Family Papers; Cohen, *Business and Politics*, pp. 45, 255, n. 9.

41. *Niles' National Register*, 20 February 1847; *New York Herald*, 12 April 1847; *New York Journal of Commerce*, 13 February 1847; *Merchants' Magazine*, 16 (March 1847), pp. 290–1.

42. *New York Journal of Commerce*, 13 February 1847.

43. *New York Journal of Commerce*, quoted in *Niles' National Register*, 20 February 1847; Quarterly Treasury Statement, 31 December 1846, 31 March 1847, in *Washington National Intelligencer*, 4 February, 5 May 1847.

44. *New York Herald*, 3 March, 2, 4, 11 April 1847; Report of the Secretary of the Treasury, 1847, pp. 74–5; Corcoran & Riggs to Elisha Riggs, 15 February 1847, Box 23, Riggs Family Papers; Robert J. Walker to James G. King & Son, 18 February 1847, E-449, p. 58, RG 53, NARA II; Walker to Matthew Morgan, 3 April 1847, ibid., p. 61.

45. Cohen, *Business and Politics*, pp. 45–7; Shenton, *Walker*, pp. 95–8; *Philadelphia Public Ledger*, 12 April 1847; *Washington Union*, quoted in *Washington National Intelligencer*, 22 April 1847.

46. 'Advertisement for Proposals for a Loan – Official', in *Washington National Intelligencer*, 10 February 1847; *Washington Union*, quoted in *Washington National Intelligencer*, 22 April 1847; *Merchants' Magazine*, 16 (May 1847), pp. 490–1.

47. Report of the Secretary of the Treasury, 1847, pp. 107–10; Cohen, *Business and Politics*, pp. 46–7; Shenton, *Walker*, pp. 95–6; *New York Journal of Commerce*, 14, 16 April 1847; *New York Tribune*, 14 April 1847; Elisha Riggs to George Peabody, 29 April 1847, Box 40, Folder 3, George Peabody Papers, Peabody Essex Institute, Salem, Massachusetts.

48. *Washington Union*, 22 April 1847; *United States Magazine*, 20 (May 1847), p. 456; *Bankers' Magazine and State Financial Register* (Baltimore, MD), 1 (May 1847), p. 621; *Philadelphia Public Ledger*, 12, 20 April 1847; *Washington National Intelligencer*, 13 April 1847; *Merchants' Magazine*, 16 (May 1847), pp. 490–1.

49. *New York Courier*, 17 April 1847, quoted in *New York Journal of Commerce*, 19 April 1847; *New York Journal of Commerce*, 19 April 1847; *New York Tribune*, 14 April 1847;

Niles' National Register, 28 April 1847; *Merchants' Magazine*, 16 (May 1847), p. 490; Shenton, *Walker*, p. 96; Cohen, *Business and Politics*, pp. 46–7.

50. Cohen, *Business and Politics*, pp. 3–17; Cohen, 'Business and Politics', pp. 8–12; I. Katz, 'Investment Bankers in Government and Politics: The Political Activity of William W. Corcoran, August Belmont, Sr., Levi P. Morton, and Henry Lee Higginson' (PhD dissertation, New York University, 1964), pp. 5–6.

51. J. A. Garraty and M. C. Carnes (eds), *American National Biography*, 24 vols (New York: Oxford University Press, 1999), vol. 18, pp. 504–6; Hidy, *Peabody*, pp. 184–6.

52. Cohen, *Business and Politics*, pp. 7–15; Katz, 'Investment Bankers in Government and Politics', pp. 5–10.

53. Cohen, *Business and Politics*, pp. 18–23; Katz, 'Investment Bankers in Government and Politics', pp. 6–8.

54. Corcoran & Riggs to George Peabody, 27 February 1844, quoted in Hidy, *Peabody*, p. 266.

55. Corcoran & Riggs to Peabody, 10 September 1845, quoted in Hidy, *Peabody*, p. 267.

56. Tick, 'The Political and Economic Policies of Walker', pp. 207–8; Katz, 'Investment Bankers in Government and Politics', pp. 7–8; Cohen, *Business and Politics*, pp. 34–9; Robert Dale Owens to Corcoran, 13 September 1846, Container 6, William W. Corcoran Papers, Library of Congress, Washington, DC; Shenton, *Walker*, pp. 96–7.

57. Corcoran & Riggs in account with James K. Polk – Account Book, 1845–1849, reel 62, Polk Papers.

58. *The Diary of Polk*, vol. 3, pp. 15–17; Polk to Corcoran, 7 May 1847, reel 58, Polk Papers; E-374, v. 50, 2, RG 53, NARA II; Cohen, *Business and Politics*, p. 255, n. 6; Inventory Conducted by J. Knox Walker and James K. Polk, reel 62, Polk Papers.

59. W. W. Corcoran to J. Knox Walker, 20 July 1847, reel 50, Polk Papers; First Auditor's Certificate, 7 April 1846, reel 45, Polk Papers.

60. Daniel Webster to Corcoran & Riggs, 30 June 1848, in *The Papers of Daniel Webster, Correspondence*, ed. C. M. Wiltse, 7 vols (Hanover, NH: University Press of New England, 1974–86), vol. 5, p. 48; Webster to Corcoran & Riggs, 19 March 1847, in ibid., vol. 6, p. 418; Webster to Corcoran & Riggs, 26 September 1846, in ibid., p. 372; Webster to Corcoran & Riggs, 2 September 1845, in ibid., p. 376; Webster to Corcoran & Riggs, 12 September 1846, in ibid., p. 384; Webster to Corcoran & Riggs, 20 October 1846, in ibid., vol. 6, p. 410; Webster to Corcoran & Riggs, 26 January 1848, in ibid., p. 432; Henry Clay to Henry Grinnell, 28 May 1851, in *The Papers of Henry Clay*, vol. 10, pp. 893–5; Clay to Corcoran, 14 September 1851, in ibid., p. 911; Clay to Leslie Combs, 14 November 1851, in ibid.; Clay to Lucretia Hart Clay, 3 March 1852, in ibid., p. 957; 'Checks drawn on Corcoran & Riggs by Abraham Lincoln', in *The Collected Works of Abraham Lincoln*, ed. R. P. Baslar, M. D. Pratt and F. Dunlap, 9 vols (New Brunswick, NJ: Rutger University Press, 1953–5), vol. 1, p. 445, vol. 5, p. 154, vol. 6, p. 380.

61. Henshaw & Sons to Corcoran & Riggs, 17, 22, 28 April 17 1847, Box 175, Riggs Family Papers; Corcoran & Riggs to Henshaw & Sons, 17 April 1847, ibid.; Matthew Morgan to Corcoran & Riggs, 24 April 1847, ibid.; Gundy & Dawes to Corcoran & Riggs, 27, 28 April 1847, ibid.; Gilbert & Sons to Corcoran & Riggs, 15 April 1847, ibid.; Josiah Lee to Corcoran & Riggs, 17 April 1847, ibid.; Jacob Little & Company to Corcoran & Riggs, 19 April 1847, ibid.; Asa Clapp to Corcoran & Riggs, 19 April 1847, ibid.; Beebe, Ludlow & Company to Corcoran & Riggs, 30 April 1847, ibid.; Cohen, *Business and Politics*, pp. 46–8, 256, n. 14. Asa Clapp was a leading merchant of Portland, Maine and President of the Bank of Maine. He also dealt in securities.

62. 'The Price of United States Treasury Notes and Stock at New York from 1 December 1846 to 1 December 1847', in Report of the Secretary of the Treasury, 1847, pp. 71–83; similarly in New Orleans, pp. 84–6.

63. Report of the Secretary of the Treasury, 1847, pp. 84–6, 71–83; Account Current – Charnley & Whelen with Corcoran & Riggs, 23 April 1847, Box 175, Riggs Family Papers.

64. Walker to Corcoran & Riggs, 14 April 1847, E-449, RG 53, p. 65, NARA II; Walker to Assistant Treasurers New York and Boston, Treasurer of the Mint, Philadelphia, and Treasurer of the United States, Washington, Collector and Depositary, Baltimore, 14 April 1847, ibid., pp. 63–5; Walker to Corcoran & Riggs, 14 April 1847, ibid., p. 67; Walker to Assistant Treasurer, New York and Boston, 16 April 1847, ibid., pp. 67–8; Walker to Assistant Treasurers in New York and Boston, Collector and Depositary, Baltimore, Treasurer of the Mint, Philadelphia, Treasurer, 20 April 1847, ibid., pp. 69–72; Walker to Treasurer of branch Mint, New Orleans, 26 April 1847, ibid., p. 73; Walker to Assistant Treasurer, St Louis, 27 April 1847, ibid., p. 74; Samuel Henshaw & Company to Corcoran & Riggs, 28 April 1847, Box 175, Riggs Family Papers.

65. Cohen, *Business and Politics*, p. 48; Henshaw & Sons to Corcoran & Riggs, 20, 22 April 1847, Box 175, Riggs Family Papers; Matthew Morgan & Company to Corcoran & Riggs, 24 April 1847, ibid.; Samuel Harris & Sons to Corcoran & Riggs, 15 April 1847, ibid.; Charnley & Whelen to Elisha Riggs, 6 August 1847, Box 24, Riggs Family Papers.

66. Report of the Secretary of the Treasury, 1847, pp. 48–54; Matthew Morgan & Company to Corcoran & Riggs, 24 April 1847, Box 175, Riggs Family Papers; Henshaw & Sons to Corcoran & Riggs, 22, 28 April 1847, ibid.; 'Register of Treasury Notes issued on Warrants', E-373, vol. 1, pp. 149–56, RG 56, NARA II; Cohen, *Business and Politics*, p. 48.

67. Cohen, *Business and Politics*, pp. 47–8; *Washington National Intelligencer*, 10 May 1847; *New York Herald*, 2 June 1847; *New York Tribune*, 29 June 1847; Report of the Secretary of the Treasury, 1847, pp. 54–62; E-373, vol. pp. 146–86, RG 53, NARA II; Corcoran & Riggs to Thomas Rogers, 19 April 1847, Box 145, Riggs Family Papers; Corcoran & Riggs to Thomas Reed, 21 April 1847, ibid.

68. Report of the Secretary of the Treasury, 1847, pp. 48–62; E-373, vol. 1, pp. 149–66, RG 53, NARA II.

69. Corcoran & Riggs to Elisha Riggs, 17 June 1847, Box 24, Riggs Family Papers.

70. Treasurer's Weekly Statement, 21 June, 26 July 1847, in *Washington National Intelligencer*, 5 July, 4 August 1847; Corcoran & Riggs to Elisha Riggs, 20 July 1847, Box 24, Riggs Family Papers; Report of the Secretary of the Treasury, 1847, pp. 57–8.

71. Cohen, *Business and Politics*, pp. 48, 257, n. 15; Corcoran & Riggs to Elisha Riggs, 17 July, 7 September 1847, Box 24, Riggs Family Papers.

72. Report of the Secretary of the Treasury, 1847, p. 40; Treasurer's Weekly Statement, 21 September, 25 October, 29 November, 27 December 1847, in *Washington National Intelligencer*, 5 October, 1 November, 4 December 1847, 3 January 1848.

73. *Bankers' Magazine*, 2 (August 1847), p. 75; *Bankers' Magazine*, 2 (September 1847), pp. 199, 202–5; Charnley & Whelen to Elisha Riggs, 6 August 1847, Box 24, Riggs Family Papers; *New York Herald*, 19 September 1847.

74. Report of the Secretary of the Treasury, 1847, pp. 79–83; *Washington Union*, quoted in *Economist*, 5 (2 October 1847), pp. 1132–3; *Economist*, 5 (2 October 1847), pp. 1132–3; *Niles' National Register*, 20 November 1847.

75. Quarterly Treasury Statement, 31 December 1847, 31 March 1848, in *Washington National Intelligencer*, 2 February, 3 May 1848; Quarterly Treasury Statement, 30 Sep-

tember 1847, in Report of the Secretary of the Treasury, 1847, p. 40; Smith, *The War with Mexico*, vol. 2, pp. 151–64.

76. E-373, vol. 1, pp. 162–8, RG 53, NARA II; Winslow & Perkins To Elisha Riggs, 1 September, Box 24, Riggs Family Papers; Corcoran to Elisha Riggs, 7 September 1847, ibid.; Peabody to Corcoran, 18 October 1847, Container 6, Corcoran Papers; Dudley Selden to Corcoran, 8 November 1847, ibid.; Cohen, *Business and Politics*, pp. 60–1, 205, n. 43.

77. Corcoran & Riggs to Elisha Riggs, 12 November 1847, 17, 19, 21 January 1848, Box 24, Riggs Family Papers; Cohen, *Business and Politics*, pp. 49, 257, n. 17.

78. Cohen, *Business and Politics*, pp. 48–9, 257–8, n. 17; Riggs & Levering to Elisha Riggs, 3, 8, 24, 30 September, 23 October, 11 November 1847, 10, 11, 12, 13, 14, 21 January 1848, Box 24, Riggs Family Papers; Larson, 'E. W. Clark and Company', pp. 450–1; J. Cooke, *Memoirs of Jay Cooke*, typescript, Cooke Papers, Baker Library, Harvard University School of Business, Boston, Massachusetts, pp. 29–31.

79. Treasurer's Weekly Statement, 27 December 1847, 24 January 1848, in *Washington National Intelligencer*, 3 January, 3 February 1848; Report of the Secretary of the Treasury, 1848, pp. 55, 72.

80. 'Proposal for a Loan', in *Washington Union*, 26 February 1848.

81. *Bankers' Magazine*, 2 (April 1848), p. 638; *Washington Union*, 8 March 1848; *New York Tribune*, 10 March 1848.

82. *Bankers' Magazine*, 2 (April 1848), p. 638.

83. Ibid.

84. *The Diary of Polk*, vol. 3, pp. 345–53; *New York Tribune*, 24 February 1848; *Bankers' Magazine*, 2 (April 1848), p. 640; *New York Courier and Inquirer*, quoted in *The Times*, 27 March 1848.

85. *Bankers' Magazine*, 2 (April 1848), p. 640; *Washington Union*, 8 March 1848; *New York Courier and Inquirer*, quoted in *The Times*, 27 March 1848; *New York Tribune*, 10 March 1848.

86. Larson, 'E. W. Clark and Company', pp. 429–45, 449–50.

87. Though Jay Cooke clearly claims too large a role for E. W. Clark & Company and himself, they undoubtedly assisted Corcoran & Riggs in selling a portion of the Washington firm's notes. Larson, 'E. W. Clark and Company', pp. 449–50; H. M. Larson, *Jay Cooke, Private Banker* (Cambridge, MA: Harvard University Press, 1936), pp. 68–71; E-373, vol. 1, pp. 175–82, RG 53, NARA II.

88. E-373, vol. 1, pp. 146–86, 269, 271, RG 53, NARA II; ibid., vol. 6, 'Register of Treasury Notes Cancelled, Summary page'.

89. The letters from the register, R. H. Gillet, and his successor, David Graham, to Walker are contained in E-585, 'Folder Related to Bonds and Certificates, 1846–1848.' Acknowledgements start 18 February 1847, RG 53, NARA II.

90. Treasury Notes Outstanding, 1 February 1847, in *Washington National Intelligencer*, 3 February 1847; *US Statutes at Large*, 9 (1847), pp. 118–22; Walker to William Selden and R. H. Gillet, 20 April 1847, E-449, p. 69, RG 53, NARA II; E-374, vol. 50, Reconciliation Sheet, RG 53, NARA II.

91. Walker to Charles Baker, 15 February 1847, E-449, p. 52, RG 53, NARA II; Reconciliation of 19 April 1891, E-374, vol. 50, Reconciliation Sheet, RG 53, NARA II.

5 Mexico's Finances

1. C. Robinson (trans.), *The view from Chapultepec, Mexican Writers on the Mexican American War* (Tucson, AZ: University of Arizona Press, 1989), pp. xx–xxii, xxvi–xxviii; Smith, *The War with Mexico*, vol. 2, p. 253; Wasserman, *Everyday Life and Politics in Nineteenth Century Mexico*, pp. 74, 77, 79; Ramirez, *Mexico during the War with the United States*, p. 83; Tenenbaum, *The Politics of Penury*, pp. xii, 56, 76.

2. Smith, *The War with Mexico*, vol. 1, pp. 157, vol. 2, pp. 253–5, 477, n. 2; Tenenbaum, *The Politics of Penury*, pp. 87, 182; Callcott, *Church and State in Mexico*, pp. 160–1.

3. Tenenbaum, *The Politics of Penury*, pp. 56–7, 182, 87; Callcott, *Church and State in Mexico*, pp. 160–1, 164.

4. Tenenbaum, 'Merchants, Money, and Mischief', p. 320; Tenenbaum, *The Politics of Penury*, pp. xiv, 76; Callcott, *Church and State in Mexico*, pp. 162–7; *Philadelphia Public Ledger*, 26 September 1846.

5. Rives, *The United States and Mexico*, vol. 2, p. 223; Callcott, *Church and State in Mexico*, p. 164; Smith, *The War with Mexico*, vol. 1, p. 214; *New Orleans Weekly Picayune*, 25 May, 8 June 1846; M. P. Costeloe, 'Church–State Financial Negotiations in Mexico during the American War, 1846–1847', *Revista de Historia de America*, 60 (July–December 1965), pp. 91–124, on pp. 92–4.

6. Smith, *The War with Mexico*, vol. 1, pp. 213–18, 223; S. V. Connor and O. B. Faulk, *North America Divided: The Mexican War, 1846–1848* (New York: Oxford University Press, 1971), pp. 140–2; R. Alcaraz et al., *The Other Side or Notes for the History of the War Between Mexico and the United States*, trans. A. C. Ramsey (New York: John Wiley, 1850), in *Western Americana* (New Haven, CT: Research Publications, 1975), microform, reel 5, item 72, p. 82.

7. Smith, *The War with Mexico*, vol. 1, pp. 218–23; *The Diary of Polk*, vol. 1, pp. 227–30, vol. 3, pp. 289–92; Connor and Faulk, *North America Divided*, pp. 141–2; W. H. Callcott, *Santa Anna* (1936; Hamden, CT: Archon Books, 1964), pp. 241–3; Rives, *The United States and Mexico*, vol. 2, pp. 308–10.

8. Rives, *The United States and Mexico*, vol. 2, pp. 309–10; Santoni, *Mexicans at Arms*, p. 166; Alcaraz et al., *The Other Side*, p. 83; *New Orleans Weekly Picayune*, 26 October 1846, 9 November 1846.

9. Santoni, *Mexicans at Arms*, p. 166; Tenenbaum, *The Politics of Penury*, p. 78.

10. Rives, *The United States and Mexico*, vol. 2, pp. 310–11; Callcott, *Church and State in Mexico*, pp. 164–5; Santoni, *Mexicans at Arms*, p. 166; Tenenbaum, *The Politics of Penury*, p. 79; Smith, *The War with Mexico*, vol. 2, p. 7.

11. *Diario de la Marina*, quoted in *New Orleans Weekly Picayune*, 21 December 1846; Tenenbaum, *The Politics of Penury*, pp. 79–81; Rives, *The United States and Mexico*, vol. 2, p. 313; Smith, *The War with Mexico*, vol. 2, p. 7.

12. *Washington Union*, 29 January 1847; Rives, *The United States and Mexico*, vol. 2, p. 314; Smith, *The War with Mexico*, vol. 2, pp. 9–10.

13. *Washington Union*, 29 January 1847.

14. Source: ibid.

15. Rives, *The United States and Mexico*, vol. 2, p. 315; Santoni, *Mexicans at Arms*, pp. 167–8; Callcott, *Santa Anna*, pp. 245–7.

16. Callcott, *Church and State in Mexico*, pp. 183–4; Santoni, *Mexicans at Arms*, pp. 168–72; Rives, *The United States and Mexico*, vol. 2, pp. 315–16.

17. Santoni, *Mexicans at Arms*, pp. 172–3.

18. *Diario del Gobierno de Mexico*, quoted in *New Orleans Weekly Picayune*, 8 February 1847; *Diario del Gobierno de Mexico*, quoted in *New Orleans Picayune*, 3 February 1847; Alcaraz et al., *The Other Side*, p. 150; Santoni, *Mexican at Arms*, p. 173; Rives, *The United States and Mexico*, vol. 2, p. 316.

19. Callcott, *Church and State in Mexico*, pp. 185–7; *New Orleans Picayune*, 3, 24 February 1847; M. P. Costeloe, 'The Mexican Church and the Rebellion of the Polkos', *Hispanic American Historical Review*, 46 (May 1966), pp. 170–8, on pp. 170–3; Rives, *The United States and Mexico*, vol. 2, pp. 316–18; Santoni, *Mexicans at Arms*, pp. 173–5.

20. Rives, *The United States and Mexico*, vol. 2, pp. 318, 320; Callcott, *Church and State in Mexico*, pp. 184–5; McBride, *The Land System of Mexico*, pp. 68–9.

21. *El Republicano Monitor*, quoted in *New Orleans Picayune*, 19 February 1847; *New Orleans Weekly Picayune*, 15 March 1847.

22. Costeloe, 'The Mexican Church and the Rebellion of the Polkos', p. 171; Rives, *The United States and Mexico*, vol. 2, pp. 318–20; Callcott, *Church and State in Mexico*, pp. 188–90: *Diario de la Marina*, quoted in *New Orleans Picayune*, 9 March 1847; *New Orleans Weekly Picayune*, 15 March 1847.

23. Costeloe, 'The Mexican Church and the Rebellion of the Polkos', pp. 171–2; Costeloe, 'Church–State Financial Negotiations', pp. 107–8; Callcott, *Church and State in Mexico*, pp. 191–2; Rives, *The United States and Mexico*, vol. 2, pp. 321–2.

24. Costeloe, 'The Mexican Church and the Rebellion of the Polkos', pp. 171–2; Rives, *The United States and Mexico*, vol. 2, pp. 322–3; Callcott, *Church and State in Mexico*, pp. 191–2; Smith, *The War with Mexico*, vol. 2, pp. 13–14.

25. Costeloe, 'The Mexican Church and the Rebellion of the Polkos', pp. 172–3; Callcott, *Church and State in Mexico*, p. 193; Smith, *The War with Mexico*, vol. 2, pp. 13–15, 25, 32–6; Rives, *The United States and Mexico*, vol. 2, pp. 392–3.

26. Costeloe, 'The Mexican Church and the Rebellion of the Polkos', p. 173; Callcott, *Church and State in Mexico*, pp. 193–4; Rives, *The United States and Mexico*, vol. 2, pp. 392–4; Tenenbaum, *The Politics of Penury*, pp. 80–2; Smith, *The War with Mexico*, vol. 2, pp. 15, 254–5; Rives, Callcott and Smith state the Church promised 2 million pesos for the repeal. The more recent works by Costeloe and Tenenbaum specify 1.5 million.

27. Tenenbaum, *The Politics of Penury*, pp. 80, 82; M. P. Costeloe, *Church Wealth in Mexico: A Study of the Juzgado de Capellanias in the Archbishopric of Mexico City, 1800–1856* (London: Cambridge University Press, 1967), pp. 119–20; Costeloe, 'Church–State Financial Negotiations', p. 108

28. Smith, *The War with Mexico*, vol. 2, pp. 50–9, 254–5, 477, n. 4; Alcaraz et al., *The Other Side*, pp. 238–40.

29. Turlington, *Mexico and Her Foreign Creditors*, pp. 91–4; Tenenbaum, 'Merchants, Money and Mischief', p. 322.

30. Smith, *The War with Mexico*, vol. 2, pp. 174–8, 180–1, 235–6, 254; Callcott, *Church and State in Mexico*, pp. 195–6.

6 Making War Pay

1. Smith, *The War with Mexico*, vol. 2, pp. 264–5; J. H. Smith, 'American Rule in Mexico', *American Historical Review*, 23 (January 1918), pp. 287–302, on pp. 287–8; *The Diary of Polk*, vol. 2, pp. 144–5; James Buchanan to the Mexican Minister of Foreign Relations, 27 July 1846, in *The Works of James Buchanan*, ed. J. B. Moore, 12 vols (Philadelphia, PA: J. B. Lippincott, 1908–11), vol. 7, p. 40; The Mexican Minister of Foreign Relations to

Buchanan, 31 August 1846, in ibid., vol. 7, p. 82; Davies, 'Assessments during the Mexican War', p. 197.

2. *The Diary of Polk*, vol. 2, p. 145; Smith, 'American Rule in Mexico', p. 288.
3. William Marcy to Zachary Taylor, 22 September 1846, in Sundry Reports, 30th Congress, 1st Session, House Executive Document 60, Serial 520, p. 342.
4. Ibid., pp. 341–3; Taylor to Marcy, 26 October 1846, in ibid., pp. 354–5.
5. Treasury Circular, 30 June 1846, in *Merchants' Magazine*, 15 (September 1846), p. 310; ibid., pp. 250–1; Treasury Circular, 16 December 1846, in *New Orleans Picayune*, 2 January 1847.
6. Smith, *The War with Mexico*, vol. 2, pp. 261–2, 483, n. 16; Shenton, *Walker*, p. 94; Tick, 'The Political and Economic Policies of Walker', p. 225; Davies, 'Assessments during the Mexican War', pp. 197–8; Walker to the President, 30 March 1847, in Richardson (ed.), *Messages of the Presidents*, vol. 4, p. 528.
7. *The Diary of Polk*, vol. 2, pp. 420–5, 437–8; Executive Order, 23 March 1847, in Richardson (ed.), *Messages of the Presidents*, vol. 4, pp. 523–4.
8. Walker to the President, 30 March 1847, in Richardson (ed.), *Messages of the Presidents*, pp. 524–9; *Washington National Intelligencer*, 1 April 1847; *The Diary of Polk*, vol. 2, pp. 442–3, 446–7; Polk to the Secretaries of War and of the Navy, 31 March 1847, in Richardson (ed.), *Messages of the Presidents*, vol. 4, pp. 529–30.
9. 'United States Tariff Regulations for Mexican Ports', 30 March 1847, in *Merchants' Magazine*, 16 (May 1847), pp. 497–505; *Washington National Intelligencer*, 1 April 1847.
10. General Order 75, 28 March 1847, in Sundry Reports, 30th Congress, 1st Session, House Executive Document 60, Serial 520, p. 930.
11. Decree of William J. Worth, Governor, 3 April 1847, in ibid., p. 931.
12. General Order 103, 10 April 1847, in ibid.; General Order 108, 12 April 1847, in ibid.; Lieutenant E. P. Scammon to William Marcy, 23 April 1847, in ibid.; Smith, *The War with Mexico*, vol. 2, p. 37.
13. William Marcy to F. M. Dimond, 19 May 1847, Container 81, William Learned Marcy Papers, Manuscript Division, Library of Congress, Washington, DC; Sundry Reports, 30th Congress, 1st Session, House Executive Document 60, Serial 520, p. 933; Sundry Reports, 30th Congress, 2nd Session, House Executive Document 47, Serial 541, p. 7.
14. *Washington National Intelligencer*, 1 April 1847; *New York Herald*, 2 April 1847.
15. *New York Herald*, 2 April 1847.
16. *Washington Union*, 4 May 1847; *Philadelphia Public Ledger*, 8 April 1847.
17. *New York Journal of Commerce*, 3, 26 May 1847; *Washington National Intelligencer*, 22 April, 18 May 1847.
18. *Albany Statesman*, 9 April 1847, quoted in *Washington National Intelligencer*, 14 April 1847; *Washington National Intelligencer*, 19, 22 April 1847.
19. Smith, *The War with Mexico*, vol. 2, p. 38; 'Proclamation to the People of Mexico', 11 April 1847, in Sundry Reports, 30th Congress, 1st Session, House Executive Document 60, Serial 520, p. 937; Marcy to Scott, 3 April 1847, cited in John Y. Mason, Acting Secretary of War, to Scott, 1 September 1847, in ibid., pp. 1005–6.
20. Quoted in Third Annual Message, in Richardson (ed.), *Messages of the Presidents,* vol. 4, p. 547.
21. Mason to Scott, 1 September 1847, in Sundry Reports, 30th Congress, 1st Session, House Executive Document 60, Serial 520, pp. 1005–6; Marcy to Scott, 6 October 1847, in ibid., pp. 1006–7; Third Annual Message, in Richardson (ed.), *Messages of the Presidents*, vol. 4, pp. 547–9.

22. *The Diary of Polk*, vol. 3, p. 56; *Merchants' Magazine*, 16 (May 1847), pp. 497–505; ibid., 17 (July 1847), p. 95; Walker to the President, 10 June 1847, in Richardson (ed.), *Messages of the Presidents*, vol. 4, p. 530; Walker to the President, 5 November 1847, in ibid., pp. 531–2; *The Diary of Polk*, vol. 3, pp. 221–3; Davies, 'Assessments during the Mexican War', p. 199.

23. *Niles' National Register*, 14 August 1847; Smith, *The War with Mexico*, vol. 2, pp. 262–3; Third Annual Message, in Richardson (ed.), *Messages of the Presidents*, vol. 4, pp. 548–9; Shenton, *Walker*, pp. 94–5; Report of the Secretary of the Treasury, 1847, pp. 4–6; Secretary of War Report, 3 December 1847, in *Congressional Globe*, 30th Congress, 1st Session, Appendix, pp. 20–1; Schedule of Mexican Tariff Collection, 31 December 1847, reel 51, Polk Papers.

24. Davies, 'Assessments during the Mexican War', pp. 198–9; D. E. Berge, 'A Mexican Dilemma: The Mexico City *Ayuntamiento* and the Question of Loyalty, 1846–1848', *Hispanic American Historical Review*, 50 (May 1970), pp. 229–56, on p. 240; C. W. Elliott, *Winfield Scott: The Soldier and the Man* (New York: Macmillan, 1937), pp. 652–3; Smith, *The War with Mexico*, vol. 2, pp. 265, 486, n. 22.

25. Marcy to Scott, 14 December 1847, in Sundry Reports, 30th Congress, 1st Session, House Executive Document 60, Series, 520, pp. 1037–8.

26. Scott to Marcy, 27 November, 17, 25 December 1847, in ibid., pp. 932–3, 1046–7, 1048; General Order 376, 15 December 1847, in ibid., pp. 1050–1; General Order 395, 31 December 1847, in ibid., pp. 1063–7; Davies, 'Assessments during the Mexican War', pp. 199–205; Smith, *The War with Mexico*, vol. 2, pp. 265–6.

27. Berge, 'A Mexican Dilemma', p. 251; Smith, *The War with Mexico*, vol. 2, pp. 188, 252, 265–6, 438, n. 32; *New York Herald*, 1 August 1848.

28. Sundry Reports, 30th Congress, 2nd Session, House Report 119, Serial 545, pp. 1–7.

29. Ibid., p. 7.

30. Ibid., pp. 24–7, 36–7.

31. *Congressional Globe*, 30th Congress, 2nd Session, pp. 635, 639, 694, 695; *US Statutes at Large*, 9 (1849), pp. 412–14; Sundry Reports, 30th Congress, 2nd Session, House Report 119, Serial 545, p. 7.

32. Sundry Reports, 30th Congress, 2nd Session, House Executive Document 47, Serial 541, pp. 7–13, 14–15, 109–11; Smith, *The War with Mexico*, vol. 2, pp. 266, 486–8, nn. 22–4.

33. Source: Sundry Reports, 30th Congress, 2nd Session, House Executive Document 47, Serial 541, pp. 7–15, 109–11.

34. Ibid., pp. 7–15, 112–14; Sundry Reports, 34th Congress, 3rd Session, Senate Executive Document 34, Serial 880, pp. 35–9; Smith, *The War with Mexico*, vol. 2, p. 488, n. 24.

35. Sundry Reports, 34th Congress, 3rd Session, Senate Executive Document 34, Serial 880, pp. 37–9; Memorandum for Captain Lay from Scott, in ibid., pp. 40–3; Scott to Third Auditor, 28 November 1854, in ibid., p. 50.

36. General Winfield Scott was the Whig candidate for president in 1852. He did not resign his position as commander-in-chief of the army. Elliott, *Scott*, pp. 652–3; T. D. Johnson, *Winfield Scott: The Quest for Military Glory* (Lawrence, KS: University Press of Kansas, 1998), p. 216; Jefferson Davis to Winfield Scott, 11 May 1853, in *Jefferson Davis, Constitutionalist: His Letters, Papers and* Speeches, ed. D. Rowland, 10 vols (Jackson, MS: Mississippi Department of Archives and History, 1923), vol. 2, p. 221; Scott to Davis, 28 May 1853, in ibid., vol. 2, pp. 228–9; Scott to Davis, 17 July 1855, in ibid., vol. 2, p. 473.

37. Davis to the President, 25 November 1854, in Sundry Reports, 34th Congress, 3rd Session, Senate Executive Document 34, Serial 880, pp. 39–40; Scott to the President, 9 February 1855, in ibid., pp. 43–4; Franklin Pierce to Davis, 3 November 1855, 12 November 1855, 19 December 1856, in ibid., pp. 44 45, 53; Davis to the President, 14 November 1856, in ibid., p. 45; Third Auditor to Davis, 12 December 1855, in ibid., p. 47; Memorandum Rejecting General Scott's Account, in ibid., p. 46; Third Auditor to Scott, 5 December 1855, in ibid., pp. 49–50; Third Auditor to Davis, in ibid., p. 51; Elliott, *Scott*, pp. 653–5.

7 The Independent Treasury at War

1. Kinley, *The Independent Treasury*, pp. 60–2; Tick, 'The Political and Economic Policies of Walker', pp. 196–7, 204; Holt, *The Rise and Fall of the American Whig Party*, pp. 234, 246–7.
2. Independent Treasury Act, 6 August 1846, in Report of the Secretary of the Treasury, 1846, pp. 39–46; *US Statutes at Large*, 9 (1846), pp. 59–66; Robert J. Walker to William C. Bouck, Assistant Treasurer, New York, 31 August 1846, E-49, 'Sub Treasury System', 15 vols, vol. 2, pp. 9–10, RG 56, NARA II.
3. Independent Treasury Act, in Report of the Secretary of the Treasury, 1846, pp. 40–1; 'Notice to Collecting, Receiving, and Disbursing Officers of the United States', 25 August 1846, in ibid., pp. 32–4.
4. Walker to Receivers of Public Money, Arkansas, Ohio, Indiana, Alabama, et al., 28 September 1846, E-49, vol. 2, pp. 25–31, RG 56, NARA II; Report of the Secretary of the Treasury, 4 December 1854, 33rd Congress, 2nd Session, Senate Executive Document 2, Serial 749, p. 256; 'Circular to Collector of Customs, Buffalo Creek, et al', 15 September 1846, in ibid., 1846, p. 35.
5. Walker to Receiver of Public Money, Arkansas, et al, 28 September 1846, E-49, vol. 2, pp. 25–31, RG 56, NARA II; 'Notice to Collecting, Receiving, and Disbursing Officers of the United States', in Report of the Secretary of the Treasury, 1846, pp. 32–4.
6. Report of the Secretary of the Treasury, 1850, pp. 3–4; Walker to the Collector of Customs, Norfolk, Virginia, 4 September 1846, E-49, vol. 2, pp. 11–12, RG 56, NARA II; Audit of Port of Newburyport, Massachusetts, 30 October 1847, E-117, (Microfilm), 'Letters Received by the Secretary of the Treasury Relating to the Sub Treasury' ('U' series), reel 3, item 181, RG 56, NARA II.
7. Walker to Cornelius W. Lawrence, Collector of Customs, New York, et al., 19 August 1846, E-49, vol. 2, pp. 5–6, RG 56, NARA II; Walker to Henry Hubbard, Assistant Treasurer, Boston, et al., 7 September 1846, ibid., p. 13; Walker to Bouck, 3 November 1847, ibid., pp. 39–40; McClintock Young, Acting Secretary of the Treasury to George Penn, Assistant Treasurer, St Louis, 24 August 1847, ibid., p. 95; Walker to Penn, 25 September 1847, ibid., p. 104; Cornelius Lawrence to Walker, 20 August 1846, E-117, reel 1, item 3, RG 56, NARA II; Bouck to Walker, 19 December 1846, ibid., reel 1, item 5; Thomas Watson to Walker, 3 May 1847, ibid., reel 2, item 301.
8. William Gouge, 'Report on the Public Depositaries', 27 November 1854, in Report of the Secretary of the Treasury, 1854, pp. 256–8; Audit of Surveyor of Customs, Cincinnati, 24 February 1848, E-117, reel 3, item 115, RG 56, NARA II; Collector of Customs, Newburyport, Massachusetts to William Meredith, Secretary of the Treasury, 2 October 1849, ibid., reel 3, item 184; Kinley, *The Independent Treasury*, pp. 56–8.

9. Circular to Each Collector, et al., 15 September 1846, in Report of the Secretary of the Treasury, 1846, p. 36; Independent Treasury Act, in ibid., p. 43; Walker to John R. McMurdo, Assistant Treasurer, New Orleans, 18 May 1847, E-49, vol. 2, p. 73, RG 56, NARA II; Walker to Bouck, 19 October 1847, in ibid., p. 110; Walker to Conway Whittle, Collector, Norfolk, Virginia, 4 September 1846, in ibid., pp. 11–12; Walker to Samuel Lincoln, Receiver, Little Rock, 25 February 1847, in ibid., pp. 58–9; Walker to John Anderson, Collector, Portland, Maine, 4 September 1846, in ibid., pp. 12–13.

10. Circular to Each Collector, et al., 15 September 1846, in Report of the Secretary of the Treasury, 1846, pp. 35–6; Independent Treasury Act, in ibid., pp. 43–4.

11. Circular to Each Collector, et al., 15 September 1846, in ibid., pp. 35–6.

12. Independent Treasury Act, in ibid., p. 45; Walker to Hubbard, 23 October 1846, E-49, vol. 2, pp. 35–6, RG 56, NARA II; Circular to Each Collector, 15 September 1846, in Report of the Secretary of the Treasury, 1846, p. 37.

13. Walker to William Laval, Assistant Treasurer, Charleston, 23 April 1847, E-49, vol. 2, p. 69, RG 56, NARA II; Walker to D. G. Bright, Receiver of Public Money and Depositary, Jeffersonville, Indiana, 11 May 1847, ibid., p. 70; Walker to Bright, 31 May 1847, ibid., pp. 75–6; Walker to Bright, 9 July 1847, ibid., p. 82.

14. M. Young, Acting Secretary of the Treasury to Patrick Collins, Surveyor of Customs, Cincinnati, 28 February 1848, E-117, reel 3, item 121, RG 56, NARA II; Collins to Young, 3 March 1848, ibid., item 122; Young to Receiver of Public Money, Chillicothe, Upper Sandusky, and Fort Wayne, 8 March 1848, ibid., item 125; John Hough, Receiver, Chillicothe, to Young, 14 March 1848, ibid., item 126; Hough to Senator William Allen, 14 March 1848, ibid., item 129; Receiver, Upper Sandusky to Walker, 18 March 1848, ibid., item 132; Receiver, Fort Wayne to Walker, 20 March 1848, ibid., item 133.

15. *Charleston Courier*, quoted in *New Orleans Weekly Picayune*, 18 January 1847; *Philadelphia Public Ledger*, 5 January 1847; Tick, 'The Political and Economic Policies of Walker', p. 197; *Washington National Intelligencer*, 20 January 1847; *Merchants' Magazine*, 16 (February 1847), pp. 184–5; *New York Journal of Commerce*, 13 January 1847.

16. Public Notice of 4 February 1847, Treasury Department, in *Washington National Intelligencer*, 6 February 1847; Treasurer's Weekly Statement, 26 July, 30 August, 20 September, 25 October, 29 November 1847, in *Washington National Intelligencer*, 4 August, 3 September, 5 October, 1 November, 4 December 1847; Shenton, *Walker*, pp. 71–2.

17. Report of the Secretary of the Treasury, 1848, p. 25; Kinley, *The Independent Treasury*, pp. 60–2.

18. Certificate of Deposit issued to James G. Holmes, Cashier of the Southwestern Railroad Bank, Charleston, 2 August 1847, E-117, reel 1, item 20, RG 56, NARA II; Circular for Each Collector, et al., 15 September 1846, Report of the Secretary of the Treasury, 1846, pp. 36, 39.

19. Walker to Bouck, 6 November 1846, E-49, vol. 2, p. 41, RG 56, NARA II; Walker to Hubbard, 7 November 1846, ibid.

20. Walker to Bouck, et al., 15 February 1847, ibid., pp. 56–7; Walker to Bouck, et al., 29 March 1847, ibid., pp. 63–5; M. Young, Acting Secretary of the Treasury to J. Ross Snowden, Assistant Treasurer, Philadelphia, 18 October 1847, ibid., p. 109.

21. Walker to Bouck, et al., 26 June 1848, ibid., pp. 158–60; Walker to Snowden, 4 August 1848, ibid., pp. 169–70; M. Young, Acting Secretary of the Treasury to Snowden, 31 March 1847, ibid., p. 123.

22. Cohen, *Business and Politics*, pp. 37–8; Walker to Bouck, et al., 30 June 1848, E-49, vol. 2, pp. 158–60, RG 56, NARA II; George Newbold to Corcoran, 27, 28 June 1848, Box

135, Riggs Family Papers; Not all of the interest was claimed. Seven months after the 1 July 1848 payment date, $975 on the 1846 loan and $2,288 on the loan of 1847 to be paid in New York remained unclaimed. Register to Assistant Treasurer, New York, Report Regarding Unclaimed Interest, 1 February 1849, E-539, RG 56, NARA II.

23. Newbold to Corcoran, 1 July 1848, Box 135, Riggs Family Papers; 'Interest Payable for the Half Year Ending December 31, 1848, in New York on Loan of 1847', E-539, RG 53, NARA II; Walker to Bouck, 26 June 1848, E-49, vol. 2, p. 158, RG 56, NARA II.

24. Newbold to Corcoran, 1 July 1848, Box 135, Riggs Family Papers; Walker to Snowden, 10 July 1848, E-49, vol. 2, p. 167, RG 56, NARA II; William Meredith, Secretary of the Treasury to George P. Kane, Collector and Depositary, Baltimore, 11 January 1850, Ibid., p. 249; Cohen, *Business and Politics*, pp. 37–8.

25. Tick, 'The Political and Economic Policies of Walker', pp. 227–9; Myers, *The New York Money Market*, vol. 1, pp. 184–5; Kinley, *The Independent Treasury*, pp. 64–5; *Bankers' Magazine*, 1 (December 1846), p. 453; Report of the Secretary of the Treasury, 7 December 1853, 33rd Congress, 1st Session, Senate Executive Document 2, Serial 694, p. 13; ibid., 1846, pp. 6–7; Sundry Reports, 33rd Congress, 1st Session, House Executive Document 42, Serial 721, pp. 1–2.

26. *New York Journal of Commerce*, 5 February 1847, 7 May 1847; Sundry Reports, 29th Congress, 2nd Session, Senate Executive Document 111, Serial 495, pp. 1–3; *New York Tribune*, July 15 1847, 6 August 1847.

27. *The Diary of Polk*, vol. 3, p. 144; Sundry Reports, 29th Congress, 2nd Session, Senate Executive Document 111, Serial 495, p. 3; General Order 103, in Sundry Reports, 30th Congress, 1st Session, House Executive Document 60, Serial 520, p. 939; Cohen, *Business and Politics*, pp. 38–9; Tick, 'The Political and Economic Policies of Walker', pp. 227–9; Myers, *The New York Money Market*, vol. 1, pp. 184–5.

28. Marcy to Walker, 13 April 1847, reel 49, item 8758, Polk Papers; *The Diary of Polk*, vol. 3, pp. 144, 146–7; Sundry Reports, 29th Congress, 2nd Session, Senate Executive Document 111, Serial 495, pp. 2–3; Walker to Bouck, 24 November 1846, E-49, vol. 2, p. 48, RG 56, NARA II; Report of the Secretary of the Treasury, 1847, p. 65; Treasurer's Weekly Statement, 30 April 1847, in *Washington National Intelligencer*, 3 May 1847.

29. Cohen, 'Business and Politics', pp. 100–1; Cohen, *Business and Politics*, p. 253, n. 29; M. Young to Corcoran, 22 April 1847, Box 135, Riggs Family Papers; Receipt for $1,000,000, E-82, vol. 32, item 356, RG 56, NARA II; Corning & Company to Corcoran & Riggs, 16, 20, 23 April 1847, Box 175, Riggs Family Papers; M. Morgan to Corcoran & Riggs, 24 April 1847, ibid.

30. *New Orleans Bulletin*, 5, 19 May 1847, quoted in *Washington Union*, 17, 31 May 1847; *New York Journal of Commerce*, 28 May 1847; *New York Journal of Commerce*, quoted in *Washington National Intelligencer*, 26 June 1847.

31. *Washington Union*, 31 May 1847.

32. M. Morgan to Corcoran, 22 May 1847, Box 135, Riggs Family Papers.

33. Corcoran & Riggs to Walker, 9 June 1847, E-82, vol. 32, item 394, RG 56, NARA II; *The Diary of Polk*, vol. 3, pp. 140–1.

34. *The Diary of Polk*, vol. 3, pp. 124, 131–4, 136–9, 140–1, 143–6, 149–51; M. Young to the President, 26, 27 August 1847, reel 51, Polk Papers.

35. Walker to M. Young, Acting Secretary of the Treasury, 23 August 1847, reel 51, Polk Papers; New Orleans Canal and Banking Company to Corcoran, 23 December 1847, Box 135, Riggs Family Papers.

36. Walker to Snowden, 3 June 1847, E-49, vol. 2, pp. 76, RG 56, NARA II; Walker to Bouck, 3 June 1847, ibid., pp. 76–7; Benjamin Marshall to M. Young, 9 June 1847, E-117, reel 2, item 254, RG 56, NARA II; Report of the Secretary of the Treasury, 1847, p. 65; Lewis Jones to Walker, 16 June 1847, E-117, reel 2, item 255, RG 56, NARA II; Receipt from Adams & Company, 16 June 1847, ibid., item 256.

37. M. Young to Bouck, 19 June 1847, E-49, vol. 2, p. 79, RG 56, NARA II; Young to Laval, 6 August 1847, ibid., pp. 90–1; Young to McMurdo, 11 December 1847, ibid., p. 120; Young to Bouck, 31 December 1847, ibid., p. 121; Young to Laval, 22 February 1848, ibid., p. 136; Young to McMurdo, 10 January, 28 April 1848, E-44, vol. 2, pp. 110, 121, RG 53, NARA II; Walker to McMurdo, 15 February, 15 March, 15 April 1848, ibid., pp. 111, 113, 119.

38. Cohen, *Business and Politics*, p. 64; August Belmont to Walker, 2 July 1847, E-119, Letters Received from Foreign Bankers, Box 2, 1847–1856, RG 56, NARA II.

39. Belmont to Walker, 3 August, 25 October 1847, 11 January, 1 March 1848, E-119, Box 2, RG 56, NARA II; Marcy to Scott, 6 August 1847, in Sundry Reports, 30th Congress, 1st Session, House Executive Document 60, Serial 520, p. 1004.

40. Belmont to Walker, 22 January 1848, E-119, Box 2, item 12, RG 56, NARA II; Memorandum of Understanding, 24 January 1848, ibid., item 13; Belmont to Walker, 3 May 1848, ibid., item 19; Davidson to Walker, 9 May 1848, ibid., item 23; Belmont to Walker, 31 May, 3 June, 14 June 1848, ibid., items, 25, 27, 28. The first $200,000 in treasury notes was part of the private sales made before the third contract was let.

41. M. Young to Belmont, 29 March 1848, ibid., item 15; Davidson To Belmont, 9 May 1848, ibid., item 23; Schedule of Payments, Adam Stewart, Paymaster, 13 June 1848, ibid., item 29; Nathan Clifford to James Buchanan, 2 July 1848, ibid., item 68; Belmont to Walker, 18 October1848, ibid., item 31.

42. Walker to the Director of the Mint, Philadelphia, 2 March 1847, 3 November 1847, E-49, vol. 2, pp. 60, 112, RG 56, NARA II; Walker to Bouck, 24 September 1847, ibid., p. 103; Bouck to Walker, 6 November 1847, E-117, reel 1, item 44, RG 56, NARA II.

43. William Meredith to John Kinzer, Receiver, Chicago, 18 July 1850, E-49, vol. 2, p. 270, RG 56, NARA II; Walker to J. Kearsley, Receiver, Detroit, 13 October 1848, ibid., pp. 184–5; Patrick Collins, Surveyor of Customs, Cincinnati, to M. Young, 3 March 1848, E-117, reel 3, item 122, RG 56, NARA II; John Hough, Receiver, Chillicothe, to William Allen, 14 March 1848, ibid., item 129.

44. Report of the Secretary of the Treasury, 1847, pp. 12–13; ibid., 1848, pp. 24–5; Tick, 'The Political and Economic Policies of Walker', pp. 202–6.

45. *Merchants' Magazine*, 18 (February 1848), pp. 181–3.

46. *Washington Union*, quoted in the *New York Journal of Commerce*, 31 August 1847; Report of the Secretary of the Treasury, 1854, p. 262; Tick, 'The Political and Economic Policies of Walker', pp. 227–9

47. Report of the Secretary of the Treasury, 1854, pp. 259–60; Kinley, *The Independent Treasury*, pp. 60–3.

48. Bray Hammond argues that the Independent Treasury was an ineffective product of a bygone agrarian era. He believes it stunted federal power and failed to provide monetary protection to the citizenry. The only beneficiaries to the system were gold handlers and speculators. Hammond, *Sovereignty and an Empty Purse*, pp. 22–3; Margaret Myers echoes Hammond's conclusions and considers the Independent Treasury the fruit of an outworn theory of government. Myers's primary objection was the loss of government interest in the economic well-being of the populace as it attempted to separate itself from

the nation's banks. The Independent Treasury protected the government's 'welfare at the expense of the whole'. Myers, *The New York Money Market*, vol. 1, p. 199.

8 The Loan of 1848

1. *Congressional Globe*, 30th Congress, 1st Session, pp. 373–4; Silbey, *Shrine of Party*, pp. 22, 183–8; *The Diary of Polk*, vol. 3, pp. 214–15, 240; Cohen, 'Business and Politics', pp. 103, 105–6; R. W. Hidy, *The House of Barings in American Trade and Finance: English Merchant Bankers at Work, 1763–1861* (Cambridge, MA: Harvard University Press, 1949), pp. 388–9; Hidy, *Peabody*, p. 299.
2. *The Diary of Polk*, vol. 3, pp. 215–17; Cohen, *Business and Politics*, pp. 49–50.
3. *The Diary of Polk*, vol. 3, pp. 213, 218, 221–2.
4. Richardson (ed.), *Messages of the Presidents*, vol. 4, pp. 532–3, 537–9, 553–5.
5. Report of the Secretary of the Treasury, 1847, pp. 2–7. Experience had shown that a $3 million reserve instead of $4 million would suffice. Ibid., p. 3.
6. Thomas Ward to Baring Brothers, 18 January 1848, reel C-1375, BPOC; *Niles' National Register*, 12 February 1848.
7. Silbey, *Shrine of Party*, pp. 22, 183–8, 253, n. 34; *The Diary of Polk*, vol. 3, p. 240.
8. Report of the Secretary of the Treasury, 1847, p. 83; ibid., 1848, pp. 55, 72; *Bankers' Magazine*, 2 (January 1848), pp. 453–6; *New York Journal of Commerce*, quoted in *Washington National Intelligencer*, 12, 8 January 1848; *Niles' National Register*, 15 January 1848; *New York Journal of Commerce*, 22 January 1848; Joshua Bates to Thomas Ward, 10 March 1848, Box 12, Thomas Wren Ward Papers, Massachusetts Historical Society, Boston, Massachusetts; George Peabody to Corcoran & Riggs, 3 December 1847, Letterbook 7, Peabody Papers; Peabody to Corcoran & Riggs, 10 March 1848, Letterbook 8, Peabody Papers; Corcoran & Riggs to Peabody, 22 March 1848, Box 12, Peabody Papers.
9. Report of the Secretary of the Treasury, 1847, pp. 2–3, 40, 45; *Congressional Globe*, 30th Congress, 1st Session, p. 312; The Treasury reported sales of 1846 treasury notes, $150,000, 1846 bonds, $111,000, 1847 treasury notes, $4,225,800, and 1847 bonds of $2,328,728 totalling $6,915,078 on its quarterly report for the period July–September 1847. Henry Cohen speculates that the error was made on purpose in an effort to increase the amount needed. If so, it was a very poor effort since the information to discover the error was clearly available in the secretary's report of 9 December 1847; Cohen, *Business and Politics*, pp. 50–1; Cohen, 'Business and Politics', pp. 104–5.
10. *New York Herald*, 31 January 1848; McClintock Young to George M. Dallas, Vice-President and Secretary of the Senate, 19 January 1848, in *NASP*, vol. 9, pp. 291–4; *Congressional Globe*, 30th Congress, 1st Session, p. 312.
11. *The Diary of Polk*, vol. 3, pp. 312–13; *New York Tribune*, 31 January 1848; *Washington Union*, 1, 2, 3, 4 February 1848.
12. *Congressional Globe*, 30th Congress, 1st Session, pp. 312–15, 322–7, 331–6, 344–8, 351–60, 363–73, Appendix, pp. 289–93, 297–302, 316–21, 325–37.
13. Abraham Lincoln to William Herndon, 1 February 1848, in *The Collected Works of Abraham Lincoln*, vol. 1, p. 447.
14. Lincoln to Herndon, 1, 15 February, 22 June 1848, in ibid., vol. 1, pp. 446–8, 451–2, 492.
15. *Congressional Globe*, 30th Congress, 1st Session, pp. 373–4; *US Statutes at Large*, 9 (1848), pp. 217–19; *Niles' National Register*, 19 February 1848.

16. *The Diary of Polk*, vol. 3, pp. 346–51, 368–9, 377–9; Calhoun to Albert Gallatin, 13 March 1848, in *The Papers of Calhoun*, vol. 25, pp. 232–3; editors' note, in ibid., p 161; Bergeron, *The Presidency of Polk*, pp. 104–6.
17. Senator C. G. Atherton, Chairman of the Senate Finance Committee, to David Graham, Register of the Treasury, 25 February 1848, E-82, item 157, RG 56, NARA II; *Congressional Globe*, 30th Congress, 1st Session, Appendix, pp. 412, 415; *New York Tribune*, 17 March 1848.
18. *New York Tribune*, 17 March 1848; Shenton, *Walker*, pp. 114–15; *Congressional Globe*, 30th Congress, 1st Session, pp. 526–7, 530–5, 549, Appendix, pp. 411–15, 472–3.
19. *The Diary of Polk*, vol. 3, p. 420; Treasurer's Weekly Statement, 21 February, 27 March 1848, in *Washington National Intelligencer*, 2 March, 3 April 1848.
20. Hidy, *The House of Baring*, pp. 382–6; Peabody to Corcoran & Riggs, 28 January 1848, Letterbook 7, Peabody Papers; Peabody to Corcoran & Riggs, 10 March, 7 April 1848, Letterbook 8, Peabody Papers; Hidy, *Peabody*, pp. 285–9; Cohen, *Business and Politics*, pp. 49–51; Thomas Ward to Baring Brothers, 30 April, 2 May 1848, reel C-1390, BPOC.
21. 'Proposal for a Loan', Treasury Department, 17 April 1848, printed in *Bankers' Magazine*, 2 (May 1848), p. 702. The winding down of the war and a reduction of the need to transfer funds to New Orleans and Mexico allowed Walker and his successor, William Meredith, to relax the requirement to deposit with the assistant treasurer nearest the bidder's residence. Corcoran & Riggs, and others, began to deposit all over the country to take advantage of exchange rates. Report of the Secretary of the Treasury, 1849, pp. 662–96.
22. Shenton, *Walker*, pp. 114–15; Cohen, *Business and Politics*, pp. 51–2; Tick, 'The Political and Economic Policies of Walker', pp. 206–7, 209–10; Hidy, *Peabody*, pp. 289–90; Peabody to Corcoran & Riggs, 14 April, 7 July 1848, Letterbook 8, Peabody Papers; Corcoran & Riggs to Peabody, 19 June 1848, Box 12, Folder 4, Peabody Papers; Elisha Riggs to Peabody, 18 June 1848, Box 40, Folder 4, Peabody Papers.
23. James G. King to Baring Brothers, 9 March, 2 May 1848, reel C-1408, BPOC; King to Thomas Ward, 3 June 1848, reel C-1390, BPOC; Ward to Baring Brothers, 5, 10, 12 June 1848, ibid.; Hidy, *The House of Baring*, pp. 383, 386.
24. King to Ward, 3 June 1848, reel C-1390, BPOC; Ward to Baring Brothers, 5, 10, 12, 13 June 1848, ibid.; Ward and King to Corcoran, 16 June 1848, ibid.; Corcoran to Ward, 16 June 1848, ibid.
25. Cohen, *Business and Politics*, pp. 259–60, n. 24; Bank of Commerce to Corcoran & Riggs, 14 June 1848, Box 135, Riggs Family Papers; John Ward to Corcoran & Riggs, 16 June 1848, ibid.; James Robb to Corcoran & Riggs, 6 June 1848, Box 192, Riggs Family Papers; Corcoran to Thomas Ward, 17 June 1848, reel C-1390, BPOC.
26. King to Corcoran, 16 June 1848, Box 135, Riggs Family Papers; Corcoran to Thomas Ward, 16 June 1848, reel C-1416, BPOC; Newbold to Corcoran, 16 June 1848, Box 135, Riggs Family Papers; Cohen, *Business and Politics*, p. 52.
27. Cohen, 'Business and Politics', pp. 109–10; Cohen, *Business and Politics*, p. 53; Report of the Secretary of the Treasury, 1848, pp. 56–63; Corcoran to Ward, 17 June 1848, reel C-1390, BPOC.
28. *Washington Union*, 18 June 1848; Report of the Secretary of the Treasury, 1848, p. 56; Walker to Corcoran & Riggs, 19 June 1848, Box 192, Riggs Family Papers.
29. *Washington Union*, 18 June 1848.
30. Ibid.; *United States Magazine*, 23 (July 1848), pp. 78–9.

31. *Washington National Intelligencer*, 19 June 1848; *New York Tribune*, 19, 20 June 1848.
32. Corcoran to Thomas Ward, 17 June 1848, reel C-1390, BPOC; Corcoran to James G. King, 17 June 1848, ibid.
33. Corcoran to Ward, 17 June 1848, ibid.
34. Ibid.; Ward to Baring Brothers, 19 June 1848, ibid.
35. Cohen, *Business and Politics*, pp. 52, 259–60, n. 24; L. S. Suarez to Corcoran & Riggs, 15 June 1848, Box 192, Riggs Family Papers; William Redmond to Corcoran & Riggs, 14 June 1848, Box 24, Riggs Family Papers; Elisha Riggs to Peabody, 18, 27 June 1848, Box 40, Folder 4, Peabody Papers; John Cryder to Peabody, 20 June 1848, Box 15, Folder 5, Peabody Papers.
36. Larson, 'E. W. Clark and Company', pp. 449–51; Report of the Secretary of the Treasury, 1848, pp. 56–8; Cooke, *Memoirs of Jay Cooke*, pp. 29–31.
37. Hidy, *The House of Baring*, pp. 386–7; R. W. Hidy, 'A Leaf from Investment History', *Harvard Business Review*, 20 (Autumn 1941), pp. 65–74, on p. 68; Ward to Corcoran, 29 June 1848, Box 135, Riggs Family Papers.
38. Corcoran to Thomas Ward, 29, 30 June, ibid.; Corcoran to Ward, 1 July 1848, reel C-1390, BPOC; Ward to Baring Brothers, 3, 4, 14, 25, 31 July, 9, 22 August, 9 September 1848, ibid.
39. Hidy, 'A Leaf from Investment History', pp. 68–9; Hidy, *The House of Baring*, pp. 386–7; Cohen, 'Business and Politics', pp. 112–13.
40. *Bankers' Magazine*, 3 (March 1849), p. 572; *Merchants' Magazine*, 15 (August 1846), p. 217.
41. *US Statutes at Large*, 1 (1792), p. 248; ibid., 4 (1834), pp. 700–1; ibid., 5 (1842), p. 496; ibid., 5 (1843), p. 607; *Merchants' Magazine*, 15 (July 1846), p. 100; *New York Herald*, 3 September 1848; L. E. Davis and J. R. T. Hughes, 'A Dollar–Sterling Exchange, 1803–1895', *Economic History Review*, 13 (August 1960), pp. 52–78, on p. 55; *Congressional Globe*, 27th Congress, 3rd Session, pp. 112–13.
42. Davis and Hughes, 'A Dollar–Sterling Exchange', pp. 52–5, 61; *Bankers' Magazine*, 3 (March 1849), p. 572; *Merchants' Magazine*, 15 (August 1846), p. 217; ibid., 15 (July 1846), p. 100: ibid., 16 (January 1847), p. 91; Perkins, *Financing Anglo-American Trade*, pp. 183–4; Hidy, *The House of Baring*, p. 387.
43. Ward to Baring Brothers, 3 July 1848, reel C-1390, BPOC; Corcoran & Riggs to Peabody, 8, 22 July 1848, Box 12, Folder 4, Peabody Papers; *Bankers' Magazine*, 3 (September 1848), p. 200; *New York Herald*, 10, 12 July 1848; *New York Tribune*, 19 July 1848; *Merchants' Magazine*, 19 (August 1848), pp. 189–90; Cohen, 'Business and Politics', p. 111.
44. Corcoran & Riggs to Peabody, 19, 20 June, 3 July 1848, Box 12, Folder 4, Peabody Papers; Elisha Riggs to Peabody, 18 June, 16 August 1848, Box 40, Folder 4, Peabody Papers; Peabody to Corcoran & Riggs, 7 July 1848, Letterbook 8, Peabody Papers; Peabody to Corcoran & Riggs, 29 September 1848, Letterbook 9, Peabody Papers; Hidy, *Peabody*, pp. 289–91.
45. Peabody to Elisha Riggs, 14, 21 July 1848, Letterbook 8, Peabody Papers; Peabody to Corcoran & Riggs, 21, 28 July, 11, 25 August 1848, Letterbook 9, Peabody Papers; Corcoran & Riggs to Peabody, 26 July 1848, Box 12, Folder 4, Peabody Papers; Peabody to W. W. Corcoran and Elisha Riggs, 26 January 1849, Box 25, Riggs Family Papers; Peabody to Corcoran & Riggs, 29 September 1848, Letterbook 9, Peabody Papers; Hidy, *Peabody*, pp. 292–3.

46. Peabody to Corcoran & Riggs, 14 July 1848, Letterbook 8, Peabody Papers; Cohen, 'Business and Politics', p. 112; Cohen, *Business and Politics*, p. 263, n. 34.

47. Report of the Secretary of the Treasury, 1849, pp. 662–96; Larson, *Jay Cooke*, pp. 69–71; Larson, 'E. W. Clark and Company', pp. 449–57; Cooke, *Memoirs of Jay Cooke*, pp. 30–1; Redlich, *The Molding of American Banking*, vol. 2, p. 350.

48. Cohen, *Business and Politics*, pp. 53, 259–60, n. 24; Report of the Secretary of the Treasury, 1849, pp. 662–6, 677–90; Cohen, 'Business and Politics', p. 110.

49. Cohen, 'Business and Politics', pp. 111–12; *New York Herald*, 1, 2, 10 July 1848; *New York Tribune*, 17, 19 July 1848; *Merchants' Magazine*, 19 (August 1848), pp. 188–9; *Bankers' Magazine*, 3 (September 1848), p. 200.

50. Cammann & Whitehouse to Elisha Riggs, 11 August 1848, Box 36, Riggs Family Papers; Account Current – Winslow & Perkins with Corcoran & Riggs, 7 September 1848, Box 198, Riggs Family Papers; Accounts Current – Charnley & Whelen with Corcoran & Riggs, 1 September 1848, Box 197, Riggs Family Papers; *New York Tribune*, 2, 12, 13 August, 1, 3, 22 September 1848.

51. John Davis to Corcoran, 10 October, 7 December 1848, Container 6, Corcoran Papers; Abbott Lawrence to Corcoran, 27 July 1848, ibid.; Thomas Ward to Corcoran, 27, 28 July 1848, ibid.; Cohen, 'Business and Politics', p. 116.

52. Report of the Secretary of the Treasury, 1848, p. 25; Corcoran to Walker, 4 August 1848, Letterbook 29, Corcoran Papers.

53. Corcoran to Walker, 4 August 1848, ibid.

54. Ibid.; Walker to Bancroft, 9 August 1848 (two letters), ibid.; Cohen, 'Business and Politics', pp. 113–14; Cohen, *Business and Politics*, pp. 54, 261, n. 28; Tick, 'The Political and Economic Policies of Walker', pp. 209–10.

55. Ward to Baring Brothers, 31 July, 7 August 1848, reel C-1390, BPOC; King to Baring Brothers, 16, 22 August 1848, reel C-1408, BPOC; Abbott Lawrence to Joshua Bates, 14 August 1848, Container 6, Corcoran Papers.

56. Joshua Bates to Ward, 18 August 1848, Box 12, Folder 3, Ward Papers.

57. Cohen, *Business and Politics*, pp. 54–5; Hidy, *The House of Baring*, pp. 387–8; Ward to Baring Brothers, 8 August 1848, reel C-1390, BPOC; King to Baring Brothers, 30 August 1848, reel C-1408, BPOC; *New York Tribune*, 16 August 1848.

58. Report of the Secretary of the Treasury, 1849, pp. 665–8, 685–92; *New York Herald*, 7 September 1848; Tick, 'The Political and Economic Policies of Walker', pp. 211–12; *Philadelphia North American*, quoted in *New York Herald*, 7 September 1848.

59. Report of the Secretary of the Treasury, 1848, p. 73; McClintock Young, Acting Secretary of the Treasury, to William Bouck, 28 September 1848, E-49, RG 56, NARA II; *New York Journal of Commerce*, 28, 30 September 1848.

60. R. Timberlake, *The Origin of Central Banking in the United States* (Cambridge, MA: Harvard University Press, 1978), pp. 78–9.

61. *New York Journal of Commerce*, 28, 30 September, 3 October 1848; Tick, 'The Political and Economic Policies of Walker', pp. 213–18; *Niles' National Register*, 11 October 1848; *New York Tribune*, 16, 23 September 1848.

62. *Washington Union*, quoted in *New York Journal of Commerce*, 7 October 1848.

63. Tick, 'The Political and Economic Policies of Walker', pp. 213–14, 216–18; *Niles' National Register*, 11 October 1848; *Bankers' Magazine*, 3 (November 1848), p. 324; *New York Journal of Commerce*, 3 October 1848.

64. Garraty and Carnes (eds), *American National Biography*, vol. 18, pp. 184–6; Hidy, *Peabody*, pp. vii–xi, 6–8.

65. Corcoran to Peabody, 1 September 1848, Container 6, Corcoran Papers; Peabody to Elisha Riggs, 29 September 1848, Letterbook 9, Peabody Papers; Hidy, *Peabody*, p. 290.

66. John Cryder to Peabody, 17 September, 3 October 1848, Box 15, Peabody Papers; Cohen, 'Business and Politics', pp. 116–17; Cohen, *Business and Politics*, p. 56.

67. Corcoran to Thomas Baring, 15, 21 September 1848, reel C-1416, BPOC; Corcoran & Riggs to Baring Brothers, 27 September 1848, ibid; Baring Brothers to Thomas Ward, 22 September 1848, Box 9, Ward Papers; Corcoran & Riggs to Peabody, 27 September 1848, Box 12, Folder 4, Peabody Papers; James G. King to Baring Brothers, 11 October 1848, reel C-1408, BPOC; Cohen, 'Business and Politics', pp. 118–20; Cohen, *Business and Politics*, pp. 56–7; Hidy, *Peabody*, pp. 290–1; *New York Tribune*, 19, 20 October 1848; Legation of the United States to Baring Brothers, 27 September 1848, reel C-1416, BPOC.

68. Cryder to Peabody, 10 October 1848, Box 15, Folder 5, Peabody Papers; Elisha Riggs to Peabody, 17 October 1848, Box 40, Folder 4, Peabody Papers; Cohen, 'Business and Politics', p. 120.

69. *Washington Union*, 13 October 1848.

70. *New York Herald*, 9, 10 October 1848.

71. Elisha Riggs to Peabody, 27 September, 17 October 1848, Box 40, Folder 4, Peabody Papers; Corcoran to Peabody, 9 December 1848, Box 12, Folder 5, Peabody Papers; Corcoran to Peabody, 5 February 1849, Box 12, Folder 6, Peabody Papers; Hidy, *Peabody*, p. 296; Cohen, *Business and Politics*, pp. 57–8.

72. Hidy, *The House of Baring*, p. 388; Hidy, *Peabody*, pp. 292–3; Cohen, *Business and Politics*, pp. 58–9.

73. Peabody to Corcoran, 29 December 1848, Container 6, Corcoran Papers.

74. Baring Brothers to Ward, 6, 27 October 1848, reel C-1430, BPOC; Baring Brothers to Corcoran & Riggs, 16, 13, 27 October, 26 November 1848, ibid.; Peabody to Corcoran & Riggs, 19 January 1849, Letterbook 10, Peabody Papers; Hidy, *The House of Baring*, p. 388; Corcoran & Riggs to Peabody, 18 December 1848, Box 12, Folder 5, Peabody Papers.

75. Peabody to Corcoran & Riggs, 6, 13 October, 17 November 1848, Letterbook 9, Peabody Papers; Peabody to Corcoran & Riggs, 1, 27 (2) December 1848, 19 January 1849, Letterbook 10, Peabody Papers; Peabody to Corcoran, 29 December 1848, Container 6, Corcoran Papers.

76. Peabody to Hope & Company, 13, 17, 27, 28, 31 October 1848, Letterbook 9, Peabody Papers.

77. Peabody to Berenberg, Gassler &Company, 3 October 1848, ibid.; Peabody to Berenberg, Gassler & Company, 12, 15, 27, 30 December 1848, 10, 23 January, 3 February 1849, Letterbook 10, Peabody Papers; Peabody to L. Lurman & Son, 16 December 1848, 4, 16 January 1849, ibid.; Peabody to Hesse, Newman & Company, 31 December 1848, 1, 10, 16 January 1849. ibid.; Peabody to Hope & Company, 31 October 1848, Letterbook 9, Peabody Papers.

78. Peabody to Corcoran & Riggs, 19 January, 9, 23 February 1849, Letterbook 10, Peabody Papers; Peabody to Elisha Riggs and Corcoran & Riggs, 26 January 1849, Box 25, Riggs Family Papers; Peabody to Corcoran & Riggs, 26 April 1849, 11, 25 May, 1 June, Letterbook 11, Peabody Papers; Hidy, *Peabody*, pp. 291–3.

79. Peabody to Corcoran & Riggs, 8 June 1849, Letterbook 11, Peabody Papers.

80. Cohen, 'Business and Politics', pp. 120–2; Cohen, *Business and Politics*, p. 58.

81. Cohen, 'Business and Politics', pp. 127–8, 137–8; Cohen, *Business and Politics*, pp. 61–2; Corcoran & Riggs to Baring Brothers, 25 June, 16 July 1849, reel C-1416, BPOC.

82. Official Announcement, Robert J. Walker, Secretary of the Treasury, 7 November 1848, E-447, item 162, RG 53, NARA II; *Niles' National Register*, 15, 29 November 1848.

83. Cohen, *Business and Politics*, p. 59; Report of the Secretary of the Treasury, 1848, p. 29; *The Diary of Polk*, vol. 4, pp. 162–3, 165, 175–6.

84. *The Diary of Polk*, vol. 4, p. 176.

85. Ibid., vol. 4, pp. 195–6; Report of the Secretary of the Treasury, 1848, p. 29.

86. George Newbold to William Corcoran, 24, 29 November, 5 December 1848, Box 135, Riggs Family Papers; Report of the Secretary of the Treasury, 1849, pp. 5, 699; *New York Tribune*, 3 December 1848.

87. Treasurer's Weekly Statement, 26 February 1849, in *Washington National Intelligencer*, 3 March 1849; Report of the Secretary of the Treasury, 1849, pp. 5, 699; Cohen, *Business and Politics*, pp. 59–61.

88. Report of the Secretary of the Treasury, 1849, pp. 5–6, 676, 697; *Bankers' Magazine*, 3 (April 1849), p. 633; *New York Herald*, 29 February 1849; E-376, Account for the Loan of 1848, vol. 94, Coupon Loan of 1848, pp. 1–149, RG 53, NARA II; ibid., vol. 95, Registered Transferrable Certificates of Loan of 1848, pp. 1–237; Redlich, *The Molding of American Banking*, vol. 2, pp. 347–55.

89. Source: Report of the Secretary of the Treasury, 1849, pp. 662–6.

9 Mexican Indemnity and Bounty Land

1. *US Statutes at Large*, 9 (1846), p. 94; ibid., 9 (1847), p. 125; ibid., 9 (1848), p. 265; Porter (comp.), 'Report on Valuation', pp. 365–7; DeKnight, *History of the Currency*, pp. 70–1, 73.

2. Sellers, *Polk, Continentalist*, pp. 230–4; Pletcher, *The Diplomacy of Annexation*, pp. 51–63; Smith, *The War with Mexico*, vol. 1, pp. 74–81.

3. *US Statutes at Large*, 8 (1839), pp. 526–32; ibid., 8 (1843), pp. 578–80; Richardson (ed.), *Messages of the Presidents*, vol. 4, pp. 197, 263, 389–91, 472–4; Pletcher, *The Diplomacy of Annexation*, pp. 56–8; Smith, *The War with Mexico*, vol. 1, pp. 79–81, 431, n. 40.

4. Polk's First Annual Message, in Richardson (ed.), *Messages of the President*, vol. 4, pp. 391–2; McPherson, *Ordeal by Fire*, p. 60; Buchanan to John Slidell, 10, 19 November 1845, in Sundry Reports, 29th Congress, 1st Session, House Executive Document 133, Serial 483, pp. 3–4; Emilio Voss to Slidell, 17 December 1845, in ibid., pp. 7–8; Slidell to Buchanan, 10 January 1846, in ibid., pp. 5–7; Tayleur, James & Company to Voss, 12 December 1845, in ibid., p. 9.

5. Richardson (ed.), *Messages of the Presidents*, vol. 4, p. 389.

6. Sellers, *Polk, Continentalist*, pp. 336–8; *The Diary of Polk*, vol. 1, pp. 34–5, 93, 233–4, 238.

7. Richardson (ed.), *Messages of the Presidents*, vol. 4, pp. 591–2; *Niles' National Register*, 22 August 1846; DeKnight, *History of the Currency*, pp. 70–1; Porter (comp.), 'Report on Valuation', p. 438; Report of the Secretary of the Treasury, 1851, pp. 25–7.

8. R. Griswold del Castillo, *The Treaty of Guadalupe Hidalgo: A Legacy of Conflict* (Norman, OK: University of Oklahoma Press, 1990), pp. 192–3; *New York Journal of Commerce*, 16 August 1848; Smith, *The War with Mexico*, vol. 2, p. 469, n. 13.

9. Richardson (ed.), *Messages of the Presidents*, vol. 4, pp. 587, 591–2, 644; Smith, *The War with Mexico*, vol. 2, p. 469, n. 13; *New York Journal of Commerce*, 16 August 1848; *US Statutes at Large*, 9 (1848), p. 265; Report of the Secretary of the Treasury, 1849, p. 26; *New York Tribune*, 1 November 1848; *Niles' National Register*, 16 August 1848.

10. *New York Tribune*, 1, 3 November 1848; *New York Journal of Commerce*, 16 August 1848; Corcoran & Riggs to Elisha Riggs, 24 August, 12 September, 29, 31 October 1846, Box 23, Riggs Family Papers; Corcoran & Riggs to John Ward & Company, 27 October 1846, Container 338, Corcoran & Riggs Stock and Bonds Records, 1843–90, Riggs Family Papers; James Robb & Company to Corcoran & Riggs, 9 December 1846, ibid.

11. 'Report of the Board of Commissioners on Claims Against Mexico', in Sundry Reports, 32nd Congress, 1st Session, Senate Executive Document 34, Serial 618, pp. 1–3; Smith, *The War with Mexico*, vol. 2, pp. 469, n. 13.

12. *Congressional Globe*, 29th Congress, 2nd Session, pp. 204–9, 214–17, 272–3, 346–7, Appendix, pp. 111–12, 122–4, 130–1, 260–1; *Niles' National Register*, 20 February 1847.

13. *Congressional Globe*, 29th Congress, 2nd Session, pp. 192–4, 204–9, 302.

14. Ibid., Appendix, pp. 122–4, 130–1, 260–2.

15. *US Statutes at Large*, 9 (1847), pp. 125–6; ibid., 9 (1850), pp. 520–1; Porter (comp.), 'Report on Valuation', pp. 367–8; Sundry Reports, 32nd Congress, 1st Session, Senate Report 350, Serial 631, pp. 1–2.

16. Report of the Secretary of the Treasury, 1849, pp. 5, 29; *American Review*, 8 (August 1848), pp. 182–3.

17. *Washington Union*, 2 November 1848; Charles Manley to Corcoran & Riggs, 18, 20, 22 September 1848, Box 197, Riggs Family Papers; Box 198 also contains documentation on numerous bounty land warrant purchases; Larson, 'E. W. Clark and Company', pp. 454–5.

18. Report of the Commissioner of the General Land Office, 13 December 1848, 30th Congress, 2nd Session, Senate Executive Document 2, Serial 530, pp. 21–3; ibid., 28 November 1849, 31st Congress, 1st Session, Senate Executive Document 1, Serial 550, pp. 28–9; Report of the Secretary of the Treasury, 1848, p. 1; ibid., 1849, p. 1; ibid., 1850, p. 1.

19. Report of the Commissioner of the General Land Office, 30 November 1859, 36th Congress, 1st Session, Senate Executive Document 2, Serial 1023, p. 173; Report of the Commissioner of the General Land Office, 1907, in *Report of the Department of the Interior* (Washington, DC: Government Printing Office, 1907), p. 259.

Conclusion

1. DeKnight, *History of the Currency*, pp. 177–9; Smith, *The War with Mexico*, vol. 2, pp. 250–2, 476, n. 31; Tenenbaum, *The Politics of Penury*, pp. 90–2, 116–17; E. Krauze, *Mexico: Biography of Power* (New York: HarperCollins, 1997), pp. 147–51; Richardson (ed.), *Messages of the Presidents*, vol. 4, pp. 587–93.

2. T. R. Irey, 'Soldiering, Suffering, and Dying', in O. B. Faulk and J. A. Stout, Jr (eds), *The Mexican War: Changing Interpretations* (Chicago, IL: Swallow Press, 1973), pp. 110–19, on pp. 110–11; E. Upton, *The Military Policy of the United States*, 3rd impression (Washington, DC: Government Printing Office, 1911), pp. 215–20; Sundry Reports, 31st Congress, 1st Session, House Executive Document 24, Serial 576, pp. 3–4; J. S. D.

Eisenhower, *So Far From God: The U. S. War with Mexico, 1846–1848* (1989; Norman, OK: University of Oklahoma Press, 2000), pp. 369–70.

3. Smith, *The War with Mexico*, vol. 2, pp. 266–7; Report of the Secretary of the Treasury, 1849, pp. 6, 8; ibid., 1850, pp. 6–10.

4. Report of the Secretary of the Treasury, 1849, pp. 6, 700; Smith, *The War with Mexico*, vol. 2, p. 266.

5. Report of the Secretary of the Treasury, 1850, pp. 6–9.

6. Smith, *The War with Mexico*, vol. 2, pp. 266–7; Eisenhower, *So Far from God*, pp. 369–70.

7. *Congressional Record*, 91st Congress, 1st session, vol. 115, part 13, pp. 18,026–7; US Bureau of the Census, *Historical Statistics of the United States, Colonial Times to 1970* (Washington, DC: Government Printing Office, 1975), p. 1140; US Bureau of the Census, *Statistical Abstract of the United States* (Washington, DC: Government Printing Office, 1936), p. 151–2.

8. *US Statutes at Large*, 9 (1848), pp. 249–50; Joint Resolution of 28 September 1850, in ibid., 9 (1850), p. 564; ibid., 39 (1916), pp. 844–6; ibid., 41 (1926), p. 587; Sundry Reports, 47th Congress, 1st Session, House Executive Document 137, Serial 2030, pp. 1–4; Sundry Reports, 56th Congress, 1st Session, Senate Document 107, Serial 3851, pp. 1–3; Report of the Secretary of the Interior, 2 December 1850, in *Washington National Intelligencer*, 3 December 1850; Report of the Secretary of the Treasury, 1850, pp. 7, 9, 78; *US Statutes at Large*, 24 (1887), pp. 371–2; US Bureau of the Census, *Historical Statistics*, p. 1145. US Bureau of the Census, *Statistical Abstract of the United States* (Washington, DC: Government Printing Office, 1964), p. 272.

9. Ibid., pp. 1140, 1145–6; DeKnight, *History of the Currency*, pp. 69–74; Report of the Commissioner of the Public Lands (1907), p. 259; Report of the Secretary of the Treasury, 1849, p. 26; ibid., 1850, p. 30; ibid., 1851, p. 22; ibid., 1852, p. 23. Under the terms of the Treaty of Guadalupe Hidalgo the United States was required to pay $15 million in principle and $1.8 million in interest. However, $908,000 of the first $3 million came from arms sales, Mexican assessment funds and army funds already expensed. The interest was also reduced by early payment. The $15.4 million was charged to the account during the fiscal years 1849 through 1852. Nathan Clifford to James Buchanan, 2 July 1848, E-119, RG 56, NARA II.

10. Report of the Secretary of the Treasury, 1849, pp. 5–6; Porter (comp.), 'Report on Valuation', pp. 365–7, 474–5.

11. Source: Report of the Secretary of the Treasury, 1849, pp. 5–6.

12. The $26.8 million consisted of the loan of 1846, $4,923,349; of 1847, $15,237,650; of 1848, $6,638,358. Porter (comp.), 'Report on Valuation', pp. 474–5.

13. Report of the Secretary of the Treasury, 6 December 1858, 35th Congress, 2nd Session, Senate Executive Document 2, Serial 979, p. 34; ibid., 1 December 1856, 34th Congress, 3rd Session, Senate Executive Document 3, Serial 874, p. 65; Porter (comp.), 'Report on Valuation', pp. 474–5; Report of the Secretary of the Treasury, 5 December 1860, 36th Congress, 2nd Session, House Executive Document 2, Serial 1093, p. 22; DeKnight, *History of the Currency*, pp. 72–4; Report of the Secretary of the Treasury, 1 December 1868, 40th Congress, 3rd Session, House Executive Document 2, Serial 1370, pp. xlv–xlix, liii; ibid., 6 December 1869, 41st Congress, 2nd Session, House Executive Document 2, Serial 1415, pp. xx, xxxv.

14. Bergeron, *The Presidency of Polk*, pp. 259–62; P. S. Klein, *President James Buchanan, A Biography* (University Park, PA: Pennsylvania State University Press, 1962), pp. xiii,

428–9; L. Gara, *The Presidency of Franklin Pierce* (Lawrence, KS: University Press of Kansas, 1991), pp. 128–32.

15. Shenton, *Walker*, pp. 124–5, 146–9, 160–1, 172–6, 192–201.
16. Larson, *Jay Cooke*, pp. 408–11, 421–5; T. Grant (ed.), *International Directory of Company Histories*, vols 1–92 (New York: St. James Press, 1990–2008), vol. 15, pp. 463–5, vol. 59, pp. 121–7.
17. Grant (ed.), *International Directory of Company Histories*, vol. 14, pp. 45–7.
18. H. Cleveland and T. F. Huertas, *Citibank, 1812–1970* (Cambridge, MA: Harvard University Press, 1985), pp. 169, 399–400, n. 46.
19. Cohen, *Business and Politics*, pp. 99–101, 208–14, 218–219.
20. Hidy, *Peabody*, p. 315; Garraty and Carnes (eds), *American National Biography*, vol. 17, pp. 184–6; Grant (ed.), *International Directory of Company Histories*, vol. 13, pp. 438–40, vol. 46, pp. 350–3; Mergent, Inc., *Mergent's Bank and Financial Manual*, 3 vols (New York: Mergent, Inc., 2000), vol. 1, p. 1551; Annual Report of PNC Financial, 2007, www.PNC.com.
21. F. Parker, *George Peabody, A Biography* (Nashville, TN: Vanderbilt University Press, 1971), pp. 67–9; V. P. Carosso, *The Morgans, Private Investment Bankers* (Cambridge, MA: Harvard University Press, 1987), pp. 44–5, 107–9; Grant (ed.), *International Directory of Company Histories*, vol. 11, pp. 427–9, vol. 40, pp. 145–51.
22. Carosso, *The Morgans*, p. 84; Grant (ed.), *International Directory of Company Histories*, vol. 16, pp. 374–8, vol. 30, pp. 261–4, vol. 46, pp. 300–2, vol. 91, pp. 273–84.
23. Parker, *Peabody*, pp. ix–x, 208–10.

WORKS CITED

Manuscripts

Baring Brothers and Company Papers, National Archives of Canada, Ottawa.

William W. Corcoran Papers, Library of Congress, Washington, DC.

William Learned Marcy Papers, Manuscript Division, Library of Congress, Washington, DC.

George Peabody Papers, Peabody Essex Institute, Salem, Massachusetts.

James K. Polk Papers (microfilm), Library of Congress, Washington, DC.

Records of the Bureau of Public Debt, Record Group 53, National Archives and Records Administration II, College Park, MD.

Records of the Department of the Treasury, Record Group 56, National Archives and Records Administration II, College Park, MD.

Riggs Family Papers, Library of Congress, Washington, DC.

Thomas Wren Ward Papers, Massachusetts Historical Society, Boston, Massachusetts.

Public Records (Printed), United States Government

Continental Congress, *Journal of the Continental Congress, 1774–1789*, ed. W. C. Ford et al., 34 vols (Washington, DC: Government Printing Office, 1904–37).

US Bureau of the Census

R. P. Porter (comp.), 'Report on Valuation, Taxation and Public Indebtedness in the United States', vol. 7 of *Tenth Census of the United States, 1880*, 22 vols (1883–8; New York: Norman Ross Publishing, 1991).

Statistical Abstract of the United States (Washington, DC: Government Printing Office, 1936).

Statistical Abstract of the United States (Washington, DC: Government Printing Office, 1964).

Historical Statistics of the United States, Colonial Times to 1970 (Washington, DC: Government Printing Office, 1975).

US Congress

Annals of the Congress of the United States, 1789–1824, 42 vols (Washington, DC, 1834–56).

Congressional Globe, 46 vols (Washington, DC, 1834–73).

Congressional Record, 91st Congress, 1st session, vol. 115, part 3 (Washington, DC).

New American State Papers, Public Finance, 32 vols (Wilmington, DE: Scholarly Resources, 1972–3).

Register of Debates in Congress, 1824–1837, 14 vols (Washington, DC).

US Congress, Report of the Commissioner of the General Land Office

1846, 29th Congress, 2nd Session, House Document 9, Serial 498.

1848, 30th Congress, 2nd Session, Senate Executive Document 2, Serial 530.

1849, 31th Congress, 1st Session, Senate Executive Document 1, Serial 550.

1859, 36th Congress, 1st Session, Senate Executive Document 2, Serial 1023.

1907, in *Report of Department of the Interior* (Washington, DC: Government Printing Office, 1907).

US Congress, Report of the Secretary of the Treasury on the State of the Finances

1828, 20th Congress, 2nd Session, Senate Document 7, Serial 181.

1829, 21st Congress, 1st Session, Senate Document 3, Serial 192.

1835, 24th Congress, 1st Session, Senate Document 2, Serial 279.

1843, 28th Congress, 1st Session, Senate Document 3, Serial 432.

1844, 28th Congress, 2nd Session, Senate Document 6, Serial 449.

1845, 29th Congress, 1st Session, Senate Document 2, Serial 471.

1846, 29th Congress, 2nd Session, Senate Executive Document 2, Serial 493.

1847, 30th Congress, 1st Session, House Executive Document 6, Serial 514.

1848, 30th Congress, 2nd Session, House Executive Document 7, Serial 538.

1849, 31th Congress, 1st Session, Senate Executive Document 2, Serial 552.

1850, 31st Congress, 2nd Session, Senate Executive Document 4, Serial 588.

1851, 32nd Congress, 1st Session, Senate Executive Document 11, Serial 614.

1852, 32nd Congress, 2nd Session, Senate Executive Document 22, Serial 662.

1853, 33rd Congress, 1st Session, Senate Executive Document 2, Serial 694.

1854, 33rd Congress, 2nd Session, Senate Executive Document 2, Serial 749.

1856, 34th Congress, 3rd Session, Senate Executive Document 3, Serial 874.

1858, 35th Congress, 2nd Session, Senate Executive Document 2, Serial 979.

1860, 36th Congress, 2nd Session, House Executive Document 2, Serial 1093.

1868, 40th Congress, 3rd Session, House Executive Document 2, Serial 1370.

1869, 41st Congress, 2nd Session, House Executive Document 2, Serial 1415.

US Congress, Sundry Reports

    27th Congress, 3rd Session, House Document 197, Serial 422.

    27th Congress, 3rd Session, House Report 120, Serial 426.

    29th Congress, 1st Session, House Executive Document 133, Serial 483.

    29th Congress, 1st Session, House Document 174, Serial 485.

    29th Congress, 1st Session, House Report 411, Serial 489.

    29th Congress, 1st Session, Senate Document 392, Serial 477.

    29th Congress, 2nd Session, Senate Executive Document 111, Serial 495.

    30th Congress, 1st Session, House Executive Document 60, Serial 520.

    30th Congress, 2nd Session, House Executive Document 46, Serial 541.

    30th Congress, 2nd Session, House Executive Document 47, Serial 541.

    30th Congress, 2nd Session, House Report 119, Serial 545.

    31st Congress, 1st Session, House Executive Document 24, Serial 576.

    32nd Congress, 1st Session, Senate Executive Document 34, Serial 618.

    32nd Congress, 1st Session, Senate Report 350, Serial 631.

    33rd Congress, 1st Session, House Executive Document 32, Serial 721.

    34th Congress, 3rd Session, Senate Executive Document 34, Serial 880.

    47th Congress, 1st Session, House Executive Document 137, Serial 2030.

    56th Congress, 1st Session, Senate Document 107, Serial 3851.

US Statutes at Large, vols 1–5, 8–9, 12, 24, 39, 41.

Newspapers and Magazines

American Review, A Whig Journal (New York).

Bankers' Magazine and State Financial Register (Baltimore, MD).

Charleston Mercury (SC).

DeBow's Commercial Review of the South and West (New Orleans, LA).

Economist (London).

Merchants' Magazine and Commercial Review (New York).

New Orleans Picayune.

New Orleans Weekly Picayune.

New York Journal of Commerce.

New York Herald.

New York Tribune.

Niles' National Register (Baltimore, MD).

Philadelphia Public Ledger.

The Times (London).

United States Magazine and Democratic Review (New York).

Washington National Intelligencer (Washington, DC).

Washington Union (Washington, DC).

Primary Sources

Alcaraz, R., et al., *The Other Side or Notes for the History of the War between Mexico and the United States*, trans. A. C. Ramsey (New York: John Wiley, 1850), in *Western Americana* (New Haven, CT: Research Publications, 1975), microform, reel 5, item 72.

Benton, T. H., *Thirty Year View*, 2 vols (1856; New York: D. Appleton & Company, 1893).

Buchanan, J., *The Works of James Buchanan*, ed. J. B. Moore, 12 vols (Philadelphia, PA: J. B. Lippincott Company, 1908–11).

Calhoun, J. C., *The Papers of John C. Calhoun*, ed. W. E. Hemphill, C. N. Wilson and S. B. Cook, 26 vols (Columbia, SC: University of South Carolina Press, 1963–2001).

Clay, H., *The Papers of Henry Clay*, ed. J. F. Hopkins, R. Seager II and M. P. Hayes, 10 vols (Lexington, KY: University of Kentucky Press, 1959–91).

Cooke, J., *Memoirs of Jay Cooke*, typescript, Baker Library, Harvard University School of Business, Boston, Massachusetts.

Davis, J., *Jefferson Davis, Constitutionalist: His Letters, Papers and Speeches*, ed. D. Rowland, 10 vols (Jackson, MS: Mississippi Department of Archives and History, 1923).

Dix, M. (comp.), *Memoirs of John Adam Dix* (New York: Harper & Brothers, 1883).

Hamilton, A., *Papers of Alexander Hamilton*, ed. H. C. Syrett et al., 27 vols (New York: Columbia University Press, 1961–87).

Krooss, H. E. (ed.), *Documentary History of Banking and Currency in the United States*, 4 vols (New York: Chelsea House Publishers, 1969).

Lincoln, A., *The Collected Works of Abraham Lincoln*, ed. R. P. Baslar, M. D. Pratt and F. Dunlap, 9 vols (New Brunswick, NJ: Rutgers University Press, 1953–5).

Polk, J. K., *The Diary of James K. Polk during His Presidency, 1845–1849*, ed. M. M. Quaife, 4 vols (Chicago, IL: A. C. McClurg & Company, 1910).

—, *Correspondence of James K. Polk*, ed. H. Weaver and W. Cutler, 10 vols (vols 1–7: Nashville, TN: Vanderbilt University Press; vols 8–10: Knoxville, TN: University of Tennessee Press, 1969–2004).

Richardson, J. D. (ed.), *A Compilation of the Messages and Papers of the Presidents, 1789–1902*, 10 vols (Washington: Bureau of National Literature and Art, 1904).

Webster, D., *The Papers of Daniel Webster, Correspondence*, ed. C. M. Wiltse, 7 vols (Hanover, NH: University Press of New England, 1974–86).

Secondary Sources

Adams, D. R., Jr, 'The Beginning of Investment Banking in the United States', *Pennsylvania History*, 45 (April 1978), pp. 99–116.

—, *Finance and Enterprise in Early America: A Study of Stephen Girard's Bank, 1812–1831* (Philadelphia, PA: University Press of Pennsylvania, 1978).

Anderson, W. G., *The Price of Liberty: The Public Debt of the American Revolution* (Charlottesville, VA: University Press of Virginia, 1983).

Balinky, A., *Albert Gallatin, Fiscal Theories and Policies* (New Brunswick, NJ: Rutgers University Press, 1958).

Bartlett, I. H., *John C. Calhoun, A Biography* (New York: W. W. Norton & Company, 1953).

Berge, D. E., 'A Mexican Dilemma: The Mexico City *Ayuntamiento* and the Question of Loyalty, 1846–1848', *Hispanic American Historical Review*, 50 (May 1970), pp. 229–56.

Bergeron, P., *The Presidency of James K. Polk* (Lawrence, KS: University Press of Kansas, 1987).

Biddy, J. F., and B. F. Schaffner, *Political Parties and Elections in America*, 6th edn (Boston, MA: Thomson & Wadsworth, 2008).

Bill, A. H., *Rehearsal for Conflict: The War with Mexico, 1846–1848* (New York: Cooper Square Publishers, 1969).

Bodenhorn, H., 'Capital Mobility and Financial Integration in Antebellum America', *Journal of Economic History*, 52 (September 1992), pp. 585–602.

—, *A History of Banking in Antebellum America: Financial Markets and Economic Development in an Era of Nation-Building* (Cambridge: Cambridge University Press, 2000).

—, *State Banking in Early America: A New Economic History* (New York: Oxford University Press, 2003).

Brack, G. M., *Mexico Views Manifest Destiny, 1821–1846: An Essay on the Origins of the Mexican War* (Albuquerque, NM: University of New Mexico Press, 1975).

Buel, R., Jr, *America on the Brink: How the Political Struggle over the War of 1812 almost Destroyed the Young Republic* (New York: Palgrave Macmillan, 2005).

Bruchey, S., *The Roots of American Economic Growth, 1607–1861: An Essay in Social Causation* (New York: Harper & Row, 1965).

Callcott, W. H., *Church and State in Mexico, 1822–1857* (Durham, NC: Duke University Press, 1926).

—, *Santa Anna* (1936; Hampden, CT: Archon Books, 1964).

Carosso, V. P., *Investment Banking in America, a History* (Cambridge, MA: Harvard University Press, 1970).

—, *The Morgans, Private Investment Bankers* (Cambridge, MA: Harvard University Press, 1987).

Chambers, W. N., *'Old Bullion' Benton: Senator from the West, 1782–1858* (Boston, MA: Little Brown, 1956).

Chernow, R. *Alexander Hamilton* (New York: Penquin Press, 2004).

Cleveland, H. V., and T. F. Huertas, *Citibank, 1812–1970* (Cambridge, MA: Harvard University Press, 1985).

Cohen, H., 'Business and Politics from the Age of Jackson to the Civil War: A Study of the Life of W. W. Corcoran' (PhD dissertation, Cornell University, 1965).

—, *Business and Politics in America from the Age of Jackson to the Civil War: The Business Career of W. W. Corcoran* (Westport, CT: Greenwood Press, 1971).

Connor, S. V., and O. B. Faulk, *North America Divided: The Mexican War, 1846–1848* (New York: Oxford University Press, 1971).

Costeloe, M. P., 'Church–State Financial Negotiations in Mexico during the American War, 1846–1847', *Revista de Historia de America*, 60 (July–December 1965), pp. 91–123.

—, 'The Mexican Church and the Rebellion of the Polkos', *Hispanic American Historical Review*, 46 (May 1966), pp. 170–8.

—, *Church Wealth in Mexico: A Study of the Juzgado de Capellanias in the Archbishopric of Mexico City, 1800–1856* (London: Cambridge University Press, 1967).

Crapol, E. P., *John Tyler, the Accidental President* (Chapel Hill, NC: University of North Carolina Press, 2006).

Curtis, J. C., *The Fox at Bay: Martin Van Buren and the Presidency, 1837–1841* (Lexington, KY: University of Kentucky Press, 1970).

Davies, T. M., Jr., 'Assessments during the Mexican War, an Exercise in Futility', *New Mexico Historical Review*, 41 (July 1966), pp. 197–216.

Davis, L. E., and R. J. Cull, *International Capital Markets and American Economic Growth, 1820–1914* (Cambridge: Cambridge University Press, 1994).

Davis, L. E., and J. R. T. Hughes, 'A Dollar–Sterling Exchange, 1803–1895', *Economic History Review*, 13 (August 1960), pp. 52–78.

DeKnight, W. F., *History of the Currency and of the Loans of the United States from the Earliest Period to June 30, 1896* (Washington, DC: Government Printing Office, 1897).

Dusinberre, W., *Slavemaster President: The Double Career of James Polk* (Oxford: Oxford University Press, 2003).

Eisenhower, J. S. D., *So Far from God: The U. S. War with Mexico, 1846–1848* (1989; Norman, OK: University of Oklahoma Press, 2000).

Elliott, C. W., *Winfield Scott: The Soldier and the Man* (New York: Macmillan, 1937).

Ernst, J. A., *Money and Politics in America, 1755–1775* (Chapel Hill, NC: University of North Carolina Press, 1973).

Ettin, E. C., 'The Development of American Financial Intermediaries', in J. V. Fenstermaker (comp.), *Readings in Financial Markets and Institutions* (New York: Appleton-Century-Crofts, 1969), pp. 241–61.

Ferguson, E. J., *The Power of the Purse: A History of American Public Finance, 1776–1790* (Chapel Hill, NC: University of North Carolina Press, 1961).

Ferguson, N., *The House of Rothschild, Money's Prophets, 1798–1848* (New York: Viking, 1998).

Gara, L., *The Presidency of Franklin Pierce* (Lawrence, KS: University Press of Kansas, 1991).

Garraty, J. A., and M. C. Carnes (eds), *American National Biography*, 24 vols (New York: Oxford University Press, 1999).

Gatell, F. O., 'Spoils of the Bank War: Political Bias in the Selection of Pet Banks', *American Historical Review*, 70 (October 1964), pp. 35–58.

Graebner, N., *An Empire on the Pacific: A Study in American Continental Expansion* (New York: Ronald Press, 1955).

Grant, T. (ed.), *International Directory of Company Histories*, 92 vols (New York: St. James Press, 1990–2008).

Griswold del Castillo, R., *The Treaty of Guadalupe Hidalgo: A Legacy of Conflict.* (Norman, OK: University of Oklahoma Press, 1990).

Hammond, B., *Banks and Politics in America from the Revolution to the Civil War* (Princeton, NJ: Princeton University Press, 1957).

—, *Sovereignty and an Empty Purse: Banks and Politics in the Civil War* (Princeton, NJ: Princeton University Press, 1970).

Haynes, S. W., *James K. Polk and the Expansionist Impulse* (New York: Longman, 1997).

Hickey, D. R., *The War of 1812, A Forgotten Conflict* (Urbana, IL: University of Illinois Press, 1990).

Hidy, M. E., *George Peabody, Merchant and Financier, 1829–1854* (New York: Arno Press, 1978).

Hidy, R. W., 'A Leaf from Investment History', *Harvard Business Review*, 20 (Autumn 1941), pp. 65–74.

—, *The House of Baring in American Trade and Finance: English Merchant Bankers at Work, 1763–1861* (Cambridge, MA: Harvard University Press, 1949).

Hietala, T. R., *Manifest Design: Anxious Aggrandizement in Late Jacksonian America* (Ithaca, NY: Cornell University Press, 1985).

Holt, M. F., *The Rise and Fall of the American Whig Party: Jacksonian Politics and the Onset of the Civil War* (New York: Oxford University Press, 1999).

Hormats, R. D., *The Price of Liberty: Paying for America's Wars* (New York: Times Books, 2007).

Horsman, R., *Race and Manifest Destiny* (Cambridge, MA: Harvard University Press, 1981).

Huffmann, S., *Politics and Banking: Public Policy and the Creation of Financial Institutions* (Baltimore, MD: Johns Hopkins University Press, 2001).

Hutchinson, T., *The History of the Colony and Province of Massachusetts Bay*, ed. L. S. Mayo, 3 vols (1936; New York: Kraus Reprint Co., 1970).

Irey, T. R., 'Soldiering, Suffering, and Dying', in O. B. Faulk and J. A. Stout, Jr (eds), *The Mexican War: Changing Interpretations* (Chicago, IL: Swallow Press, 1973), pp. 110–19.

Johnson, T. D., *Winfield Scott: The Quest for Military Glory* (Lawrence, KS: University Press of Kansas, 1998).

Kammen, M. G., *Colonial New York: A History* (New York: Charles Scribner's Sons, 1975).

Katz, I., 'Investment Bankers in Government and Politics: The Political Activity of William W. Corcoran, August Belmont, Sr., Levi P. Morton, and Henry Lee Higginson' (PhD dissertation, New York University, 1964).

Kilbourne, R. H., Jr, *Slave Agriculture and Financial Markets in Antebellum America: The Bank of the United States in Mississippi, 1831–1852* (London: Pickering & Chatto, 2006).

Kinley, D., *The Independent Treasury of the United States and its Relationship to the Banks of the Country* (Washington, DC: Government Printing Office, 1910).

Klein, P. S., *President James Buchanan, A Biography* (University Park, PA: Pennsylvania State University Press, 1962).

Krauze, E., *Mexico: Biography of Power* (New York: HarperCollins, 1997).

Kuhn, R. L., *Investment Banking: The Art and Science of High-Stake Dealmaking* (New York: Harper & Roe, 1990).

Larson, H. M., 'E. W. Clark and Company, 1837–1857: The Beginning of an American Private Bank', *Journal of Commerce and Business History*, 4 (July 1932), pp. 429–60.

—, *Jay Cooke, Private Banker* (Cambridge, MA: Harvard University Press, 1936).

Lee, S. P. and P. Passell, *A New Economic View of American History* (New York: W. W. Norton, 1979).

Levine, R., and S. Zervos, 'Stock Markets, Banks and Economic Growth', *American Economic Review*, 88 (June 1998), pp. 537–58.

McBride, G. M., *The Land System of Mexico* (New York: National Geographical Society, 1923).

McCoy, C. A., *Polk and the Presidency* (Austin, TX: University of Texas Press, 1960).

McGrane, R. C., *Foreign Bondholders and American State Debt* (New York: Macmillan Company, 1935).

McPherson, J. M., *Ordeal by Fire: The Civil War and Reconstruction*, 2nd ed. (New York: McGraw-Hill, 1992).

—, *Battle Cry of Freedom: The Civil War Era* (1988; New York: Oxford University Press, 2003).

McSweeny, D., and J. Zvesper, *American Political Parties: The Formation, Decline and Reform of the American Party System* (London: Routledge, 1991).

Markham, J. W., *A Financial History of the United States*, 3 vols (Armonk, NY: M. E. Sharpe, 2002).

Merk, F., *Manifest Destiny and Mission in American History* (New York: Alfred A. Knopf, 1963).

Mergent, Inc., *Mergent's Bank and Financial Manual*, 3 vols (New York: Mergent, Inc., 2000).

Michener, R. W., and R. E. Wright, 'State, "Currencies" and the Transition to the U. S. Dollar: Clarifying some Confusion', *American Economic Review*, 95 (June 2005), pp. 682–703.

Morgensen, G., and C. R. Harvey, *New York Times Dictionary of Money and Investing* (New York: Times Books, 2002).

Myers, M. G., *The New York Money Market*, 4 vols (New York: Columbia University Press, 1931).

—, *A Financial History of the United States* (New York: Columbia University Press, 1970).

North, D. C., *The Economic Growth of the United States, 1790–1860* (1961; New York: W. W. Norton, 1966).

Parker, F., *George Peabody, A Biography* (Nashville, TN: Vanderbilt University Press, 1971).

Perkins, E. J., *Financing Anglo-American Trade: The House of Brown, 1800–1880* (Cambridge, MA: Harvard University Press, 1975).

—, *The Economy of Colonial America* (New York: Columbia University Press, 1980).

—, *American Public Finance and Financial Services, 1700–1815* (Columbus, OH: Ohio State University Press, 1994).

Pletcher, D. M., *The Diplomacy of Annexation: Texas, Oregon and the Mexican War* (Columbus, MO: University of Missouri Press, 1973).

Ramirez, J. F., *Mexico during the War with the United States*, trans. E. Scherr (Columbus, MO: University of Missouri Press, 1950).

Ratner, S., J. H. Soltow and R. Sylla, *The Evolution of the American Economy: Growth, Welfare and Decision Making* (New York: Basic Books, 1979).

Redlich, F., *The Molding of American Banking: Men and Ideas*, 2nd edn, 2 vols (New York: Johnson Reprint Corporation, 1968).

Remini, R. V., *Andrew Jackson and the Bank War: A Study in Presidential Power* (New York: Norton, 1967).

Rives, G. L., *The United States and Mexico, 1821–1848*, 2 vols (New York: Charles Scribner's Sons, 1913).

Robinson, C. (trans.), *The View from Chapultepec, Mexican Writers on the Mexican American War* (Tucson, AZ: University of Arizona Press, 1989).

Rosseau, P. L., 'Jacksonian Monetary Policy, Specie Flow, and the Panic of 1837', *Journal of Economic History*, 62 (June 2002), pp. 457–88.

Santoni, P., *Mexicans at Arms: Puro Federalists and the Politics of War, 1845–1848* (Fort Worth, TX: Texas Christian University Press, 1996).

Scheiber, H. N., *Ohio Canal Era: A Case Study of Government and the Economy, 1820–1861* (Athens, OH: Ohio University Press, 1969).

Seager, R., II, *And Tyler Too, A Biography of John and Julia Gardiner Tyler* (New York: McGraw-Hill, 1963).

Sellers, C. G., *James K. Polk, Jacksonian, 1795–1843* (Princeton, NJ: Princeton University Press, 1957).

—, _James K. Polk, Continentalist, 1843–1846_ (Princeton, NJ: Princeton University Press, 1966).

—, _Market Revolution: Jacksonian America, 1815–1846_ (New York: Oxford University Press, 1991).

Shenton, J. P., _Robert John Walker: A Politician from Jackson to Lincoln_ (New York: Columbia University Press, 1961).

Silbey, J. H., _Shrine of Party: Congressional Voting Behavior, 1841–1852_ (Pittsburgh, PA: University of Pittsburgh Press, 1967).

Smith, J. H., 'American Rule in Mexico', _American Historical Review_, 23 (January 1918), pp. 287–302.

—, _The War with Mexico_, 2 vols (New York: Macmillan Company, 1919).

Stabile, D. R., _The Origins of American Public Finance_ (Westport, CT: Greenwood Press, 1998).

Studenski, P., and H. E. Krooss, _Financial History of the United States_, 2nd edn (New York: McGraw-Hill, 1963).

Sylla, R., 'Forgotten Men of Money: Private Bankers in Early U. S. History', _Journal of Economic History_, 36 (March 1976), pp. 173–88.

—, 'Monetary Innovations in America', _Journal of Economic History_, 42 (March 1982), pp. 21–30.

—, 'Shaping the United States Financial System, 1690–1913: The Dominance of Public Finance', in R. Sylla, R. Tilly and G. Tortello (eds), _The State, the Financial System and Economic Modernization_ (Cambridge: Cambridge University Press, 1999), pp. 249–70.

Sylla, R., R. Tilly and G. Tortella, 'Introduction: Comparative Historical Perspectives', in R. Sylla, R. Tilly and G. Tortello (eds), _The State, the Financial System and Economic Modernization_ (Cambridge: Cambridge University Press, 1999), pp. 1–19.

Temin, P., _The Jacksonian Economy_ (New York: W. W. Norton & Company, 1969).

Tenenbaum, B. A., 'Merchants, Money and Mischief: The British in Mexico, 1821–1862', _Americas_, 35 (January 1979), pp. 317–39.

—, _The Politics of Penury: Debt and Taxes in Mexico, 1821–1856_ (Albuquerque, NM: University of New Mexico Press, 1986).

Tick, F., 'The Political and Economic Policies of Robert J. Walker' (PhD dissertation, University of California at Los Angeles, 1947).

Timberlake, R., _The Origin of Central Banking in the United States_ (Cambridge, MA: Harvard University Press, 1978).

Turlington, E., _Mexico and Her Foreign Creditors_ (New York: Columbia University Press, 1930).

Upton, E., _The Military Policy of the United States_, 3rd impression (Washington, DC: Government Printing Office, 1911).

Wasserman, M., _Everyday Life and Politics in Nineteenth Century Mexico: Men, Women and War_ (Albuquerque, NM: University of New Mexico Press, 2000).

Watson, H. L. *Liberty and Power: The Politics of Jacksonian America* (New York: Hill & Wang, 1990).

Weinberg, A. K., *Manifest Destiny: A Study of Nationalist Expansion in American History* (Baltimore, MD: Johns Hopkins University Press, 1935).

Wilentz, S., *The Rise of American Democracy: Jefferson to Lincoln* (New York: W. W. Norton, 2005).

Williamson, J. P. (ed.), *The Investment Banking Handbook* (New York: John Wiley & Son, 1988).

Wright, R. E., *Hamilton Unbound: Finance and the Creation of the American Republic* (New York: Praeger, 2002).

—, *Wealth of Nations Rediscovered: Integration and Expansion in American Financial Markets, 1780–1850* (Cambridge: Cambridge University Press, 2002).

—, *The First Wall Street: Chestnut Street, Philadelphia, and the Birth of American Finance* (Chicago, IL: University of Chicago Press, 2005).

Wright, R. E., and D. J. Cowens, *Financial Founding Fathers: The Men Who Made America Rich* (Chicago, IL: University of Chicago Press, 2006).

Ziegler, P., *The Sixth Greatest Power: A History of one of the Greatest of all Banking Families, the House of Baring, 1762–1929* (New York: Alfred A. Knopf, 1988).

INDEX

For Product Safety Concerns and Information please contact our EU
representative GPSR@taylorandfrancis.com
Taylor & Francis Verlag GmbH, Kaufingerstraße 24, 80331 München, Germany

www.ingramcontent.com/pod-product-compliance
Ingram Content Group UK Ltd.
Pitfield, Milton Keynes, MK11 3LW, UK
UKHW021613240425
457818UK00018B/544